# The Art of Managing Software Development People

# The Art Of Managing Software Development People

**Paul S. Licker**

The University of Calgary
Calgary, Alberta, Canada

JOHN WILEY & SONS

New York / Chichester / Brisbane / Toronto / Singapore

**Library of Congress Cataloging in Publication Data:**

Licker, Paul S. (Paul Steven), 1944–
The art of managing software development people.

Bibliography: p.
Includes index.
1. Computer programming management. 2. Electronic data processing departments—Management. I. Title.

QA76.6.L515 1985 001.64'2'068 84-25619
ISBN 0-471-89024-3

Printed in the United States of America

10 9 8 7 6 5 4 3 2 1

*To Marilyn and the boys*

# PREFACE

This book had its roots in the mid 1960s, but wasn't actually begun until 1980, when I began to see that others besides myself needed to take heed of what is going on in data processing. Even a cursory look now at trade publications like *ComputerWorld, Datamation,* and *Byte* will alert anyone in the software development industry to the epidemic of bad experiences in managing software development. The pages of these journals relate analyses, solutions, and tales of woe and success, but no one seems to be able to do much about the sorry state of programming management.

Worse yet, no one is really sure of the scope of the problem or even that the problem lies with management, as opposed to something else, such as the programmers, the economy, the DP industry, or the stars. In fact, judging from the interest in the past few years in the topic of programmer productivity, the industry seems ready for the promulgation of some racist theory about the inherent inferiority of programmers. Concepts such as "programmer shortfall," "productivity increasing tools," and "professionalism" come and go with the supply of programmer bodies, but the questions remain: do we really *have* problems? And where are they?

The thesis of this book is that yes, there are problems, and no, we cannot point our fingers in specific directions. Yes, there are many problems with software development. These problems range from the simple (it takes too long to make a piece of software) to the complex (organizations have little conception of what software is and what it can do for the firm). On the other hand, no one specific person or group is at fault here. Instead, we are observing, in programming, the continuation of a trend that began in the early 1960s and that will probably not terminate until the fading years of this century: the maturation of programming as a vocation.

It is important to explain this, since the idea of a vocation maturing may seem odd, although in fact, we have seen many vocations and industries mature during the last 75 years. If the nineteenth century was the era of political maturation, which culminated in the great wars of the first half of the twentieth century and the subsequent formation of international leagues, the twentieth is the era of technological maturation, and we shall not see the end of this until the middle of the twenty-first. We have seen many new vocations arise in the early years of this era: management consulting, financial planning, psychology, electronics engineering, and computer programming. With few exceptions, these professions have blended well within families of similar professions: most, but not all, of these professionals know their places.

Vocations are born, they mature, and ultimately die. We may be seeing the tail end of certain manufacturing vocations, especially in the automobile industry and to an extent in aeronautics. It is natural for any system to grow, then reach a peak, and die. What of programming?

Programming is the newest of the professions in the twentieth century to reach mass proportions. Already there are many hundreds of thousands of people in North America making their livings programming computers. Their numbers are sure to grow. But programming is an *immature* profession. It has no code of ethics. It has no unions. It has no great traditions. Almost no one has retired from programming; the average age of programmers is younger than other nonathletic vocational groupings. Its literature is found in the mathematics section in the Dewey Decimal system for library cataloging and in the library science, office systems, and mathematics sections in the Library of Congress system. Most lawyers, doctors, nurses, accountants, biologists, aeronautics engineers, and psychologists know where to go to find their literature and can read adjacent sections' books. Most programmers have only a passing interest in mathematics and almost no exposure whatever to science.

In other words, programming is an adolescent profession and the industry that employs programming talents is therefore an adolescent industry. In a way this metaphor is fitting, too, in a psychological sense. Many who manage programmers often feel they are dealing with adolescents. My personal experience is precisely that, since I became a programmer at the tender age of 20. The best programmers in our shop were 13 and 15, respectively—they were so young we couldn't pay them, but they worked for free, anyway. High jinks, playful sabotage, and insubordination were their daily bread, and I joined in, too. My most vivid memory of 1967 is that of observing a baseball game played in our programmers' "enclosure" beside the machine room. The pitcher was 18, the catcher, 15. The batter, wielding rolled-up listing paper, was 13 and he was taking mighty swings at wads of balled-up listings while the rest of us (average age around 22) cheered. What the users thought never entered our minds; our managers had graciously absented themselves for the afternoon.

If this experience was typical in some ways it is atypical in others. Most programmers, like most doctors and ditchdiggers, care about their work. They like their paychecks, dislike their managers, and feel that it would be great if they could be left alone to get the work done. But there is an undercurrent of immaturity found almost uniquely in programming. The undercurrent flows through management ranks as well as through the cubicles of the kids in the basement.

Not only is programming an immature profession, it also represents a transition profession, in many ways echoing the science-fiction stories that programmers love. For while the 19-year-old (lately 29-year-old) hero or heroine is discovering some inherent nobility (à la Luke Skywalker), the cosmos of employment is undergoing a rapid revolution under the influence of the very technology our programmer employs. For programming is both the last of the third-generation jobs and the first fourth-generation job.

The three generations of jobs civilization has experienced are roughly these: farming, artisanry, and manufacturing, with their attendant supervisory positions and support "staffs." We don't include gathering, soldiery, and administration here; somehow these "jobs" seem to be impervious to technology, planetary cataclysm, and generation gaps. Programming is the last of the manufacturing jobs because it doesn't seem to be working right under the typical regimen of the "shop." It doesn't lend itself well to the kind of planning that manufacturing requires. It doesn't deal in raw materials. Its semifinished products are useless and in many cases unstable (structured design and testing are ways of trying to retrofit programming to a manufacturing environment). Its employees cannot be made to punch any clocks. It seems like a managerial level job, but its employees are increasingly nearly illiterate and incapable of the type of planning that has always been demanded of managers. And the managers of programmers seem even worse. *Their* abilities to supervise are limited, *their* delivery schedules are comical, *their* concerns are not those of general management. Calling a software unit a "shop" is like calling interstellar space a crystalline structure.

But programming is also the first of the new, fourth-generation jobs that, like a shock wave, are pushed forward before the information revolution rocket. Programmers have that basic understanding of control and technical planning that has traditionally been denied line workers, whose daily schedule is often planned to the minute. Programmers, and their managers, work artisan-like exclusively on single-item manufacture, in a manufacturing environment barely removed from the sweatshop.

The mental environment, however, is almost pure science-fiction. No other workers, except perhaps government planners, spend such a large proportion of their time on multilevel metastructures of information and control. Programmers, resembling bureaucrats, speak glibly in abstract terms like virtual memory, linked lists, relational data bases—terms that have almost no physical representation and no analogues in daily life. Unlike bureaucrats, however, programmers and their managers never see the "real" world. Increasingly, programmers are denied access even to the machines they work on. Instead they are issued an account code, a password, and a green screen. They, like their users, view their abstract world only through a small window.

It is this attribute, the viewing of a large articulated world of abstract objects through a small window, that I think defines the world of fourth-generation work. The first generation consisted of a large view of real agricultural objects. The second generation consisted of a small view of real crafted objects. The third generation consisted of a restricted view of parts of real objects. The fourth generation will view work in an as-yet undefinable way through a complex of layers of work-defining information processors. The ultimate texture of this world is as-yet inexpressible, but trends such as database management, program development environments, and office automation are rapidly building those layers now.

Thus the need for this book. Managers of programmers, or MOPs for short, need help in surviving the coming dislocation, of which the past 20 years have been but a symptom. Fighting the contributing forces of the rapid growth of technological advancement, the increase in work-defining layering, and personal obsolescence as managers move into their middle years at the end of this century, MOPs are curiously unarmed to survive the revolution they lead. Changes in organizations and how they function are being evidenced as the West pulls out of its worst economic downturn since the Great Depression. The newer, leaner, more specialized, more highly automated organizations are in the vanguard of the march toward the fourth generation of workers. Where are their MOPs?

At the human level, the programming and programming management cadre is aging more rapidly than any other profession, but little is being done to help managers cope with the changes that personal maturation brings. Career planning, personnel development, and the development of fourth-generation management philosophies are not in general being promulgated through the MOP ranks. The change in function for management that the fourth generation of work will necessitate is not being foreseen by MOPs, who more and more are being left to drift through life managing as though they were factory foremen.

It simply will not work. The gap between theory and practice is growing daily. Each issue of important academic journals develops interesting theories of management that *can* be applied to programming shops, but aren't. Research into software engineering, general systems theory, programmer personality traits, job satisfaction, alternative management styles, and the application of human relations training in the shop are simply being ignored. Usually the excuse is lack of time, pressure to produce, lack of resources. Only software engineering seems likely to help. "Programmerless programming" may help, too, but few of us really want to see that trend become a habit. This book attempts to alert managers who find the time to read it to the wealth of research on software development management that they can tap.

The curious thing is that not only is programming the last of the third-generation jobs, it seems also to be skipping, third-world fashion, some of the experience that other third-generation jobs had. In particular, there has been little attempt to apply general management techniques in a serious way to the software shop. Granted, programming may be so much a fourth-generation job that none of the techniques hold water, but it is curious that they haven't been tried. Excuses here range from "they're unmanageable" to "they're inscrutable" to "who's got the time?" In fact, the problem is that the relative immaturity of the field and the pressures of the transition to fourth generation have simply not brought anyone out, guru-like, to apply these techniques. Where is the Drucker of the digital shop and the output Ouchi? Why have no micro McGregors and half-duplex Hackmans appeared? Why haven't the various interesting systems approaches to management been applied to those who construct the systems? The answer is clearly that the time was inappropriate, the ground infertile for the propagation.

While this writer can scarcely claim Druckerhood, this book is a first attempt to bring together what is known from personnel management, career planning, human resources development, organizational behavior, and general management to the software shop. If it seems contradictory that I should wish to apply some well-chosen third-generation management techniques to the new fourth-generation jobs, the reader will have to live with that contradiction, for no one knows how the fourth generation will happen. Maybe 5, maybe 15 years from now, a set of how-tos can be compiled for fourth-generation managers. For now, all we can do is look at some of the more advanced management techniques and hope that they can be applied to software development.

Chapter 1 goes into some more detail about the new profession of managing programmers and raises a number of issues that look at the problem of managing programmers in a new way. Chapter 2 explores technical management, a topic that MOPs will find familiar, but does so in a fresh way that looks at the challenges of managing individuals who produce abstract objects. Chapter 3 is concerned with work management and the productivity question, one that will mean less in the fourth generation of work but that oppresses software shops everywhere now. Personnel management is the topic of Chapters 4 and 5; a variety of theories are presented and their possible applications discussed.

Prospering within any organization presents difficulties, but seemingly more so for programmers. Although they have some commonalities with other technical, scientific, and research workers, one important quality that stands out for MOPs is the ignorance and antagonism the software shop and the firm seem to have for each other. Chapter 6 looks at this and proposes a number of solutions.

Career planning in an immature field is almost impossible. As programming matures, however, it is becoming imperative for the maturing MOP to begin planning careers into, through, and out of DP management. The information revolution is providing opportunities for MOPs that did not exist 10 years ago and MOPs can and should take advantage of them. This is the topic of Chapter 7.

Finally, Chapter 8 makes some clearer prognostications about the final two decades of programming and programming management. The trends, rather than the specific predictions, are what MOPs should be alerted to. The revolution that will proliferate fourth-generation jobs is now gathering steam. MOPs are uniquely prepared to lead this revolution, yet they remain solidly, and usually willingly, frozen in early twentieth-century manufacturing molds, curiously ready to follow precisely what the rest of society is apprehensively waiting for them to lead. The final notes of this book are a call for leadership. Perhaps this call is naive, but then so are the followers of all leaders in all our history.

The preparation of this book owes a debt of gratitude to many third- and fourth-generation people. John Francis Lubin, of the University of Pennsylvania's Wharton School, was my first employer—and the first to call me a "professional" in public. It was in his shop that the baseball game I've mentioned was played. Amanda Poor (née Rasinski) was my first skilled manager. The others with whom I worked during these five years each contributed to the growth of my fourth-generation hypothesis.

To Sol Worth, who was my thesis supervisor and who died tragically young, in 1977, a posthumous thanks for introducing me to anthropology and helping channel my bit-ridden energies into the proper study of mankind. Over the years, others have contributed in measures of varying sizes, but Sol, and Klaus Krippendorff, mentor, teacher, and friend at the Annenberg School of Communications, had the greatest influence on me.

Many thanks to John Mahaney, who was the general editor for this manuscript, and to the many reviewers he prodded into service critically looking over this project. His faith in the value of this book and the reviewers' insightful comments helped shape a lump of bytes into a tightly linked list of text elements. Nina Lewis provided the original "New York Connection" and Elias Awad much encouragement along the line. Students who survived my courses in Systems Analysis, Systems Design, DP Management, and my seminars in the Management of Programmers at the University of Calgary contributed far more than I to this project.

Finally, I'd like to thank the beautiful and gracious Marilyn Miller of Montreal, my consort and social-science consultant for this book. Marilyn, my wife, has taught me everything I know about people in social systems. Adeptly aided by her three lab assistants, Andrew, Sandy, and Aaron, our attempt at direct programming of a human being has been successful and now I do everything they instruct me to do. Considering that I am one of the third generation of Lickers this side of the Atlantic it is appropriate that I thank the fourth generation for their help in keeping my spirits up while preparing the manuscript. I hope it will help them at the end of this century.

Reader, I take no credit for any good ideas you derive from this book. University teaching experience demonstrates that learners teach themselves. If you are confused, send me an angry letter and I'll prepare a fourth-and-a-half generation version. If I insult any programmers, I hope none of them bytes me. Logout.

PAUL S. LICKER

*January 1985*
*Calgary, Alberta*

# CONTENTS

# The Art of Managing Software Development People

CHAPTER ONE

# MANAGEMENT OF PROGRAMMERS
## A New Profession

In the 40 years since the invention of the electronic digital computer, two human generations have passed. In technical parlance, four "generations" of computers have evolved; there is even talk of a fifth. But with respect to the management of software development, with little exception, technique lags in generation one or two. Unlike, say, management in engineering or construction, two other industrial areas heavily modified by technology, the technique of management of human resources in the data processing software shop remains very much as it was in the 1950s.

This book is a response to a need that is apparent in software development. "Over schedule and over budget" is the rule rather than the exception. Except for brief periods during the worst recessions, turnover is rampant, and loyalty to the employer is almost nonexistent among programmers. From the employees' viewpoint, too, there is much to be desired from management. While the software they develop becomes increasingly sophisticated, relations between programmer and manager remain shockingly primitive. Every issue of *ComputerWorld*, *Datamation*, and *Data Management* contains a disproportionate share of articles with titles like "How to Motivate Your Employees," "DP Productivity Shocking, Says Consultant," "How XYZ Manufacturing Gets Along Without Any Programmers," "Shift Program Development to Your Users." What is the basic problem here? How can the industry respond to a 40-year "crisis" seemingly getting worse yearly? Most important, how does the new software manager or the programmer or analyst who desires to become a supervisor cope with these problems? This book addresses these and related questions.

Three major areas are addressed; the highlights are presented in this chapter and more details given in the following ones. First, although programmers share many of the characteristics of other technical workers (notably engineers), there are a number of important differences for which allowance should be made. This book contends that programmers are the vanguard of a transition to "fourth-generation employees."

Second, the technology has outstripped not only the application of computers but also the ability of technically minded individuals—those most likely to become supervisors of programmers—to cope with development pressures in the traditional project environment. This is changing rapidly, but not in a way very favorable to the development of good management practices.

Third, in the past, there has been little emphasis on management in software development. It has been almost as though the technology was so good that, no matter how bad the management, something profitable would result. Now, however, there are a number of incompatible responses to this need. New environments for software development have been designed. Some firms are moving software development to the user side. Others respond by severely restricting programmer latitude through development tools. Still others now purchase their software from other users or buy general packages that a small software staff customizes. A market for project management packages has grown in the last five years. Some of them replace important supervisory functions with mechanical procedures.

These three trends are the focus of the book. Essentially they boil down to changes in personnel management and development, a drastic change in resource and technical management within the organization, and increasingly important changes in project and work management. These trends have important implications in the recruitment, development, day-to-day activities, and career progression of managers of programmers. This book chronicles these changes and provides some pointers on how to move with them.

In the book we use the term "MOP" as an acronym standing for "Manager of Programmers." This term has been coined only for this book. Other terms, notably "Lead Programmer," "Chief Programmer," "Programming Supervisor," "Head of Software Development," and "Director of Programming" are used, and some have particular nuances of meaning. Here a MOP is anyone with at-least-supervisory authority in a software shop, but does not typically include the person often called "Head of Data Processing" or "Data Processing Director." Thus the emphasis here is on supervisors rather than on current middle management, on operations rather than on strategy. These other regions of management and their activities are very important, but the problems are different and lie within different spheres.

## 1.1. A NEW PROFESSION

Our interest here is in a new application of technical management. The application is so new that we may almost speak of a "new profession," and the evidence is very much that there is a new profession in the making.

The electronic professions, such as programming, engineering of computers, the sales and maintenance of the equipment, and the administration of these functions are relatively new. Compared with civil engineering, accounting, and law, which derive from precivilization roots, the electronic professions are all less than 75 years of age. They derive from the great inventions of the first half of the twentieth century, from a time when, seemingly, it was more important to create than to understand what to do with the creation. ENIAC was born from a need to defend the Free World, but when the world was defended, few felt the computer would have much use, that more than a few dozen would ever be created and sold.

Therefore the electronic professions seldom strayed very far from their origins in engineering and sales. To this day, the technology far outstrips the application, and applications far outstrip the ability of organizations to manage the innovation. The example of office automation stands as mute evidence. Little of the problem in evolving toward wide-scale introduction of automated offices stems from either the technology or application. The major barrier is managing that introduction. Trade magazines devote an inordinate amount of space to the "DP/WP War" for control of office computer resources. Obviously management expertise is not in place to guide the application of the technology. Instead, office automation is being managed as though it were the typing pool, the telephone switchboard, or, in some cases, the production software shop.

Why has this management problem occurred? There are several reasons. First, the origins of data processing management are generally in office operations. This is not traditionally a place for innovation. The office is an overhead item, not a producing profit center. Second, software development itself has its roots in the engineering laboratory. The "Gyro Gearloose" mad scientist—or more appropriately, the whiz-kid second-year-graduate-student-turned-data-processing-director—ran the show. High security, high cost, and a technical jargon all its own made data processing off-limits to general management. Third, while the technology evolved at a whirlwind pace, users and managers became even more estranged from control and then interest in what happened in a DP shop. In response to this, and not entirely blamelessly, those working in a DP shop grew increasingly arrogant about their aptitudes, far out of proportion to their traditional importance to the firm. Fourth, as actual importance increased, a new business discipline—Management Information Systems (MIS)—developed, again with its own jargon, rules, goals, and management spirit. And again, there was decreased contact, formalized through the cult of the Systems Analyst—a kind of high priest or priestess who translated between the computer jargon and the jargon of work. Systems analysis,as a discipline, has its origins in industrial engineering and operations and methods (O & M)—these latter are the ranks of the feared efficiency experts.

Finally, this isolation has brought about strong inbreeding. DP managers are taken exclusively from within the DP shop itself. While this is seen as both necessary (who else speaks our language?) and good (it develops the team in the back room), it is the most powerful determiner of the lack of success in data processing management generally and software development management in particular. As we discuss in great detail in Chapters 4 through 6, there is little in programming and not much more in systems analysis that prepares a technical person to become a manager, and little in the typical DP shop that enables a worker to develop a broad organizational view so necessary to success in management.

Therefore, while programmers achieved the so-well-deserved name of "computerniks," their managers, who were mostly the better and somewhat older programmers, earned the labels "inefficient" and "ineffective" from users. Couger and Zawacki's (1980) book *Motivating and Managing Data Processing Personnel* details well how programmers and their managers respond to the situation by substituting a need for the technology (termed by Couger and Zawacki "growth need strength") for a need for people (which Couger and Zawacki call "social need strength").

We are now into the modern times (after 1965) of the so-called "third generation" of computing. Programmers still have a reputation for being hermits and wacko individualists. Their managers still have the reputation of being poor planners and terribly expensive users of corporate resources. Electronic data processing (EDP) management generally is given huge budgets. Why not? Every project, whether it be for automating order entry or improving the performance of the typing pool, seems to meet with success. This occurs while other departments scream for funds, people, and resources. The Golden Boy of the corporation is universally hated.

Three aspects of the growing pains of the programming profession are these: (1) DP as a whole will develop its own traditions; (2) the definitions and career paths for DP professionals will stabilize; and (3) the technology will eventually slow down in its speed of change. While programming is not yet a "mature" profession—not yet completely defined, not yet fixed in management techniques, not yet well-defined in terms of career paths—it is typical of the new *fourth generation* of jobs. The farmer, the artisan, and the factory worker produce physical products that can be directly experienced during production. The fourth-generation "knowledge" worker comprehends the product only through the means of an electronic digital tool, which describes it to him or her. Each successive generation of worker has found both narrowed field of vision over the product and increased control over production. The programmer is typical of the fourth-generation worker who can claim total control over production of the products. The field of software engineering attempts to remove the final traces of chance from software production.

Programmers represent the first workers whose products lie within this fourth generation. Is it surprising that traditional management techniques and measures are inappropriate? Should one expect programmers to work as though they were in a factory?

In this book, we're concerned with helping MOPs survive the transition, for most programmers are treated as third-generation, factory workers. In many important ways they are not. The MOP has to know what the differences are if the transition to fourth-generation status is to be survived.

## 1.2. THE MANAGER OF PROGRAMMERS

Who is the MOP? What are the responsibilities of this person? What background, skills, attitudes, and goals should this person have? What is the typical day of the MOP like?

The MOP is typically a promoted programmer, someone with 2 to 10 years of experience in programming, and typically quite good. There have been several studies of programmers and their qualities. Studies of MOPs are rare. Often we may extrapolate from what is known about programmers to MOPs simply because we know that the majority of MOPs achieved their positions because of excellence as programmers.

In a recent study of skills required of programmers, analysts, and information systems managers, a number of interesting things were discovered. When asked to indicate how important certain skills were for these three vocational groupings, information systems managers generally noted that technical skills were important for programmers and analysts while people-oriented skills were crucial for managers. There was little correlation between those skills seen as necessary for successful programming and those necessary for successful management. But most MOPs are promoted "successful" programmers! How can they be successful as managers?

We return to that crucial question soon. In order to "manage programmers," the MOP must concentrate efforts in three areas: resource or technical management, product or project management, and personnel management (see Figures 1.1 and 1.2).

*Resource management* includes the planning and procurement of software development resources, successful allocation of these resources to projects and groups, accounting for the resources and review of resource maintenance requirements. These resources might be software development tools (compilers, packages, design

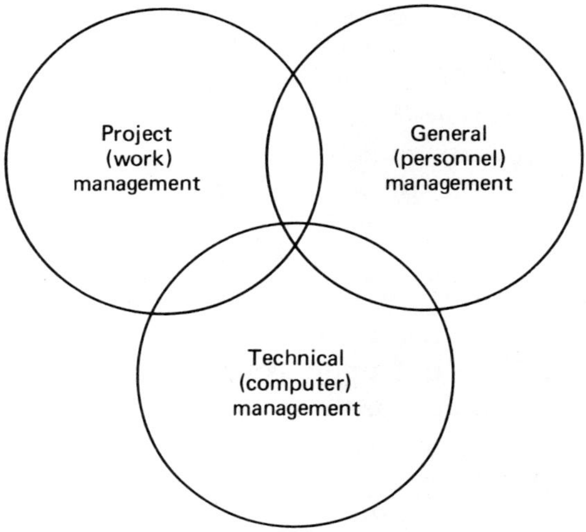


**FIGURE 1.1** Three components of management of programmers.

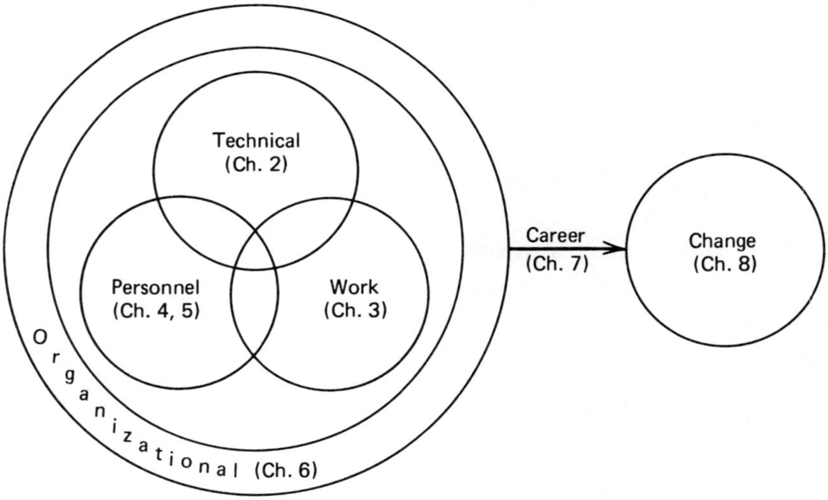


**FIGURE 1.2** Interlocking managerial functions in this book.

tools), computer hardware (terminals, modems, disk and memory allocations), system resources (account codes, CPU time, microcomputers, passwords), or management resources (access to managers' time, meetings, reports, forms). Resource management is discussed in Chapters 2 and 3.

*Product management* may occupy a large percentage of the typical MOP's time. Usually this occurs because the managerial aspects of the job are secondary to the need to produce software products, and the MOP must supervise this effort closely. A part of Chapter 2 is devoted to project management.

*Personnel management*, or what others have termed "general" or "human resource management," constitutes the bulk of the time a MOP spends outside technical discussions. Personnel management activities include hiring and developing staff, controlling work, directing activities, providing guidance and counseling, arguing, convincing, and deciding upon courses of action. Research has shown that the average executive spends from 40 to 90% of each working day in oral conversation with others. In first-level managerial jobs the proportion is smaller. Still, whether comfortable or not, the MOP can expect to spend over half the working day speaking with people face-to-face, in meetings, or on the telephone. Aspects of personnel management comprise the major part of this book. Chapters 3 through 6 examine these activities in great detail. Chapter 7 looks at the career of a MOP, providing some guidance for career planning.

A MOP can therefore be seen as a person who manages software development resources, who undertakes and controls projects to create software products, and who manages people who happen to be programmers. On the other hand, there are a number of things that a MOP is *not*.

A MOP is first and foremost not a programmer. True, the manager of programmers might have been the best programmer around two years ago. The chances are large that the MOP is no longer even a passably good programmer. Nor should the MOP consider programming something that should be undertaken by himself or herself. Although all technical employees appreciate a manager who can empathize and understand the activities and difficulties at a technical level, they simply do not like—and the MOP can ill afford—to have a manager look over their shoulders, perhaps competing with them. The problem of *delegating* responsibilities and *trusting* programmers to carry them out is a common one.

The MOP is neither a consultant nor a chief programmer. A consultant is a person brought into the organization from outside or someone occupying an important, and neutral, position inside the organization. The MOP can be fair and polite, but there is no way the

MOP can remain neutral and employed. A consultant is hired for specific, usually technical, skills to apply to a single problem area. The MOP is required to be a generalist who understands the technical area well. Consultants are often tied to single projects; the MOP manages several in various stages. The chief programmer is the person recognized for superior program development skills. A MOP probably has excellent skills as a programmer, but is expected to take a far broader organizational view.

Although the MOP manages some of the system's resources as they pertain to programming, the MOP is not a system manager. That is an operations job. Instead, the MOP represents the software development group to DP management in pursuit of a fair proportion of the system's time and resources and fair access to these resources *consistent with the system manager's operational plans*. Usually there are disagreements (i.e., there are too many requests for the scarce resources represented by the system), and the MOP has to present arguments convincingly that the software development group needs specific resources. This is one important reason why a broader view is necessary.

Finally, a MOP is not merely a supervisor, someone who "rides herd" on projects and programmers, making sure the work is done. This *is* a crucial responsibility. But it is not the only one. The MOP is also responsible for planning—short-term as well as long-term—policy in software development, team development, and organization. Directing and controlling work is but one aspect of the MOP activity package.

## 1.3. THE CHALLENGES OF MANAGING PROGRAMMERS

Five challenges face the MOP. These are:

1. The uniqueness of programmers as workers.
2. The uniqueness of programming work itself.
3. The short supply of programmers relative to the funds to pay them.
4. The difficulty of managing change in an organization.
5. The problem of career development.

Programmers are similar to other technical workers. But there are some important differences. Recent survey research has demonstrated that programmers, as well as other DP personnel and their managers, demonstrate a very low need for socialization. As previously cited, this social need strength (SNS) is the lowest of any professional group—in fact, given the way the survey was conducted, an immediate interpretation of the results is that programmers are actually on the average "indifferent" to the presence of others. Their managers score little higher, while other managers scored quite high. In addition, programmers, compared with other professionals tend to feel that their jobs entail lowered responsibility and provide less feedback. In other words, although programmers do not see their *jobs* as being much different from other technical work, they do feel differently about *themselves* in their jobs when compared to other professionals.

The research merely puts numbers on the long-standing stereotypes about programmers: they love their machines, but not their co-workers, managers, and users. Research has not yet shown us where this set of attitudes comes from. However, several possibilities exist.

Programmers tend to be quite young, as are their managers. Programmer training has tended to emphasize technical skills such as programming languages, use of packages, logical problem solving, and the like. University education in MIS or DP has emphasized long hours of debugging COBOL programs and very few hours of argument, negotiation, and understanding. Most MIS programs and the bulk of DP programs (the difference between the two may be academic!) require only the minimum university education in literature, history, the arts, and the social sciences, areas in which human relations are paramount.

The selection process for programmers again stresses only computer-related skills. It is reasonable to expect that social skills would be at best only as good as those in other professions and, given the strong selection on computer programming language proficiency, probably a great deal lower. This in turn leads to the image of the profession as one involving service to the machine, dissuading those who might enter it for social reasons such as working with other people. The vicious circle, when augmented by the *actual* isolation of DP and programming from organizational channels for learning about people and the organization, can only lead to a natural selection of technicians over gabbers, of machine-tenders over comforters.

Other work on motivation and job satisfaction among programmers points out that technical challenge in the form of learning about the computer overwhelms the motivation to work with others. Programmers, like engineers, like to build, but they may not like talking about their products very much with anyone.

Programming work is also unique in several ways. To start with, there is the programming language, and the technical jargon in project management has tended to fragment the work so that almost no interaction among programmers is needed, heightening the tendency to work alone. A great deal of the technical supervision of a project is left to software development tools, primarily compilers, database management systems, and operating systems monitors. Intervention by a supervisor for difficult problems is seldom feasible, for the supervisor is probably no longer expert in the problem area.

An even greater difficulty is that, until quite recently, the programmer's product was invisible. The famous "90% complete" diversion used for years by programmers to keep managers off their backs has now fallen into disfavor. But there is still the difficulty that programmers must document their programs before anyone can understand what the program is or does—and documentation is not seen as profitable labor by most programmers. It presents no technical challenges and provides no opportunity for learning. Furthermore, no one will cheer reading documentation, especially the manager, who will probably find problems with it. Reintegrating the programming group and providing a common language for conversation other than COBOL is the primary team-building problem facing the personnel manager.

The economic dislocation caused by the severe shortage of programmers and other DP personnel is well known to all DP managers. Starting salaries for programmers are inflated out of all proportion to programmers' actual contribution to a firm's profit or function. Twenty years ago a programmer might point proudly to a 95% gain in productivity in a clerical area owing to a specific program. Now, complex programs with complex interfaces to managers and other professionals cannot be so easily credited with observable productivity gains. Until recently DP represented a cost-reduction opportunity. DP departments were not profit centers. With prototyping, decision-support systems, and end-user software generation, the DP department itself is under scrutiny, and the work of a programmer may no longer justify hiring one. Evidence of this is the effect of charge-back policies on the backlog of DP requests. In one firm, the backlog dropped from three years to zero with the simultaneous introduction of an Information Center and a charge-back policy that established a cost of $475 daily for a senior programmer and $225 for a college co-op student.

Turnovers in the range of 30 to 50% annually were common until recently, and seemingly acceptable to those in charge of software development. The trade literature abounds with articles on turnover, its effects, and its prevention. This book argues that turnover is a symptom of the demographics of the software workforce and of the total lack of any coherent career pathing for programmers. Instead of providing true careers *within* an organization, management seems satisfied to string a programming career *across* organizations. The resulting lack of firm loyalty is seen as worth the gain a firm gets in not having to promote anyone. Chapter 7 discusses career pathing in detail.

Another implication of the short supply of programmers is the low esteem in which the DP Department is held in most firms. Until quite recently, DP was a cost center, and a greedy one at that. Now the department is asked to justify its costs not only in terms of cost reduction elsewhere in the firm, but also in terms of how DP contributes to income. This is a difficult proposition. With programmers in short supply, there is little chance of selecting programmers who might rise through the hierarchy in DP and elsewhere to carry that important technical expertise to the boardroom to help meet this challenge.

Finally, as is the case with doctors and lawyers, programmers and other DP workers are both the beneficiaries and the victims of pervasive myths about computers in society. In legends, those who tend the gods are priests or priestesses, conduits of our wishes and pledges to the All-Powerful ones. Programmers are seen in society as having some of these qualities. Since programmers speak COBOL, APL, and SIMSCRIPT, they can talk to computers and make our wishes known to them.

Unfortunately, being able to speak COBOL doesn't qualify one to understand an errant vehicle registration system or the motorist whose license has not been renewed because of an error. And equally unfortunately, this aura of mathematical virtuosity discourages many otherwise qualified individuals from seeking work in the field.

Tests have shown that math is only one, small, aspect of a programmer's skill repertoire. General symbolic aptitudes, such as found in architects and engineers, but also in musicians, poets, and anthropologists, are far more important. Until programming is thought of and taught as a *communication* skill rather than a mathematical one, it will continue to attract those of one particular bent and discourage those who might provide additional, and needed, attitudes.

The MOP works with individuals in a period of great change. Coping with this change may take all of a manager's time. Not only is a manager instantly obsolete with regard to programming the moment of promotion from the programming ranks (except those who continue to program), but there is no time to "retrofit" afterwards. Two-thirds of a manager's day is spent gathering information, not making technical decisions. The higher a manager goes in the hierarchy, the greater the long-range, nontechnical responsibilities. Managers do not read manuals; they do not read the magazines and tech report services they subscribe to; they have little time to attend seminars. Instead they attend meetings, often ill-prepared for the slick sales pitches from vendors and uninformative staff meetings called by their own managers or by themselves. At these meetings and in these conversations, they must interpret the rapidly changing needs of the organization for information in terms their rapidly changing staff can understand to produce software to run in a rapidly changing machine environment. An example is that make-or-buy decisions often become moot. By the time the decision has been taken, someone has already made it for lease or purchase.

Finally, there is the problem of the day after tomorrow: a career. Given a turnover of 40%, it is statistically likely that, over a four-year period, only 20% of your original staff remains employed by you. Four out of five will have chosen to make their careers in other organizations. What do you do with those left? In four years, almost everything they know is out of date. You have surely changed mainframes or operating systems (or gone through four to ten releases of the operating system) and probably have installed at least two major development-related packages such as database management system, a programmer's toolkit, or a project management system such as SDM/70, SPECTRUM, or the like. But few of the 20% remaining may ever be promoted. You may give them increased responsibilities in project management (typically control of timesheets), and some of them can help you plan, but primarily they spend all their time chasing after the technology you have helped introduce. They *say* they feel satisfied. After all, you have provided technical challenges. Meanwhile, none of them can become systems analysts unless by chance they have become specialized in a particular application area for programs (this can happen—you should encourage it). More likely, however, they will specialize in a bit-and-byte area: understanding language X's peculiarities, doing I/O in assembler-level routines, telecommunications packages, figuring out how to program for a now-obsolete piece of equipment, or fancy code. Many will develop and market their own software tools within the programming group, approaching you only at the last minute to have it adopted as an aid, never mind as a standard. When things slow down a bit (they never do), you might send one or two of them on a course. They'll be two weeks behind when they return.

Most firms publish "ideal" career paths for programmers. There are two conceptions, the career ladder and the dual path system. The first provides increasing organizational responsibilities and technical breadth (programmer/analyst/operator manager/DP executive). The second provides increasing technical responsibility for those without management futures (junior programmer/programmer/senior programmer/chief programmer). Neither helps the firm much or profits the employee in the long run. Historically most programmers progress along the lower tier system and eventually are shuffled into a project management position, without any chance for meaningful advancement into management or analysis. They know that they don't have the skills for management or the in-depth user knowledge required for systems analysis. Those who follow a career ladder become MOPs, sometimes without appropriate training except experience from another untrained MOP who muddled through. The MOP, too, knows that the broad organizational view and experience necessary for an executive position is hidden from view in the bowels of the DP department despite its organization-wide mandate. What to do the day after tomorrow is rarely a consideration of the harried MOP, but when one is faced with the possibility of a lot of free days, one has to consider it.

## 1.4. MEETING THE CHALLENGES OF PROGRAMMER MANAGEMENT

These five challenges are not insurmountable, but they are difficult. Organizations change slowly, more slowly than the people and technology they employ. It is likely that you are reading this book because you are faced with one or more of these challenges and feel that *you* must change to meet them. This section provides general background material on where these challenges can be met and discusses some way to meet them. The remaining chapters of the book give details.

To repeat the challenges in one sentence, the MOP is faced with managing a unique kind of worker doing a unique kind of work in a rapidly changing technological environment with an undersupply of these workers in an unsure organizational climate for advancement.

The uniqueness of programmers is indeed a challenge, but since the MOP is probably a former programmer, at least there is a great deal of empathy already established between management and the employees. Build upon this empathy. After all, *you* had to learn half a dozen arcane languages, *you* had to put up with frequent and seemingly arbitrary system changes, and *you* had to put up with error-ridden specs, users with no knowledge of computers, and an organization that seemed unconcerned with your special technical abilities.

If programming work is indeed isolated, fragmented, and relatively invisible, programmers are not. It is possible to create teams and develop a team spirit even among hermits. Many of the newer techniques involve meetings and reviews of code and designs. These encourage the development of communication skills and a spirit of cooperation in the programming staff. Research in motivation and job satisfaction vividly underscores that relations with managers are typically poor. You must take the initiative here, since all the cues in the work environment convince the programmer to back off. The major component of poor relations with management is lack of feedback on work progress and lack of feedforward of work plans. There is no reason to keep the former secret. There is no reason not to share the latter. In fact, the two-way flow of information upward and downward through you is the only way the programming group is going to participate in the organization's activities. Communication is the primary tool you have to meet the challenge of work styles.

DP managers toss and turn in their beds at night having nightmares about "programmer productivity." The concern arises because of the shortage of programmers and the high cost of software. Although there are many measures of productivity (and we review several), the issue is primarily a red herring. Of far more importance are the estimation of software development costs and providing feedback to the programmer on work progress. While these are, of course, related to productivity measurement, they go beyond the issue of "Are programmers producing (enough)?" to the issue of "What does it mean to have a producing programmer on staff?" Productivity *per se* is only vaguely related to the value of the product. Ten thousand lines of COBOL code may cost you $10,000; you may be able to purchase the same code in firmware for $500.

Data processing management presents the unique problem of managing rapid change. Academic work on this topic reassures us with its results. Change can be managed and people can be managed in a changing environment. The role of the MOP and, as well, the role of the data processing shop is undergoing swift but coherent change, when seen from a distance. From a service group that tinkers with hardware, the DP shop is transmogrifying into a profit center. Management of technological change in a profit center appears different from management of change in a service organization. This is so because instead of focusing upon the need to keep up with the technology in order to produce more, better, faster, the profit center focuses upon the nature of the product produced and plans to acquire appropriate tools. Detroit was caught with its pants down in the face of the Robotics Revolution, and so far DP management appears heading down the same embarrassing path. However, DP product management can be planned coherently with the appropriate software development tools and management techniques borrowed from marketing and finance.

Finally, the challenge of the career in data processing cannot be met only by rational career planning. This kind of planning is easy only in a stable vocation, and data processing has not yet stabilized. This is evidenced by predictions every five years that in five years there will be no more programmers. In fact, however, the astute MOP will view a career as embracing, but not being limited to, data processing. Traditional "careers" in data processing do not yet exist. However, management is a profession in its own right, and one can see data processing management in general and programmer management in particular as merely one exotic flavor of management. With this view, it is possible to construct a career plan for an individual MOP. Chapter 7 looks at this question and provides a career planning model.

## 1.5. IDEALS AND PRACTICALITIES

The ideal MOP is a technical person who has managerial skills and a broad organizational view with respect to computer-based products. That is, the ideal MOP knows the technology (hardware and software), understands people and what motivates them, and can translate the needs of the organization for the software development group's products into terms the MOP's employee can relate to.

The ideal MOP is, however, an ideal. In order to meet this ideal, one would have to acquire a bag of skills that cannot be collected in only one or two places. Consider this list deemed necessary in one description of a MOP:

1. Is responsible for work under his or her direction.
2. Reviews and accepts program specs.
3. Prepares time and cost estimates.
4. Participates in hardware and software evaluations.
5. Advises management on programming and related matters.
6. Defines programming staff functions.
7. Directs programming staff functions.
8. Initiates and directs system performance appraisals.
9. Recommends, develops, and enforces standards.
10. Is in charge of maintaining existing programs.
11. Specifies training requirements.
12. Recommends hiring and firing.
13. Coordinates group efforts.
14. Seeks improved methods for programming.
15. Develops departmental policies.

This 15-year-old job description places little emphasis on supervision of employees, but it is apparent that in order to carry out these tasks, the ideal MOP must be a technical whiz as well as an all-round-nice-guy and politician. Considering that the MOP speaks for up to 20 or more people who speak only COBOL to an organization that is only concerned (typically) with cost control, the responsibilities are onerous. No wonder the job is hard.

The reality is different. You have maybe a university degree in computer science or business, but it is equally as likely that you have an Associate degree or even a certificate in DP. You may have entered your current position through promotion, but possibly you came from another firm, having found your challenges not worth the perks there. More than likely, this is your third job in five years and you've got far more contact with your colleagues in ASM or DPMA than you do with anyone working for your current employer outside the shop. Over these five years you've picked up a lot of COBOL and APL to complement the BASIC and basic COBOL you learned in earning your sheepskin. You've adapted to two or three machine environments and as many or more operating systems. In five years you became an "expert" at something—let's imagine it's file layouts for a particular mass storage device or retrieval packages using a DBMS. You feel comfortable with the technology, but you're tired of swimming in currents you cannot control. In five years you've had three supervisors, and while one was OK, two were terrible. Anything you've learned about supervision has been by bad example. Your interaction with users has been good, though. In one project, maybe, a user understood your need to interpret the technology and guided you skillfully in making that interpretation. In another project, you dealt with a particularly intelligent user, who wanted to learn, learn, learn—and let you know you'd done a good job. Your strong background in one application area let you see more of how the firm worked and how important software was. When a MOP job came vacant in another company, you took your applications experience, your DBMS expertise, and your five years of successful employment, and got a job managing others.

In other words, you have no training for your job and little opportunity to learn from it while you struggle to "direct, review, prepare, advise, define, initiate, develop, enforce, maintain, specify, hire, fire, coordinate, improve, and train." The practical facts are that all you know about management is that you shouldn't manage like your former boss. The new organization is different from the old one, and the Director of Data Processing has some really super ideas about hardware expansion—which translates into one heck of a lot of work for the Software Development Department. The users are the typical bunch: ill-informed, pressured, and demanding. Your 10 employees are turning out code by the bushel basket, but you haven't the time to look at it, even if they'd let you. Two are leaving next month and two aren't talking to you because you don't know FORTRAN and that's what they know. Today a user phoned and said that the sorts came out backwards and he followed the instructions and the analyst said to call you because it had to be a software problem, and what are you going to do about it? Read this book.

## 1.6. TWO CASES IN MANAGEMENT OF PROGRAMMERS

The following minicases represent the range of challenges facing the MOP. The first case looks generally at the question of coping with managing a team of programmers. The other wonders aloud whether or not you can take the kid out of programming without taking programming out of the kid.

### *Case 1. "Manage? I Can't Even Cope!"*

From Frank's point of view it was no laughing matter. For seven months Frank's tried managing his small shop of programmers, charged mostly with maintaining a fair-sized marketing and sales analysis system. Everything went well until the time for his first weekly departmental status report. Since he had been a programmer himself, he understood that most of what he asked for was difficult to get. But he couldn't get his workers to play along. Then there was the problem of Julie's time off. She couldn't have it because the department would have been short-handed and she's being very prune-faced about it. And Ted! Sure, Frank understood that specs were "only" guidelines, but did Ted have to ignore them so completely and so publicly? It was embarrassing to have Ted show up at code reviews with code no one recognized.

Karen, too, had her quirks. You can't criticize anything about her work. She's *so* sensitive. And lately she's been after Frank for advanced communication courses. There's no use for any of those packages in Frank's shop, but it's in vogue at most of the large banks and retail establishments in the region. Is Karen "shopping around"? Maybe it's that awful performance review Frank did with her last month. Or could it be the way Ted treats her at staff meetings? She is so outspoken for such a sensitive person. Maybe that's why Ted is such a pill.

They're all pills, even Frank's old friends from Systems Analysis, where Frank worked before being promoted to Software Development Manager. Gosh, those analysts really throw their weight around, thought Frank. Manage? I can't even cope! □

Frank's got a number of things to learn about management before he can begin to cope. Programmers aren't machines; they are people with the usual (and some *un*usual) problems. Frank's experiences as programmer and analyst have only barely begun preparing him for life as a supervisor. Those status reports may have been silly and difficult for him as a worker, but he's got to motivate his staff to fill them out correctly now. Julie's pouting is her problem, not Frank's; she's got to be assisted in seeing that it is the survival of the *team* that is foremost on Frank's mind now. Ted's shenanigans only damage Ted; Frank will have to provide leadership to Ted, and Julie too. Since neither Ted nor Julie—nor probably Frank either—has much of an appreciation for the firm and its goals, it is unlikely that their attitudes will die easily of their own accord.

Karen's sensitivity stems naturally from her self-appointed role as prima donna programmer. Frank's suspicion of her motives in wanting courses is blinding him to Karen's need to excel and be rewarded by recognition. This is only compounded by Frank's obvious inability to judge the performance of his workers well. It is clear that Frank tolerates inappropriate behavior and poor interpersonal relations because he's enamored of the product (software) and not necessarily the producers (programmers). This all contributes to Frank's confusion about his ever having left systems analysis.

Meanwhile, his former colleagues see him properly as the representative of the programming group. The usual tension between programming and systems analysis strains the strong bonds of collegiality that existed in the past. Frank no longer sees himself in any proper role. He's not a programmer, not an analyst, and not a manager—at least not yet! Meanwhile, the analysts have to get on with the job, however confused *Frank* is.

It is likely that, without training in management, Frank will adopt a mechanical approach to the management of programmers that so often characterizes others' responses. Frank wants weekly status reports, smoothly functioning staff meetings, rigid adherence to specs, loyal employees, and close relations with other departments. Unless he discovers how to get these skillfully, he will end up demanding them or else. As we see in Chapter 5, legitimate power (the power to order others to work) is the weakest of all a manager's powers. Frank needs to utilize his *expert* power, derived from his knowledge of the firm and his group's role in it.

To build loyalty, Frank should learn team-building and provide the rewards programmers crave, such as recognition and a chance to learn. If Frank is going to improve interpersonal relations among his staffers, he will have to learn how to conduct reviews and meetings in a nonthreatening way, how to present himself to his staff, and how to create an atmosphere of cooperation rather than competition.

In order to maintain good relationships with other departments, Frank will have to understand the role of the software group vis-à-vis other groups in DP and in the firm. He will come to see "influence" not as "weight" but as organizational communication. In short, Frank will learn how to cope when he learns how to manage.

### *Case 2. Managing from Afar*

Rita Northcott is a recently appointed Manager of Software Development for a Government Department that analyzes statistical business data. Rita really is not a programmer—all she knows is what she learned in one course in BASIC and a semester of COBOL with business applications. Both were required courses in her graduate business program. She got her job because of her superior management skills and her experiences as a user of statistical software. Her seven years as a statistical analyst, an MBA from an outstanding school, and an unblemished record of accomplishment in producing reports and analyses on-time and in understandable terms made her a good bet to put Software Development on the right track. A somewhat unorthodox choice, to be sure, but a solid one.

Eight months into the job, Rita's turned the group around, built up its morale, and raised its credibility with the department's management. But several members of the group have resisted being managed by an "outsider." Stuart Thackery, for example, has six years as a coder, programmer, and programmer/analyst. He knows COBOL, assembler, APL, CICS, a dozen packages, and three methods of structured design. He cut his teeth on two different Univacs and single-handedly implemented a time-sharing monitor for a mini. Stu, in short, is a technical whiz. And in the past, Stu has had the run of the place, but now . . . he's not so sure.

Others, too, feel that while Rita is a good administrator, it would be nice if she knew a few packages. They have a lot of trouble relating to her at meetings. They want to talk shop and Rita insists upon discussing setting milestones and meeting them.

For her part, Rita wonders if her "success" is not merely a honeymoon period, and more a function of her personal style than any long-term change in the way the group works. She is certain that she is a better representative of the group to the outside world because of her user orientation. But she's having difficulty making her management activities carry any weight with her workers. □

Here's a typical example of why managing programmers is maddening sometimes. Because programming is an extremely technical job and because *esprit de corps* is essentially built around shop talk, MOPs without a strong programming background can easily feel left out. Resentment of MOPs who don't know the technology from the inside can accumulate with time no matter how well the MOP does at presenting the programming group's face to the rest of the firm. Programmers who have a very limited view of the firm and its goals simply do not understand why it is important, perhaps more important than demonstrating technical skills, to feel comfortable in the role of representative.

Most technical jobs are organized about the concept of service. That is, technicians are expected to keep the machinery going. Programmers, too, have this orientation, but since the machinery is changing under their fingers at the keyboard, they feel that they command it. The very language of programming ("instructions," "commands," "control") reinforces this image. A MOP who cannot provide this service and who cannot command the technology deserves only limited esteem in their eyes.

On the other hand, the narrow, specialized view of the career programmer is insufficient for the MOP who must not only *advocate* (i.e., argue for) the programming group, but also must *represent* the group as one among equals. A manager is not a foreman. The foreman sits atop the work and understands it so that the work can be forced through the assembly line at an appropriate rate. The manager plans the work, negotiates for it, and defends it to the customers. Thus the MOP needs organizational skills in addition to technical ones.

Rita has what Frank (Case 1) didn't have: knowledge about organizations and about the firm and its goals. Frank has what Rita doesn't have: detailed technical knowledge about the programming group and its products. Who is the better MOP?

So long as no one outside the programming group makes difficult demands on it, Frank will experience fewer major problems. He has competent, if somewhat difficult, employees, and they will continue to turn out programs almost "on command." In fact, however, they manage themselves with the advice and consent of Frank. Frank will crumble at the first tremors of dissent. If Karen actually does leave, if Ted actually fails to code correctly, if Julie decides to take time off anyway, Frank will fail miserably.

Rita has no problem handling threats to the group from outside, but she lacks the confidence necessary to deal with technical people at a technical level. On the other hand, resentment is an emotion with which Rita is capable of dealing. Rita understands that programmers need to be recognized as technical experts. She can arrange for this recognition in a number of ways. She is not the only one who is available to recognize talent, and forums such as conferences, demonstrations, and classrooms may provide arenas for recognition of the type Karen, Ted, and Julie obviously need. Meanwhile, Rita can withstand almost anything the firm throws at the group. It is likely that Rita can teach her group many skills of management; they can teach themselves programming.

Does this mean that the Franks of this world are doomed to be poor managers? No, not if they acquire and practice *management* skills. What, after all, does Rita have that Frank doesn't? Neither the MBA nor the user orientation are hers by birthright; Frank can study the same things. But Frank has to lose his narrow-minded viewpoint on the role of the programmer and acquire a broad, organizational perspective before he can be an effective manager. Rita, on the other hand, can merely learn PSA/PSL and impress the pants off her staff. Frank's got the harder job, because he cannot manage effectively in a turbulant environment so long as he doesn't understand how people and organizations function. If you empathize with Frank, read on. If you are a Rita, read on, too, for you need to understand what programmers want out of their jobs and managers.

CHAPTER TWO

# TECHNICAL MANAGEMENT

In this book, we distinguish between managing programmers and managing programming. The literature on the use of processors such as compilers and DBMS is large and only of peripheral concern in this chapter.

The management of the programmers who produce the software products is more difficult and less well documented, however. Aspects of technical management that look at how programmers work with resources form the content of this chapter. For instance, we are not concerned with how well a *compiler* works, but rather how well a *programmer* works with the compiler.

Technical management may be defined as matching tools, tasks, and resources with workers. By "matching" we mean planning, supplying, monitoring, and adapting the tools, tasks, and resources to the workers and their needs. As an alternative, we may also consider training workers in how to use the tools. For instance, one of the roles a technical manager has in the software shop is obtaining clear specs for the workers. This chapter looks at technical management as *obtaining appropriate resources for workers in order to get programming work done.*

There are three aspects to this. First there is *managing software development and maintenance*. This includes negotiating specifications, handling users and analysts, and settling disputes over software quality and maintainability. Since maintenance work forms such a large part of programming, MOPs will have to attend to maintainability aspects such as code clarity, documentation, and code conventions. In these areas, of course, technical management looks a lot like managing programming itself, and it is this interface between the code and the coder that often provides the most satisfying managerial challenges.

The second aspect is *the use of management resources*. These are the people, plans, and systems that enable a manager to allocate the firm's resources effectively. Standards, languages, meetings, and documentation are some of these resources.

The last aspect is *project management*. Since volumes are available on the topic, we do not cover specific project management techniques. Instead, we focus upon the boundaries of responsibility that project management necessitates in the software shop. Also of concern are organizational considerations and the "texture" of work in a project setting. We explore some alternatives to project organization and the impact of these alternatives on management style and technique.

## 2.1. MANAGEMENT OF SOFTWARE DEVELOPMENT AND MAINTENANCE

Managing software development efforts resembles management of any construction effort. Managing maintenance resembles other maintenance work in that it is often messy and rarely rewarded well. The differences are in the type of work and the way workers behave. An added factor is the nature of the product. Software is not like concrete, steel, or a leaky pipe—at least not usually.

There is little confusion in the traditional DP shop about what programming is. However, recent trends in off-loading software production to users through information centers and end-user developed software have blurred the definition somewhat. Since programming is only a part of the system development process, recently developed techniques for managing DP product delivery have also tended to blur the distinction between programming and systems analysis on the one hand (by the use of prototyping and end-user developed software) and operations on the other (through architecture-based—i.e., screen-driven—development and information centers).

We adopt, therefore, a relatively restricted definition of programming:

> *Programming is that set of activities that an individual performs to develop, test, deliver, and maintain computer software according to verbal and written specifications.*

Two major software development management goals arise from this definition:

1. Getting the software produced or maintained for delivery (the *production* goal).
2. Certifying that the software produced is in fact the desired product (the *certification* goal).

The first is the common factory aim of keeping production levels high. Managing software production is made all the more difficult in that the product is relatively intangible and unique. Programmers have unique programming styles—after all, the task is termed "writing" programs, not "fabricating" them—and MOPs may have difficulty obtaining the needed resources such as CPU time, port access, and terminals for their workers.

The second goal relates also to the intangibility of the product. Like a hammer, its value is known only when it is used. Unlike a hammer, however, it is a unique tool, one that probably has never existed before and that may be valuable only to a small group of peculiar and untrained individuals. Not only are there problems in testing a program, but there are difficulties in determining whether or not the specifications drawn up by the analysts are correct, correctable, acceptable, or implementable.

While some of these problems are technical and a knowledge of computer science or of specific machinery will be needed to puzzle them out, others are purely managerial. A common example is the sudden appearance of a high priority project that, because of time limitations, appears on the MOP's desk with the word *rush* across the title page, but that is incomplete and has an attached note indicating a delivery date of tomorrow. Is it worthwhile or even possible to complain? To whom should the MOP complain? What can the MOP say, anyway?

### 2.1.1. Technical Challenges

These aspects of software development and maintenance imply a number of technical challenges:

| Challenge | Implications | Solutions |
|---|---|---|
| Need to reduce backlog | Skimming, need for new management skills | New development procedures |
| Increased user involvement | Hiring more personnel | Develop human resource skills |
| Desire for accountability | Less time for planning, organizing | Delegation |
| Need for more feedback to programmers | More time spent with employees on their problems | Better human resource skills |
| Many more vested interests | More people around to interfere | Role clarification |
| More special work | Unique products | Standardization |
| Packaging of products | Increased pressure on maintenance | Shop standards, managing for maintainability |
| More worker variety | Decreased efficiency in resource use | Technical management skills needed |
| More project variety | Increased pressure on skill pool | Learn new organization techniques |
| Tighter budgets | More paperwork | Better plans, delegation |

Some of these challenges are discussed in more detail below.

There is an increasing backlog of requests for software development in large firms. This necessitates that the firms explore alternatives to software development, alternatives such as end-user development, prototyping, information centers, and fourth-generation languages. From the MOP's viewpoint, these strategies imply that the easier projects will be skimmed off, and the more difficult, less-well-defined, more arguable work will remain for the software development group. This implies a greater need for programming skill and management expertise.

Projects are moving perceptibly closer to the end user. Research has shown that product quality is enhanced with user involvement. But users also want to get involved now because they recognize the cost of ignorance. Managing a multidisciplinary team may prove fatal to the traditional technically minded MOP, however.

Programmers are requiring closer supervision, both on a personal basis and through the usual paperwork. Larger software staffs, greater demands on still inadequately staffed units, incrementally more difficult projects, and a general shift from computer whiz staffs to "employees" put an enormous burden on MOPs. Administrations are demanding more accountability at precisely that moment when MOPs have less time and fewer resources to do the accounting.

Projects are becoming more expensive. They are no longer merely in-house efforts using a couple of programmers and some computer time. Now projects use very expensive computer resources of a complex nature. Users have understood the grave implications of poor systems, too. They know what "down time" means and how it affects them; this awareness increases the pressure on budgets. Packages, vendor time, and borrowed equipment also appear in most major projects. Interested bystanders from government and industry regulators, clients, and auditors will check in from time to time and want to know how the dollars are being spent. The typical MOP may not be aware of these people until the first major project. When privacy legislation and copyright laws mature, the software shop may seem like a branch of the county courthouse.

Software projects are unique items. Unlike projects to build bridges or set up government welfare programs, programming usually produces a unique product: a single accounting system, a single inventory system. Rarely is experience on the previous system transferable; rarely is there much to build on. Parts of the old system cannot often be salvaged. While many staffers may have previously worked on accounting or inventory systems, it is only their experience, not their product that can be tranferred. In maintenance—on the opposite side of the coin—the emphasis is upon retaining or recovering the original design without creating a lot of disturbance.

These extremes make the job of supervising programmers difficult.

Other work may require revising software by customizing, tuning, front-ending, or back-ending.

MOPs are also expected to supervise an inordinately wide range of projects, both in size and type. These range from a one-line enhancement of a subroutine to the design and installation of a completely new on-line accounting system with—or without—the assistance of analysts or cooperative customers. Different techniques may prove appropriate for projects of such widely disparate sizes. Few MOPs have direct experience to tap for such endeavors.

Programmers, likewise, come with a wide variety of skills, attitudes, and backgrounds. They range from co-op students through apprentice coders and programmers to senior programmers. Some know only one language; other know ten—none of them well. The MOP has to supervise a shop in which these skill levels coexist. While this is a problem all managers face, it is usually easier to judge the difference in the finished product. Software is such that even the greenest apprentice coder can turn out a masterpiece given appropriate resources and documentation. The most seasoned veteran can create elegant garbage. Making certain appropriate resources are available is the MOP's main task.

The "in-house or buy" decision is another major technical challenge. Many packages are available in completely usable form for common business applications—it is no longer necessary to build most accounting, purchasing, inventory, forecasting, or scheduling software. Yet the temptation is strong to build rather than purchase because of the attendant problems in tailoring packages to specific business situations. Knowing when it is worthwhile to buy rather than build is a technical challenge that MOPs must face. These decisions depend critically upon the MOP's ability to forecast expenditures and the ability of the DP department to understand an application fully. Even then, the MOP may be faced with a bewildering array of completed software, software generators, or database managers with which to satisfy a need.

### 2.1.2. Strategies

These challenges must be met with general strategies. Three such general strategies prepare the MOP for detailed technical tactics. These are (1) obtaining adequate system specifications, (2) interfacing properly with the user, and (3) negotiating accountability for performance.

System specification depends greatly upon the project management system employed in a shop. Martin points out, in *Application Development without Programmers,* that many project management systems are inflexible, not allowing for important deviations such as prototyping, developmental approaches involving non-DP personnel, and informal consulting. Specs tend to be rigid and difficult to meet. An adequate system specification details (see Figure 2.1):

1. What software is to be delivered (traditionally, "the specs").
2. How well the software is to perform.
3. Who is to work on the software (both user and development personnel).
4. Which procedures will be followed to change specs.
5. When software will be certified (sign-off schedule).
6. Which resources are controlled by whom (where authority lies).

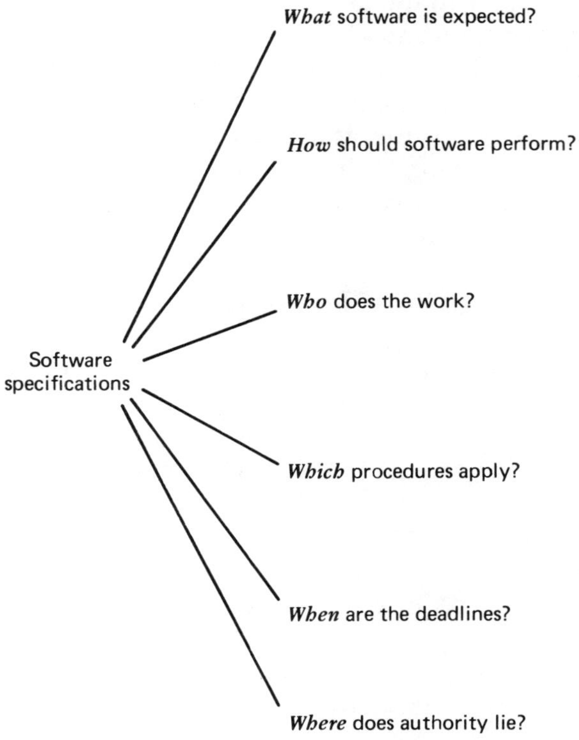


**FIGURE 2.1** Components of software specifications other than code.

A second strategic point is proper interfacing with the user. Typically the user group follows a procedure requiring a great deal of documentation before resources are committed to a project. This begins with the user filing a request for DP services. Often, later, the ultimate "client" is not this user or even a user from the requesting department. It is imperative that the MOP know and have access to an appropriate, informed, concerned, and authorized individual in the requesting organization. One way to assure this is to develop contacts outside the specific context of the project, perhaps through high-level user seminars, either pre-project or as part of a general DP education. Other shops have experimented with integrating users in with development groups. These individuals become more dedicated to the project, but they may not have much appreciation for the difficulty of working on software.

A final strategic point is negotiating accountability for performance. Specs may clearly read "Processes 5000 transactions per hour," but there are many reasons for failure to meet performance goals. These are listed in Figure 2.2. These, and other, factors may reduce performance in the field from that in the development "laboratory." Programmers and MOPs may be required to maintain packages and systems that previously passed acceptance testing but that now look like dogs. Accounting for the responsibility to make the needed changes is an important aspect of technical management. MOPs should be aware of these when specs are being negotiated. Realistic performance goals, rather than idealized ones, should be written into the contract.

### 2.1.3. Technical Role Problems

MOPs also face challenges in fulfilling their personal roles. Not only is the MOP the supervisor of the programming group, but the MOP also represents "software" as a concept to the firm. Since "software" is rarely understood outside the DP organization, role conflicts can arise when the MOP is called upon to perform miracles in nontechnical spheres.

*Responding to market pressures* occupies a large part of the MOP's day. Whether this be in the form of having to refuse interesting projects because of time pressures or in having to accept uninteresting maintenance projects because they are upper management pets, MOPs are part of a marketing effort that the DP organization carries on implicitly.

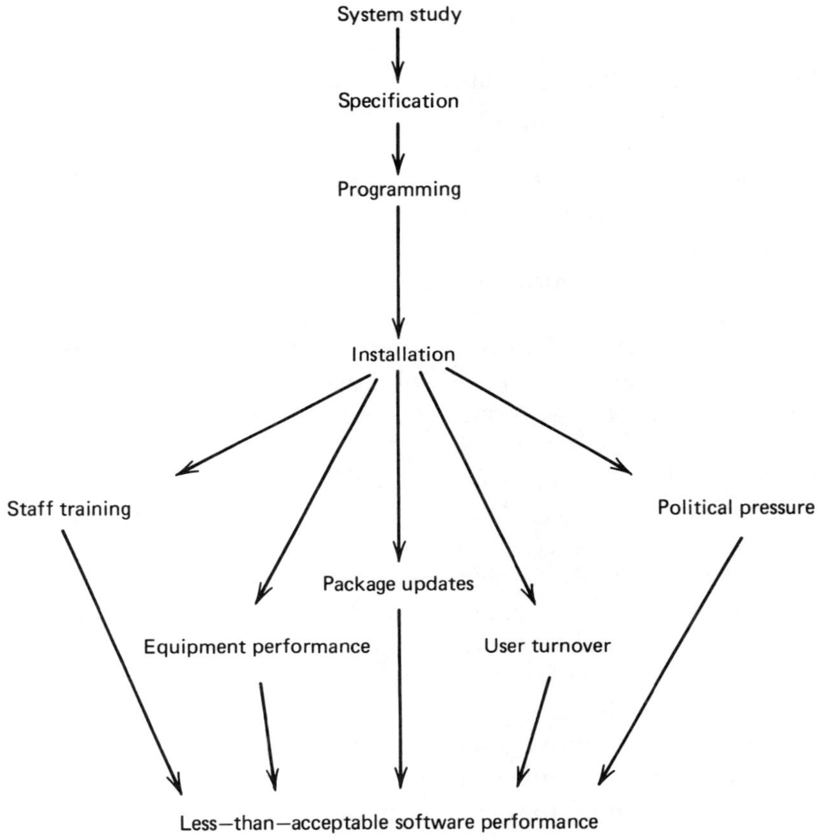


**FIGURE 2.2** Factors leading to less-than-acceptable performance in accepted software.

In the words of a popular song, "You gotta know when to hold up, know when to fold up, know when to walk away, and know when to run." No one is yet arguing that the DP Department isn't worth having, but like other service organizations, it is constantly trying to live up to false high expectations and to meet deserved and undeserved criticism. On the other hand, DP, like other organizations, usually perceives that the alternative to growth is extinction. New users have to be located and convinced to participate, as well as to pay the very high charge-back rates now in vogue. Others have to be dissuaded from taking interesting work outside the firm to an information center or doing it themselves. Often there is no individual in the DP Department charged with this responsibility. Sometimes the

MOP will have to meet with irate or impatient current users or confused and doubting potential customers.

Responding to these pressures is made easier if the MOP retains contacts outside the DP Department while remaining cognizant of—and an active participant in the development of—DP goals. Chapter 6 details the process of "organizational politicking" for the MOP and spells out in some detail how to go about developing and maintaining these contacts.

Another way to respond to market pressures is to anticipate them or create your own. The entrepreneurial role for the MOP is new, but will grow as alternative design strategies percolate upward in the organization and as more middle- and upper-level managers become familiar with computers. Again, this is discussed in Chapter 6 and—in the context of furthering DP careers—in Chapter 7.

Another technical role problem for the MOP is *anticipating* future system needs. That is, MOPs should be able to project into the future, prognosticating the need for technical resources at specific future dates. Part of this is the systems analyst's responsibility. However, MOPs should be able to understand, too, how systems grow, mature, and die. Software "wears out" in peculiar ways.

Coordinating present and future maintenance efforts, too, is an important technical role problem. Given the need for maintenance, MOPs often have to make a fix-or-rebuild decision for systems with many Band-Aids. An out-of-date system may merely require new documentation. Or it may need to be rewritten. Sometimes the MOP may decide to reverse the normal flow of analysis-design-implementation when a maintenance effort appears too difficult or expensive. A program with a fix is a program with a fix that will have to be maintained. Knowing when to hold up (refix) and when to fold up (rebuild or replace) is going to become the most important aspect of the MOP's work as we make the transition to the fourth generation of programming effort. Martin points out in his book that many firms are moving toward maintenance proportions of 80 to 100% of software development budgets. Obviously this represents a transitional situation. However, MOPs must be able to understand and anticipate this trend in preparing for increased maintenance of "jalopy" systems.

In summary, technical management aspects of the MOP's job include not only working with the machinery but also providing an organizational climate within which to work profitably. MOPs have to plan and work toward smooth procedures for obtaining specifications and certifying programs. Part of this work includes managing for maintainability, responding to internal market pressures, and anticipating future system needs. Increasingly, MOPs find themselves interfacing with users and working in modes to which the system development life cycle doesn't apply. Responding to these challenges requires careful planning and understanding of where these challenges come from.

## 2.2. MANAGING PROGRAMMING RESOURCES

This section concentrates on the resources a MOP controls, which are necessary to the completion of work. The list includes compilers, debuggers, and specifications as well as machine time, consumable resources, design tools, and benchmarks. In addition, MOPs control other resources that enable them to manage effectively and correctly. These include project management books, shop standards, shop objectives, and meetings.

### 2.2.1. Resources as Costs

The *human* resource is the primary concern. This is usually measured in employee-months or employee-days. One of the most critical aspects in this expenditure is the decision to accept a project and the risks involved.

Programming costs may be either *direct* or *indirect*. Direct programming costs include labor and resources that are consumed (such as paper or connect time) or set aside (such as permanent mass storage and tape usage). Indirect and shared costs are the costs of resources that must be acquired (for example, compilers, terminals, packages, or telecommunication equipment) but that can be prorated over several projects or departments. In addition, indirect expenditures include opportunity costs for other work not accepted because of lack of personnel and transfer losses from other projects because they may be late or completed with less expertise.

Many of these are difficult to figure. In particular, opportunity costs and transfer losses may be difficult to figure and argue for. It is far easier to see that the cost of two more terminals can be spread over a number of projects than it is to see the cost of removing an expert coder from one project to another. Many of these costs are absorbed into a general DP department or software group overhead figure, which serves to boost charge-back fees uniformly. This only increases the problem of accountability. MOPs should be aware of the sources of these overhead costs. Often costing algorithms apportion part of all machine costs to the programming department rather than to operations, inflating apparent development costs and thereby skewing the choice of projects.

Other costs are often buried in overhead. These include the following:

1. *Staff Training.* Most programmers require at least some introduction to shop standards, specialized languages, and packages; in some shops, training is considered a "perk" for good performance.
2. *Staff Burn-in.* There are no figures on the amount of time it takes a programmer to become familiar with a shop. Many firms figure on three to six months.
3. *Maintenance.* Each program written has to be maintained. Maintenance costs are often far higher than can be effectively charged back.
4. *Debugging.* Certain projects seem easier to debug than others. One rule of thumb adds a factor for each item of equipment added. There are no hard-and-fast rules here; count on surprises.
5. *Documentation.* If a project book is used, a certain factor, up to 100%, has to be added for writing in English. These costs, however, have to be balanced against the greater costs of failure to document.
6. *Testing.* Apart from debugging, the higher levels of testing may require special equipment or the training and attendance of operators or observers. These costs are hard to anticipate and calculate.
7. *Intrusion.* The sudden appearance of the company President, the user VP, an important customer, or a school tour cuts down on performance. Political pressures may result in twice as many user design reviews as are really necessary. Each new piece of equipment brings in schedule changes, service personnel, and a host of system faults, not to mention a flock of systems programmers. Every system change, however minor, is an ulcer for the MOP.

Each of these may increase actual costs and lead to a decision to reject work.

### 2.2.2. Management Resources

In addition to development resources, the MOP has use of a number of resources specifically intended to help the MOP manage. These include a project book, shop and documentation standards, and meeting times.

Some of these items are more or less standard for all shops. That is, most shops have developed a project book that outlines the steps by which projects will be executed. Most have shop standards that may range from how to generate variable names through when to use assembly-language subroutines to which version of a compiler is to be used for released software.

Others of these resources are not commonly treated as such. For instance, most firms do not consider the authority to call meetings a management resource. Yet it is very much so. Meetings should be kept to a minimum, but they prove necessary in specific cases. Each meeting is a costly venture for the firm, just as is each hour of CPU time. Considering meetings a management resource is an important step in the direction of sensitive and effective technical management.

This section does not demonstrate how to develop a project book or create shop standards. What is important here is the role of these resources in good technical management practice. How are these resources going to help the MOP be more effective? How will they affect the style and authority of the MOP? What are the dangers to be alert for?

*The project book* may be of two types: purchased or developed in-house. Small shops may not have a formalized book or "bible" for project management. Informal procedures may have grown up over a period of time. Perhaps no procedures exist because small DP shops respond to perceived needs on a rapid and on-call basis and do not have time or money to develop fixed procedures.

Where a project book doesn't exist, the MOP is on shaky grounds at each step in the development process. As Martin points out, however, it is possible to overdo it, too. The happy medium between an overbearing burden of pressed tree pulp and total chaos is difficult to achieve. The priorities are:

1. Determine and include standard work-allocation forms so that

programmers can find out what they are supposed to be doing and what they are committing themselves to.

2. Determine what documentation is necessary for official hand-over of software to users.
3. Develop procedures for certification and hand-over.

These priorities insure that programmers and customers understand what is happening during development with regard to responsibilities. Many packaged project management systems leave these considerations for the shop to handle in any case. The exercise is also valuable in alerting DP management in a small shop to potential problems of responsibility. Many firms have recently been introduced to DP and have unjustifiably high expectations of, and perhaps justifiable fears about, DP products. Looking first to hand-over procedures and documentation is a good step toward grappling with these emotions.

Larger shops may wish to commission a task force to produce project books. This is especially important if informal practice has built up considerable project folklore over a several-year period. Project folklore is fine for a small shop with low turnover. Quickly, however, a growing shop of relatively mobile programmers can perpetuate procedures that only specific individuals liked or tolerated. Programmers find themselves doing things they don't understand as though it were ritual. This situation is less than desirable. A task force, led by an individual with organizational skills and a good knowledge of projects in the shop, can create the necessary project book. It also can serve as a unifying and morale-increasing catalyst for the shop. Done poorly, however, this exercise may prove divisive.

In this case, an off-the-shelf project management system can be purchased. Systems such as SDM/70 and SPECTRUM are highly articulated, expensive, and require a great deal of training. Others may be simple project tracking systems and require little in the way of resources. The benefits of off-the-shelf systems are two: there is no development time (but the cost may be high) and the purchased system is one everyone can criticize without fear of hurting a programmer's feelings!

*Shop standards* are typically developed by accretion or through an active standards project (see Figure 2.3) or committee set up by the MOP or the Director of DP. In most medium-sized shops with many small maintenance projects, shop standards may remain informal. In

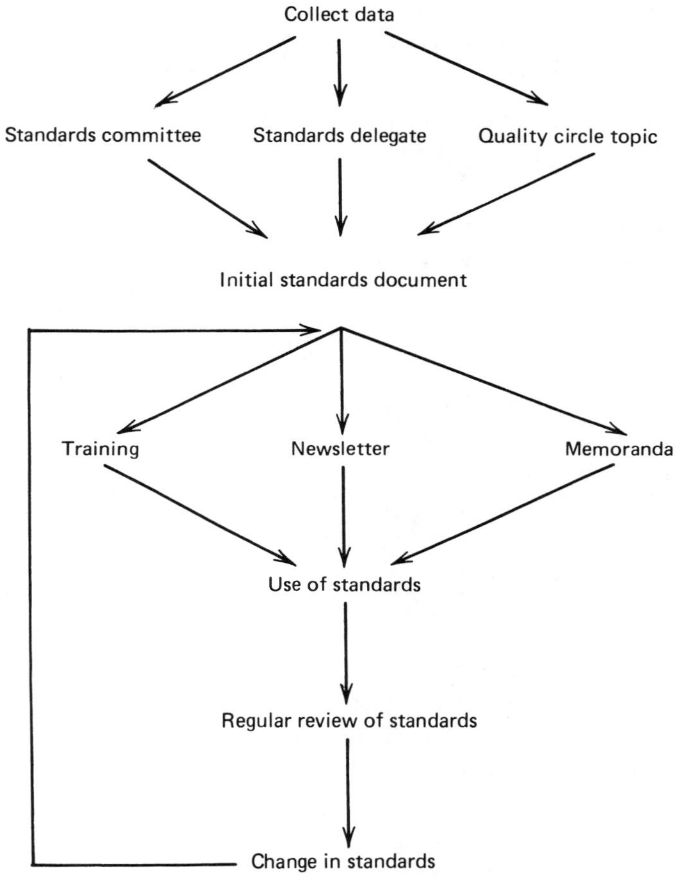


**FIGURE 2.3** The process of standards development.

larger shops or in shops with large or long projects, standards inevitably arise to meet the need to coordinate work. Frank Brooks (1975) points out (in *The Mythical Man-Month*) that the costs of adding labor resources to a late project invariably make the project even later. Each additional person added to the project incurs added training, familiarization, and coordination costs.

Preexisting shop standards can reduce this cost in several ways:

1. In addition to knowing how to code, programmers added to a project also already know how to code for this project.

2. Standards provide ease of communication among programmers and between programmers and users and systems analysts.
3. Effective standards reduce MOP supervision time, releasing it for handling tougher human resource and technical resource management problems.
4. Excellent standards may reduce the incidence of bugs, although Murphy had something to say about that.

Software standards lie in four areas: language choice, coding, documentation, and testing. Although most shops have little freedom in language choice, in shops where several languages are available, it is necessary to know which will be used for which purposes, if only to facilitate maintenance. Where a single language is used, such as in "COBOL shops," there are subsets and levels among which to choose. Some are more learnable, maintainable, and permanent than others. In addition, there are always dialects and versions.

From time to time, the MOP may be given the opportunity to choose a new language. This is akin to being the executor of a will: an important task for which no common mortal is prepared and about which no one really wants to talk anyway. Language choice in these cases may prove traumatic because of the long-term implications.

Large languages like PL/I and COBOL require careful decisions among choices of subsets, since it is not always clear that there will be an expert around to debug seldom-used features. Other languages, like BASIC, exist in several sometimes-incompatible versions.

In addition, command and job control "languages" need to be standardized. Again, there may be little choice. "Ici, on parle JCL" reads the sign outside the systems programming group's offices. But there is JCL and JCL as it is used. One version may be appropriate in a given shop and other not so appropriate.

Language and coding standards include a variety of restrictions and desiderata ranging from the use of structured versus spaghetti coding down to simple variable-naming conventions. On the structured programming issue, it seems apparent after almost a decade of argument that the debate is not resolvable. It is in fact likely that the move to nonprocedural languages may make the debate moot. Another move, that to DBMS, may make variable-naming conventions moot too. But note that there is still a person, now called the "Data Administrator," who makes these decisions, thereby forcing a *de facto* convention.

Shop standards don't appear by magic. There are four major considerations here: development, publicizing, enforcement, and change.

Development of shop standards is most effectively carried out by a task force as a responsibility delegated to an individual with research and writing skills. The MOP and the Director of DP will have to approve all standards. But where there is both the appearance of participation as well as actual involvement of staff in writing of standards, the job of enforcing and publicizing them is made easier.

The best route for publicizing standards is through having programmers participate in creating them. Beyond this, a philosophy of standards-awareness, motivated by the MOP, will make the job easier. In the areas of program registration and checkout and intermodule communication, these standards can be publicized at meetings and by the personnel directly involved. Standards can also be publicized through electronic mail or through a "help" facility in the operating system. When purchasing software development environments and project management systems, the idea of standards publicity should be kept in mind. A system that allows standards to be directly queried during development is superior to one that requires looking them up in a book. One solution would be a semimanual system involving a hot-line to a standards individual; often the Data Administrator can serve in this role.

Probably the most difficult task is enforcement of standards. After all, anyone can write a standard and put it in a notebook. Telling a programmer to meet standards, to rewrite a module, to resubmit a job, or to redo a week's work is not easy. The manager has to walk the narrow line between overbearing management by the book and the too-easy bending of standards that, after all, were written to make work more predictable and manageable.

Enforcement of standards is easier if the following points are kept in mind:

1. Standards are not developed to make the manager's life easier; they come about in response to a need to make work more rational, predictable, and manageable for everyone.
2. Participation in standards-writing is a path toward an interest in standards and standards-awareness; it is part of a general quality-control program.
3. Most of enforcement is an educational function; the need to discipline workers or redirect work in a major way will occur rarely.

4. Standards are changeable. A spirit of experimentation may make adherence to standards more reasonable in the minds of programmers. In particular, a standards review committee serves as a sign of the flexibility inherent in standards.

The MOP can check on standards in a variety of ways. Spot-checking code had the odor of *1984*, although the MOP does have ultimate responsibility for code integrity. The review process, and particularly structured walk-throughs, may focus upon standards and produce informal standards reports as part of procedures.

Careful attendance to documentation of bugs provides a lot of data that can be used to judge standards adherence. Few firms maintain this data—keeping it can be expensive—and even fewer analyze it. A simple form (see Figure 2.4) may assist in collecting the data, which can be passed to the standards committee for analysis.

Another technique that has proved useful in quality control is a newsletter or column in a newsletter that concentrates upon results of this type of research or on spot-checks of standards. The newsletter can, if produced sensitively, build morale and standards-awareness among the group. Again, this is a cost that will have to be justified.

Finally, training in standards—apart from the usual training in languages—is a proactive technique that seeks to avoid problems. One-day seminars or a series of half-day meetings on standards can assist both the veteran programmer and the novice in understanding shop standards and the procedures for development and change. This can also be part of a general quality-control campaign. What after all is "quality" in a software shop but meeting standards?

### 2.2.3. Meetings as a Management Resource

The final resource controlled by the MOP is meeting times and content. Many meetings are associated with programming work; these are detailed in Chapter 3. Controlling meeting times is critical in project execution. As a general guideline, managers should call meetings only if (1) the same activity has to be performed by a number of people simultaneously, (2) they can be brought together quickly but with sufficient notice, and (3) physical presence is absolutely required.

Many meetings are unnecessary in all but extreme situations. These include customer project status meetings, weekly staff meetings, and group consultations to solve software problems. But MOPs

Bug Description

Seq. No. _____-_____ Project/System ______________

Programmer ________________________ Date __________________

Apparent Problem:

---

Action Taken

Check one of the following:

__ Fixed (See below) on ____________

__ Specifications changed on pg(pp) __________

__ Not a problem

Description of Fix:

FIGURE 2.4 Bug documentation.

call these meetings often and regretfully. Why do we say they are unnecessary?

This is so because they serve no constructive purpose. They don't accomplish work. They don't solve problems that individuals couldn't solve themselves. They inform, but in an expensive and uncomfortable way. Instead they provide an arena for programmers, users, analysts, and you to spar, looking for trouble. Meetings such as these fail because few arrive prepared for constructive work, because almost everyone has a stake in getting others upset, and because most important business is carried out either before the meeting or after it.

In particular, weekly staff meetings may serve no purpose other than to keep insecure MOPs falsely comfortable. Someone will always find a way to waste the hour or two devoted to these meetings. There will be a fight, a bit of grandstanding, and you will be compelled to give a lot of gratuitous advice.

The guidelines for effective meetings include:

1. Schedule the meeting well enough in advance so that invitees can be prepared and have settled their other business *before* the meeting.
2. Limit those invited to those who have a direct interest in producing something from the meeting; observers and interested bystanders are forbidden in constructive meetings—they can read the reports.
3. Limit the time for the meeting by preparing an agenda with time limits for each topic; distributing this in advance, perhaps electronically, will help prepare others for the meeting.
4. Having made an agenda and distributed it, stick to the timetable; not everything has to be *on* the agenda, but what *is* there should be covered.
5. Call meetings only in order to produce outcomes; calling them to assuage guilt, to establish contact, or to calm fears and insecurities is asking for trouble.
6. Use audiovisual aids (AVs) liberally; use the computer itself for preparing and distributing materials; distribute these, too, well in advance.
7. Prepare the room, disallow interruptions, allow no incoming phone calls or interruptions for phone calls; make sure everyone stays for the whole meeting.

8. Work toward consensus; the only reason you've brought all those people together is to capitalize upon group dynamics; this means that consensus rather than agreement is important.
9. Be a strong, fair chairperson—or hire or draft someone who is; the meeting is for your benefit, but if you are unfair or weak, then no one will profit.
10. Create an action agenda by the end of the meeting—this is a list of things to be done before the next meeting.
11. Evaluate each meeting afterwards to see whether or not you've accomplished your goals; this implies that you have measurable goals for each meeting.

Timing of meetings may vary, but generally a meeting prepared by an agenda and predistributed materials can accomplish almost anything within an hour. These 3.6 ksec should be carefully planned. A six-person meeting costs $200 to $400 per hour to conduct (i.e., significantly similar to CPU costs). Is your meeting worth it?

What meetings *are* essential? The list below illustrates several essential meetings, their formats, the appropriate chairperson, a reasonable time limit, typical outcomes, and invitees. Note that all meetings have restricted attendance. None is scheduled for over two hours, although some demonstrations may require a lengthy time period spread over several sessions.

A final note on meetings is that many can be replaced with nontraditional formats, especially audio and video teleconferencing, computer conferencing, and electronic mail. Audio teleconferencing in particular is very effective in technical discussions when augmented by on-line data transmission, facsimile, slow-scan TV, or a graphics tablet. A simple system for coupling terminals through a virtual operating system and a basic screen editor can be very effective when used in conjunction with common telephone features or speakerphones, as illustrated in Figure 2.5.

Computer conferencing is an extension of electronic mail. Here messages are directed usually to a topic rather than to individuals. To participate in the conference, only a registration key (usually a name) and a list of topics is needed, plus the ability to type. The participant indicates the desired conference(s) and proceeds to read the conference transcript. Comments are added to this transcript or directed to specific participants. Some systems, such as EIES, allow the creation

| Meeting | Format | Chaired By | Time/Frequency | Attendees | Outcome |
|---|---|---|---|---|---|
| Project status | Reports | MOP or project leader | 1 hr/month | Chair, project staff | List of problems to be handled, agreement on next steps |
| Customer project status | Questions and answers | Customer | 30 min/rare | Customer, MOP, senior project staff | Agreement that stated problems actually aren't |
| Milestone meeting | Checkoff | MOP or project leader | 30 min/each milestone | Chair, project staff | Disposition of project phase, praise to staff, release of resources to next phase |
| Technical Review(s) | Walk-through | Peers | 1 hr/session | Peers | Quality control |
| | Code review | Peers | 1 hr/session | Peers | Quality control |
| | Technical design or review | MOP | 2 hr max/special change or hand over | MOP, project staff or analysis staff, and manager | Deployment of staff to specs |
| Demonstration | Demonstration | MOP or project leader | Varies/each item or system | I. Programmer, project leader | Delivery of module |
| | | | | II. Programmer, project leader | Delivery of function |
| | | | | III. MOP, project leader, maybe analysis staff | Delivery of system |
| | | | | IV. MOP, maybe DP Director, customer, senior project staff | Operational test, acceptance |
| Sign-off | Handshake | MOP or DP Director or customer | 30 min/delivered product | MOP, DP Director, customer or delegate | Formal acceptance of the product |

of subconferences and private notebooks. Advanced features include voice annotation, message forwarding, and the saving of messages in private files for later reading or incorporation into other documents via word processing.

Electronic mail can be used for off-line or real-time meetings, depending upon local facilities. Many larger computer centers use electronic mail facilities to handle requests for casual consulting. A user can "mail" an entire program or listing to the consultant, with whom a voice conversation can be conducted to find out whether or not the problem is in the user program, the operating system, or the system documentation. If such a system is now available, it should not prove difficult to conduct more complex meetings this way. Since programmers like to work late or from home, these kinds of meetings will prove increasingly useful in the future.

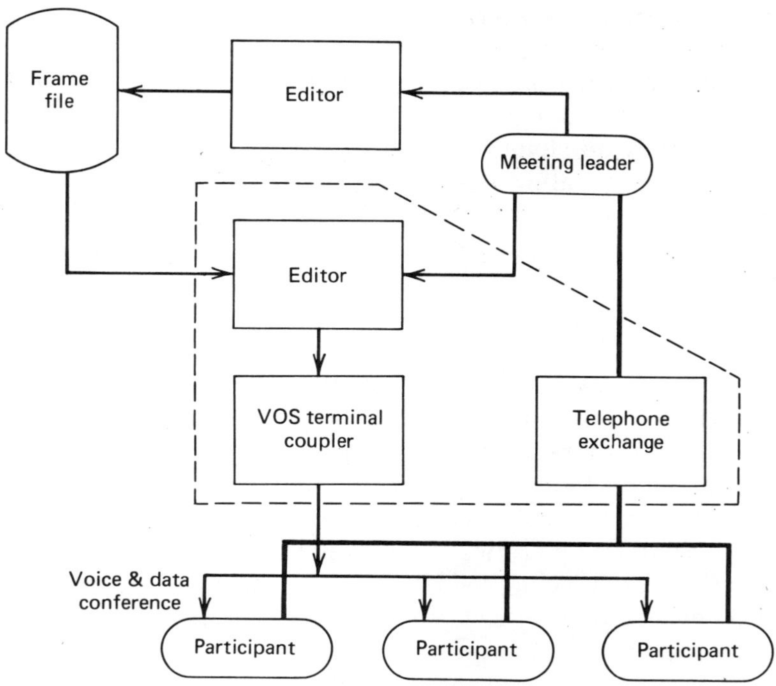


**FIGURE 2.5** Using a virtual operating system (VOS) and the telephone to conduct a meeting.

## 2.3. WORKING IN A PROJECT ENVIRONMENT

A project is a temporary organization of individuals working on a single product or system for a specific customer. A project is limited in its use of time and other resources, the scope of the work, and the clientele. The centerpiece of the system development life cycle (SDLC), the project is one of the more well-documented DP concepts. The SDLC has its champions and its foes, but until we are into fifth-generation computer work, it will continue to dominate both the system development literature and the activities of software development and maintenance managers.

There are a number of ways of organizing work other than projects. Lately, alternatives to projects have been successfully introduced. In specific cases, such as prototyping and some forms of screen-driven development, they may be preferable. The information center and end-user-developed software may well replace much—and the least difficult—software development by the end of this decade. Until then, MOPs will have to live with and prosper in a project environment.

Essentially an engineering management technique, the SDLC is supposed to carry large-scale building enterprises from plans to completion in a finite length of time, during which time few changes are to be expected. Labor, computer, and management resources are expected to be available at specific moments and in specific proportions. A complex web of interlocking activities is planned at the outset of the project to insure this.

Needless to say, troubles always develop. Most software projects are late and over budget. The fine art of estimating budgets is just that, a fine art, about which much has been written and little is known. Regression analysis and laboratory experimentation have been used in attempts to derive formulas, some of them humorous, to predict time and labor requirements for projects.

It is this writer's view that such formulas may be red herrings. Not only is software by its nature exquisitely plastic—and therefore constantly begging to be changed—but the industry itself is in a state of flux, moving from the third to the fourth generation of workers and languages, peopled with a changing pool of talent and attitudes. The type of software written is changing, too, as ideas become increasingly complex and more expensive to implement. In other words, the kind of estimation that projects require simply cannot be performed readily.

The problem is not only that a project can't get good estimates in advance, but that projects actually *need* these estimates. Again, this relates to the engineering heritage of the SDLC. If we are to build a bridge, we cannot get approval to spend the funds unless we can guarantee a price and a ready supply of raw materials. If our price is flexible, the customer is asking for huge cost overruns. If the supply of materials is at risk, the customer can expect lengthy delays. The smart customer wants guarantees, not gambles.

When software was built like bridges, the customer was entitled to the same respect a bridge authority gets from a contractor: a firm bid and a promise of delivery. The SDLC promises this by conducting a quick preliminary study, producing firm cost and schedule figures, and then detailing activities into a network built about a critical path.

Clearly this doesn't work for software now, and it never really worked well in the past. Software, in any event, is no longer constructed like bridges. It's handcrafted and changes are supposed to be made in it. Several versions of a program may be available simultaneously through parameters. Imagine a driver pulling up to the toll booth of the George Washington Bridge and choosing which lane to drive in, which surface (asphalt, concrete, astroturf, Bonneville Flats sand) would be nice, how many turns (turns!?!) would be interesting, and whether or not the ride will be made upside down. Software provides these options; tomorrow it can provide others. Bridges can't be built this way.

Thus there is movement in some production efforts toward alternatives, which would reflect this flexibility without engendering complete chaos. This is a natural response to the unmanageable aspects of building software using the SDLC.

Others are working on the SDLC itself. Structured techniques, especially structured analysis, aim toward lengthening the pre-budget period. Here a more detailed system study produces almost machine-readable specifications that are reduced, Taylor-like, to the least common implementables.* Structured programming techniques are valuable since each structure is in one of three or four distinct types. Hence costing *may* be easier.

*Frederick Taylor introduced the technique of work analysis over half a century ago. He standardized tasks and tools, thereby increasing efficiency by making the proper match. He also routinized work tremendously. "Taylorism" is the management practice that stems from these early attempts. Often the term is applied derogatorily, implying that those who use Taylor's techniques, or later refinements, dehumanize work and those who perform it.

Interestingly, structured advocates rarely convert their *techniques* into *operational terms* for MOPs to use in costing out projects. MOPs may find, too, that using structured programming simply makes estimating even more difficult. There is no way yet known to turn structured specs into labor estimates. Without a scale, there's no way to determine the price either of software lasagna (structured programs) or spaghetti (unstructured programs).

## 2.3.1. The Role of the MOP

Let us consider only the case of the MOP who is not simultaneously a project leader. In many shops, matrix management (see Figure 2.6) assigns individuals to specific projects either part-time or full-time, temporarily or for the duration of the project. MOPs remain as "discipline" directors, individuals who know software management and administration. Programmers report also to project leaders, who are usually either promoted lead programmers or seconded systems analysts, the latter more common in a true matrix-managed DP shop. Often other individuals are seconded from the rest of the DP shop: librarians, consultants, operations personnel, and even PR personnel may be assigned to specific projects.

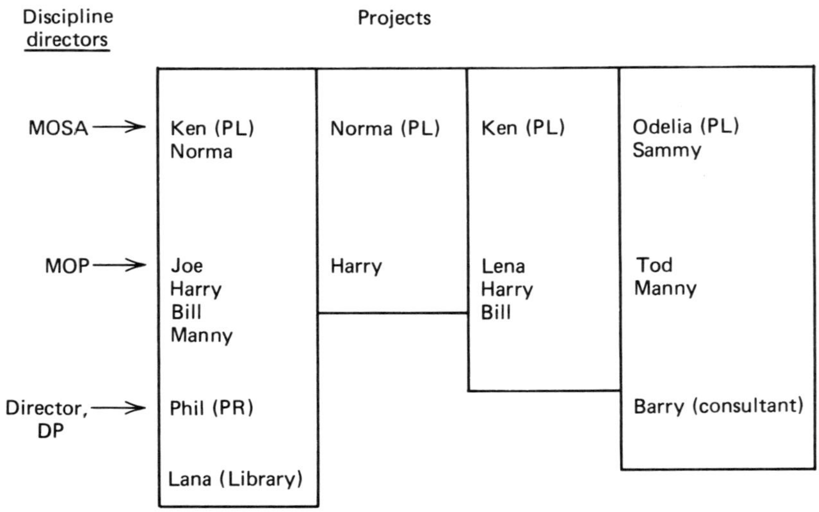


**FIGURE 2.6** Matrix management in a project environment. PL = project leader, MOSA = manager of systems analysis.

Given that the MOP may have little day-to-day involvement in a given project in this environment, what role is the MOP supposed to play? After all, MOPs in these situations will not be reviewing code, making labor assignments, checking out programs, or assisting in debugging. It is unlikely, too, that the MOP will be invited to the sign-off meeting for a large, integrated system. What does the MOP do?

Five general responsibilities are left to the MOP in this situation:

1. *Acceptance of specifications from the analysis group.* General development responsibilities when there is no analysis group.

2. *General direction of development in the shop.* This is accomplished through control of tools and development environments on the computer. In particular, the MOP is the advocate of the software shop to the DP Director in making a case to obtain a new compiler, an upgrade to a development system, a new or additional terminal, and so forth.

3. *Officiation at hand-over "ceremonies."* These ceremonies are where major reallocations of labor resources are made. These events include project initiation and termination and project phase transitions as well as any major project reorganization—such as a reassignment of project leadership.

4. *Arbitration of disputes.* This usually means calling in the MOP when a programmer feels overworked or bored or when a programmer feels the work is impossible or the project leader feels the programmer is inadequately prepared or motivated for the work. The MOP acts with the best interests of the software development group at heart.

5. *Maintenance acceptance and delivery.* A project isn't finished when the active development phase is terminated. The MOP has to certify, formally or otherwise, that the unit is willing to maintain the software. No project leader can give that certification. Short-term or long-term, only the MOP has the authority to make labor commitments.

Gatekeeper, facilitator, judge, arbitrator, and owner are the roles for the MOP in a strictly project-oriented, matrix-managed shop. This tends to restrict MOPs to administrative work: meetings and reports. Most managers spend 50 to 80% of each working day in meetings; here is an instance in which meeting planning may prove important. Experience with computers to maintain paperwork will come in handy, too. Note that what is missing here is coding, debugging, and testing of programs—MOPs in project-oriented shops may never see code again.

A project has been defined as a temporary organization of individuals working on a single product or system for specific customers. Projects play unusual roles in organizations because of this. In many organizations, especially in DP shops in which costs are charged back directly to customers, projects are assigned numbers to which resource expenditures are charged. In particular, labor time, computer use, and capital and lease costs are charged to these projects. Large projects are assigned budgets just as departments are. Where a shop is exclusively project oriented, all costs, including training and holidays, are billed to a project number. In one absurd situation I am aware of, a large resource firm charges back every microsecond of DP staff time. DP staffers cannot serve on task forces simply because there are no project numbers to charge.

Projects have limited life spans and limited budgets. But they do not necessarily have limited organizational impact. For instance, a change in the payroll system affects everyone in the firm. A project to automate even the company library has organization-wide implications. A small maintenance project to interface an existing DBMS to an imported database brings new information to everyone in the firm.

Furthermore, since individuals in a project are not usually involved in it for life, they are not seen as totally identified with the project in the way a department can be seen as identified with service to the firm. After all, six months down the line the project will terminate. Who does the user complain to if the project members don't care? And more important, who will even listen to the complaint five years from now when the project is only documented memories but the software is continuing to proliferate errors in life insurance claims files?

Thus there are problems of authority, responsibility, continuity, involvement, scope, and influence. These problems are not exactly the same as those facing more permanent organizations such as the DP Department itself or the software unit, although managers in these groups are usually faced with the problems. The problems that *organizations* face in these regards are discussed in Chapter 6. What about *projects*?

The project is the creature of the SDLC, and thus is properly the responsibility of the DP Department as a whole. Unfortunately, the

DP Department may not see it that way. Traditionally, the DP management style is hands-off, letting workers do their own things on company time because they are so unmanageable, and because there is so little time to get involved. The time has obviously come for changes in the way the SDLC is handled in the DP shop. As has been stated, recent trends are blurring the distinction between the phases of the SDLC, and the value of the methodology itself is now in doubt. In most cases, too, the project's authority is improperly delegated to it by the DP Director. That is because the Director assumes that in most cases the MOP and the MOP's counterparts in operations and systems analysis will accept real responsibility for projects. This is, however, rarely so. It's a dishonest attitude, which can only harm projects and relations with customers. In fact, project leaders tend to exercise very little real authority, and MOPs either avoid it or are unsure that they have it.

Again, the SDLC is at fault, because its basic premise is that the only problems a project can encounter after its flawlessly crafted plan is drafted would be technical ones. In fact, most of the problems are managerial and entrepreneurial, and these problems are not effectively covered in the implicit contract between MOP and project leader, which defines a project.

What is to be done, then? MOPs should insure that authority is properly delegated when projects begin:

1. Who has responsibility for handling which problems?
2. When can specific individuals exercise this authority?
3. Whom does person *X* complain to about person *Y* or spec *Z*?
4. Who has the right to call a staff meeting to explain the problem and change the mandate of the project?
5. Can the customer butt in?
6. What are the specific responsibilities of the project leader vis-à-vis personnel management?

These are tough questions, but they have to be settled before a project begins.

The critical times during a project's life are, of course, project commencement and project end. But the truly frightening moments occur when projects assume gargantuan proportions in the eyes of the firm ("We've just got to have that system next month, Joe," said the VP for Finance to the MOP), when the project champion or client is promoted, or has a change of heart ("Well, Joan, I'm sorry, but we can't commit to this project since Harry left; the funds have to go into increased sales force admin support. Sorry."), or when one project is folded into another ("Joe, we're putting the patient database project in with the payroll project—to save money and because they both run on the computer"). At times like these it's no longer clear who is the constituency for the project. A department, after all, can look to its mandate, but a project needs a continuing sponsor, a customer, a champion.

Most projects are canceled either for nondelivery—such as failure to meet milestones—or for political reasons. The second is our concern here. Political reasons for canceling projects range from loss of a client to a new popular concept ("MIS is out, DSS is in, Joan"), a new market thrust ("We're now looking at a terminal on every desk by 1987, Joe, so your batch system's got to go"), to a change in DP philosophy ("Joan, we just don't support piecemeal systems development any longer now that Betty's taken over—she really wants integrated office systems."). None of these should surprise a MOP. It is, in fact, one of the MOP's major responsibilities to be in on conceptualization, marketing of DP ideas, and development of a DP philosophy, as discussed in more detail in Chapters 5 through 7. MOPs shouldn't have projects canceled out from beneath them for these reasons.

Other reasons for canceling projects may be economic in nature. These are like "acts of God" to MOPs, although a trend toward the marketing of DP projects may give the MOP a bit more control, or at least feedback, here. On the other hand, a MOP should never accept a project with a large economic risk. The reality, of course, is that there is often no choice in this matter. Instead, part of the negotiation for specifications and resources should include an at-least-yearly allocation of funds and reasonable milestones designed around the delivery of salvageable products on that schedule. In the event the project is canceled, some work of a maintainable quality already done may be useful yet to the firm.

### 2.3.2. Managing People in a Project Setting

Chapter 4 covers personnel management in some detail. But there are some considerations arising from working in a strongly project-oriented environment that should be kept in mind while reading Chapter 4:

1. Training for projects is not exactly the same as training for employment. Project needs are typically more urgent and more intense. Skills needed for projects are usually highly technical and related to the content of the work. Many skills acquired for specific projects are not transferable to others.

2. Staff mobility is affected by project organizations. Not only are skill requirements likely to imprison talented individuals in single projects for lengthy time periods, but the need for specific skills may also force a firm to hire or promote individuals when they would otherwise not be hired or promoted. Working on a heavily telecommunications-oriented project may only qualify a programmer to work for another firm when this project is completed. MOPs should be alert for the ways in which project skill demands affect employee marketability and mobility.

3. The demands on the MOP for counseling and discipline may increase in project environments simply because the short-term nature of the project magnifies workforce needs and shortfalls. What does the MOP do if a key project person is found selling the firm's software to competitors? What if a programmer starts drinking and this affects staff morale? Behavior tolerable over the long run is likely to create a short-term schedule difficulty that can endanger a project.

4. Performance appraisal should be keyed to projects rather than to calendar or fiscal years (except, of course, for the situation in which a "maintenance" programmer has a work repertoire consisting exclusively of short, fix-up maintenance work). Most performance appraisal exercises ignore this principle. MOPs should work hard for relief from this regimen; the exercise is difficult enough without having to compare February's oranges with October's apples.

In addition to these differences, MOPs should keep their own career considerations in mind. Four questions are uppermost in accepting and completing project work with regard to career options:

1. Is movement between projects good for a MOP's career? Yes, so long as the MOP is successful! By definition, "management" is a generalist vocation and one needs a wide range of experience (see Chapter 7).

2. How many projects should a MOP supervise? That depends on a number of project factors. Ten is almost surely too many. Organizational pundits point out that most supervisors would be most comfortable with between two and seven projects of a non-

maintenance nature. Of course, a single very large project can absorb several MOPs. As Chapters 4 and 5 point out, effective delegation is more important than a specific number of projects.

3. What does a MOP develop in a project-oriented shop? Patience, judgment, and tact, plus a sense of humor!

4. What about the future? It is definitely moving away from the SDLC. By the time programmers are truly fourth-generation workers, no one will remember what a project, in the SDLC sense, was. No one will plan today's kind of development work more than a month in advance . . . and such plans will make little sense in an era of user-driven, information-center assisted development. More is said on this in Chapter 8.

### 2.3.3. Conclusions

This section has examined the effects of the project environment on MOP-management efforts. The MOP's role in a strictly project-oriented matrix-managed shop is that of administrator. Severely restrictive bounds are placed on MOPs in these environments. These require strategies of an organizational nature. Within the organization, the project has a life of its own; this affects MOPs, especially as regards work and personnel management. These are the topics of Chapters 3, 4, and 5.

CHAPTER THREE

# MANAGING PROGRAMMING WORK

Creating software products occupies the bulk of the programmer's day, yet this seemingly innocent statement is the cause of ulcers for many MOPs. Why? That is, after all, what programmers are hired to do—create programs. The answer is both simple and complex.

The simple answer is that programming is still a difficult task, requiring hard-to-find skills, and as the kinds of programs MOPs need to produce become more complex, it becomes more difficult to meet a schedule. This has led a number of researchers, vendors, and even programmers to explore the possibilities of alternative programming means. That is, if the job of programming is too complex, we should build some tools to make the job easier. The extreme view is to automate the task completely (termed "programmerless programming" by James Martin).

The complex answer to the problem of programmer productivity is that, while we have an idea that programmers are not working up to our standards, programming productivity is extremely difficult to measure and control. Regardless of how difficult the task of programming is, management has the even more difficult job of supervising work it finds difficult to measure. If that is so, then some of our basic assumptions about what programming work is may be part of the barrier to improved productivity.

This chapter looks at work management, at how to supervise work and the products of work in a software shop. Our approach is as follows:

1. Define work units.
2. Define work goals and productivity measurements.
3. Provide the tools for production.
4. Use the goals and measures to control work.
5. Manage for maintainability.
6. Seek reasonable appropriate alternatives to traditional programming methodologies.
7. Develop supervision skills in the workers.

Briefly, this approach is an example of management-by-objectives applied in a software shop. Management-by-objectives—or MBO—is a systematic approach to management that provides management with the means to judge performance based on concrete objectives. It gives the employee relatively more freedom to pursue the means of making programs in unique fashions. While MBO has its detractors, it has proven useful in a wide variety of job situations. One variation, called performance data and development (PDD), takes MBO a step further by having manager and programmer cooperatively define the kinds of behaviors that exemplify "good performance." The manager and the employee need only agree on appropriate behaviors rather than on what a specific program will look like.

These behaviors may be similar to the following:

1. Delivery of specific documentation within a certain time period.
2. Certification of testing at a specific level by a certain time.
3. Adherence to shop standards for coding, documentation, meetings, and so on.
4. Use of specific tools for development.

## 3.1. DEFINING WORK UNITS

Programming work exists at several levels: line of code, function, module, system. This view of work focuses upon the physical product. Another way of viewing programming work is to look at the social environment of work: individual, team, unit, shop, department, division, company. Still another view of programming work concentrates upon the level of the software activity itself: user interface, transaction, data management and database management, system interface, hardware. Each of these schemes attempts to structure programming work into different levels. This makes it easier to judge the difficulty of development, testing, and documentation. Different skills are necessary to succeed in working at these different levels.

However, the effective MOP takes a more sophisticated view of work. Factors that influence work management include these:

1. Size of project.
2. System development methodology.
3. Amount of user/programmer interaction required.
4. Abilities of programmer.
5. Availability of resources.
6. Timetable considerations.
7. Testing considerations.

For instance, for a small project requiring a great deal of interaction with the user over a short period of time, the appropriate work unit may be the prototype system version. A large system involving a number of resources but requiring the services of several novice programmers over a period of time is best handled using functions as the physical unit and the individual programmer as the entity whose performance is being judged. A still larger system may further subdivide units by which aspect of the system is involved in the coding: user interface, transaction, database, and so forth. The table in Figure 3.1 graphically illustrates the appropriate choices for units to be managed in a variety of situations.

One overriding factor in work management is the choice of system development methodology. Since structured design is in vogue, the tool of the structure chart will be used to illustrate the importance of the choice of development process on work management.

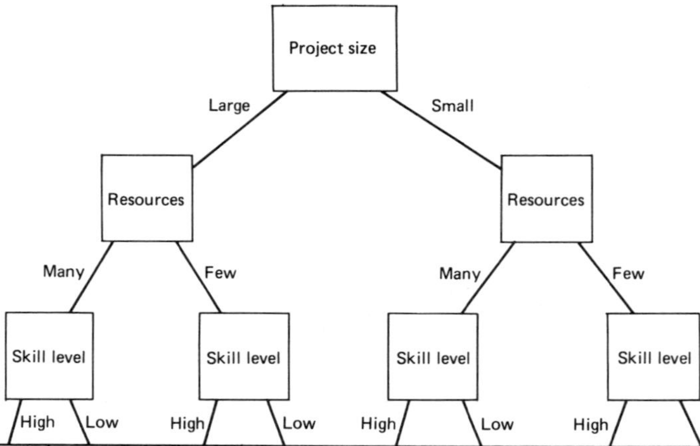


| Large / Many / High | Large / Many / Low | Large / Few / High | Large / Few / Low | Small / Many / High | Small / Many / Low | Small / Few / High | Small / Few / Low | |
|---|---|---|---|---|---|---|---|---|
| System by unit | System by team | System by team | System by individual | System by team | Subsystem individual | System by team | Module by individual | SDLC |
| Function by individual | Function by individual | Module by individual | Module by individual | System by individual | Function by individual | Function by individual | Module by individual | Prototyping |
| Module by team or unit | Module or line by individual | Line by individual or team | Line by individual | Function by individual or team | Module by individual or team | Module by individual | Line by individual | Packages |
| Module by individual | Module by team | Module by individual | Line by individual | Function by individual | Line by individual | Module by individual | Line by individual | Maintenance |

**FIGURE 3.1** Principles of work assignment based on project size, resource availability, and worker skill level.

Figure 3.2 illustrates a structure chart for a large project. Note that, although the chart indicates which modules invoke others, it does not necessarily imply any order to development. In *top-down* development, the highest level modules are coded first, often by a senior programmer. Dummy modules or *program stubs* are created for the next level down. As development progresses, testing is naturally integrated, and as the lowest levels of the structure chart are implemented, the system starts to process live data in "natural" environments.

*Bottom-up* development is based on the assumption that existing, independently developed modules can be integrated into functioning units at higher levels. While bottom-up development has the advantage of reutilizing existing software, it requires a great deal of extra coordination and very, very detailed documentation to insure that the fit is perfect. However, bottom-up development and imple-

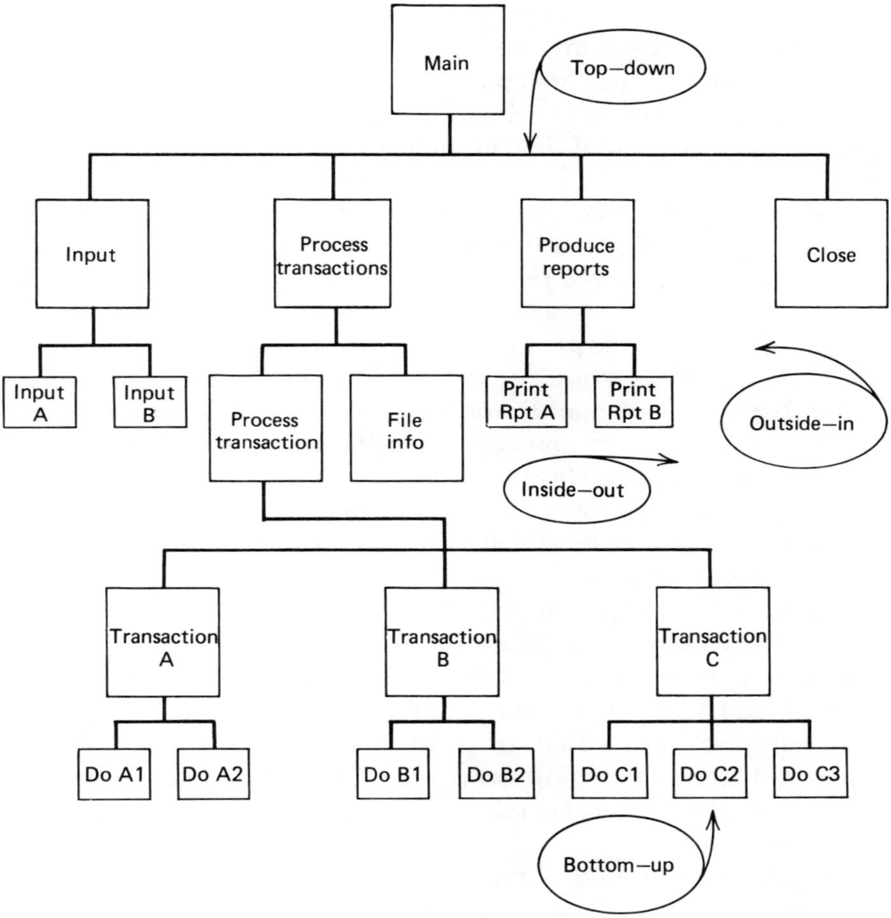


**FIGURE 3.2** Structure chart for large system, showing four development strategies.

mentation can be effective if management is willing to invest the effort in maintaining standards and testing interfaces.

*Inside-out* and *outside-in* development begin either from the inside of the structure chart or from the top and bottom and work toward complete integration. Inside-out development is appropriate in *retrofitting* an existing system to a new operating environment (say, for instance, within a new division) and to new data requirements (as when a database management system is used to access data). Outside-in development is appropriate when both operating modules and higher-level defining modules are already available, but a new "middle" needs to be created. This is analogous to installing a new instrument panel in an existing airplane. Most maintenance work is outside-in. Incremental development, as in prototyping, is inside-out.

*End-user-oriented development,* in which a user works with an analyst, a programmer, or a menu to develop applications, has introduced a variety of development environments for the programmer. In true *architecture-based development,* the programmer does not directly create applications. Instead the programmer must supply all the necessary drivers and processors, which can be combined via menu displayed commands and other screen-based operations.

A prototyping environment requires the programmer to work with an ever-changing specification list and a piece of hardware that is difficult to program—the user! The appropriate units here are not predictable; therefore the MOP may have to examine the schedule of delivery of prototypes.

One final "development" environment is *maintenance.* "Managing for maintainability" is a slogan that has meaning only if we define what the maintenance environment might be. Unlike the automobile repair industry, software maintenance is not based upon a catalog of interchangeable parts that are held in stock for the inevitable replacement. Instead, maintenance rests upon a different set of assumptions. Parts (modules) don't wear out, but uses (applications) "wear in."

Software is subjected to more and more stresses and "unusual" (i.e., unanticipated) applications by a larger pool of users. Ultimately a situation arises within which the software cannot function, and the program-maintenance group is contacted. No stock items are installed. Instead the maintenance programmer becomes a physician. Depending upon the diagnosis, the programmer may prescribe surgery (replacing a module), abstinence ("Avoid using the A/R program on accounts more than 360 days in arrears"), or medicine and rehabilitation ("You know you're not supposed to run this program on Tuesdays; it says so right here in manual—why don't you train your dispatchers properly?"). Since maintenance may produce such a variety of outcomes, the appropriate unit may be the problem worked upon, rather than a line of code, a module, or a system. The problem may encompass an entire department too.

## 3.2. WORK ASSIGNMENT

The principles of *work assignment* provide for the matching of work, workers, and work environments. Seven principles stand out:

1. *Make the delivery of the work unit measurable.* Time, date, place, documentation, testing level of acceptance, test data, and performance characteristics such as speed and response time are all measurable.

2. *Match work units with programmer skills.* A skilled programmer may work at a higher design level, such as a system or module, while a novice programmer may work on a function within a module. Programmers with good human relations skills can be "turned loose" on the users; others may require some supervision in their dealings with users or may work only with understanding or knowledgeable users. Programmers who are familiar with human factors may appropriately be expected to deliver tested user interface units, while programmers unfamiliar with the operating system cannot be expected to code operating system interfaces correctly without assistance.

3. *Adopt a certifiable testing discipline.* Black-box approaches, top-down testing, a morphological approach, functional testing, and performance auditing are accepted testing disciplines, which need only be adapted to the specifics of the shop. Without a testing discipline, the statement "90% bug-free" or "tested" is meaningless. Most testing disciplines are tightly related to documentation systems, too.

4. *Insure inter-unit communication through standards.* Many firms have adopted a system development methodology because of fear of loss of control over system development staff rather than from a desire to control quality. Work assignment is useless unless a system development methodology insures that integration of the assigned work units can proceed smoothly, reliably, and rigorously.

5. *Schedule resources so that the work can be done.* Few things are more frustrating to MOP and programmer than waiting for work or a tool. Machine time, manuals, disk space, and the installation of the new operating system may cause delays. Hardware has a way of appearing "some time in the next few weeks," which makes testing of modules requiring the hardware difficult to schedule.

6. *Utilize project management tools.* These include project books

and system development methodologies, automated and semiautomated project management systems for recording and computing work assignments and progress toward goals (such as AMPS), and the tools of management science such as PERT, CPM, and others for tracking progress and predicting resource requirements. Without them, the MOP is in the curious position of ignoring the tool being prepared for users, namely the computer.

7. *Assign for maximum maintainability.* Because systems tend toward increasingly more difficult, if fewer, errors, a development plan that takes this into account assists those who must maintain the software later, when the hard bugs appear. Thus an early work assignment may fall to a senior programmer who will attempt to determine the failure conditions of the system and how to note them.

These seven principles should be the primary focus of work management. An instrument in this is the computer itself. While it is possible to overdo computer use in work management, it is unusual to find a MOP who uses the computer as an integral tool of work assignment and management. As late as 1979, research by Lehman (1979) pointed out that the great majority of software shops ignore the use of the computer in making work assignments and tracking work progress. Most of the major project management methodologies (like SPECTRUM and SDM/70) treat the computer as an interesting, but nonintegral, adjunct to project management. Here is an opportunity for improvement that MOPs cannot afford to ignore.

## 3.3. THE PRODUCTIVITY QUESTION

There are few controversies in the area of management of programmers that have attracted the attention of the DP public as much as the productivity question.

There may be reason to believe the productivity of programmers is indeed low, as many have asserted. This is especially defensible when industrial measures of productivity are used. Despite the large number of tools a programmer uses, productivity has scarcely improved since the early 1960s in these terms. Some say that the number of debugged lines of code produced per day is relatively constant over languages and environments. Other workers who use computers to the extent of programmers—word processing clerks, for instance— have demonstrated productivity gains over their manual counterparts in the order of hundreds of percents. Yet a programmer is still rewarded for producing a few lines of code per hour.

On the other hand, no one has demonstrated what an adequate level of performance might be for *specific* situations for *specific* programmers. Many formulas are available (see Bartol, 1982, detailing work measurement and estimation techniques). But there is no real theory that indicates what appropriate production levels might be in particular situations. (Chrysler has an intriguing formula that must be incorrect in any single circumstance. There are also several "metrics" around for estimating program complexity—and by extension, codability. See Halstead's (1977) work on this.)

In other words, the formulas available are either extrapolations from other specific situations or are systematized rules of thumb that disguise our lack of knowledge.

It is true that published experiences have demonstrated that in some situations performance as measured by output volume (such as lines of code or modules per day) can be dramatically increased. On the other hand, as several writers have noticed, merely assigning an *expert* programmer to the job can usually account for all the increase. Low productivity may only be the symptom of an industry in which almost everyone is a hacker.

The following are examples of techniques that many claim can improve productivity in the industrial sense. No one has shown, however, either that (1) these techniques will *generally* increase productivity, or (2) the improvements are permanent, low in total costs, or achievable across all organizations. With these *caveats,* consider this list:

1. Chief programmer teams (CPT).
2. Structured programming (SP).
3. Human relations training (HRT).
4. Programmer productivity tools (PPTs—the term is from Yourdon, 1982).
5. Top-down design (TDD).
6. End-user software development (this, of course, eliminates the programmer, reduces *programmer* time and cost to zero, and thereby increases productivity artificially—training costs and start-up costs are seldom factored into the formula).
7. Software generators.

8. Fourth-generation languages (4GLs—actually a form of end-user software development).
9. More education for programmers (this is the one that truly accounts for increased productivity in most situations).

There are four theories that attempt to pinpoint the source of low productivity in the software shop:

1. Poor human relations.
2. Economic considerations.
3. Lack of appropriate tools.
4. Problems with the measures of productivity themselves.

A number of *human relations theories* begin to explain why productivity among programmers may appear to be low. In particular, the low need that programmers apparently have for the company of others is offered as an explanation as to why they become prima donnas and react poorly to direction, criticism, and suggestions on the whole. Note that this research is statistical in nature and says nothing about the personality or behavior of an individual programmer or MOP. Other human relations problems, discussed in Licker (1983a and b), imply that output from the software shop can be increased by assisting MOPs through human relations training. Understanding workers and making allowances for their foibles as well as directing their work intelligently can, in some cases, increase motivation and loyalty. These, in turn, influence productivity in complex ways.

A second theory of productivity is that the output of programming work is greatly influenced by the availability and educated use of appropriate tools. Howden (1982) lists a number of tools that can increase productivity in programmers. The details are in his paper. His lengthy list is valuable because Howden recognizes that tools need to be appropriate both for the environment and for the stage of evolution of a shop. He suggests that a shop might first acquire a text manager, an automated source code manager, cross-reference tools, and then—as projects grow—obtain machine-readable program test plans, automated configuration managers, and source code formatters. In still more mature and larger environments, programming archiving tools become necessary.

Tools, however, can themselves become significant actors in the

MOP's theater, taking up much of the manager's time with acquisition, training, and control. Attempts to raise productivity by raising the number or power of such tools may swap a short-term increase in productivity for a long-term decrease in managerial effectiveness. In one small microcomputer shop with which this writer is involved, over six months have been spent researching and acquiring tools for a single programmer to use. Factoring this expenditure (and subsequent ones involving training and dissemination) into the productivity formula seriously decreases imputed gains.

A third theory of productivity in software development relates the perceived low productivity to economic and social factors in the marketplace and in society generally. Specifically, low productivity is attributed to the inflation of salaries and perks for programmers on the one hand (i.e., too much money offered for product delivered) or, on the other hand, to lack of training and motivation (i.e., too little product delivered for the price). Certainly programmers receive handsome salaries, although the relatively high starting salaries are not matched by correspondingly higher salaries over the programmer's entire career. Salaries have not grown as rapidly, either, during the most recent three years. Programming salaries, however, are assumed to reflect less the quality of the product, than the low supply of excellent programmers. In a phrase, it's still a seller's market for programming talent. This theory, or prejudice, is offered by no single pundit, but is systematically voiced through the columns of the trade literature and letters to the editors. If it isn't true, it at least reflects a folk wisdom that programmers have too much "power."

More important, many new workers are attracted to the profession simply because it *is* seen as a relatively highly-paid profession. This dilutes skills among those who are in it for the money rather than for the thrill of coding. Phillip Kraft (1977) points out the danger in this trend. He feels that the relative lack of skill in newcomers, compared with the computer whizzes of the 1960s and 1970s, will create a two-class software society. Training alone is not the solution either, since it isn't clear what sort of training is needed. What seems to be required is a cadre of language-skilled programmers who know when a program *feels* right as well as when it is *running* right. This cadre is not now being produced by our technical schools and therefore, according to this theory, productivity is low.

A final theory attributes low productivity to a mirage. Productivity, in this theory, only *appears* low. This is so because we have poor measuring devices for programming products. We compare apples and oranges when we say that this programmer is unproductive because code is delivered late or that one because code is incorrect. The "mirage" theory of low productivity implies that in measuring "productivity" we are looking for products and that software is not a product in the usual sense.

There is something to this idea. Certainly the experts are weaning us from "lines of code per day" to other, more complex, measures of productivity. These measures include learnability, maintainability, and documentation quality. The idea that there is a single, simple measure of how much software a programmer produces is slowly dying out.

However, there also seem to be few good, numerically based candidates to replace lines of code per day. The value added by a program—that is, the value to the purchaser organization—is realized only at the time the program is successfully installed and run. Merely translating specs to COBOL is insufficient. In other words, software production is not an industry in the sense that manufacturing ball bearings is—not yet, anyway.

The value-added concept is a good one to use though, and we return to it later. Let's first look more closely at the *industrial* conception of productivity and see how this blends with what we know about programmers and their products (see Figure 3.3).

Industrial productivity measures rest upon the idea of a single, tangible, countable product. Productivity is measured by the *efficiency of transformation* of raw materials into finished product over time. For programmers, this would naturally seem to be lines of code per hour. Note that there is no true "transformation" here, however, since products are in essence built out of nothing but ideas.

Most software production and all maintenance illustrate the very high cost of the first "product" and the very low cost of subsequent products identical to the first. Unfortunately, there is usually no subsequent production of software, especially for maintenance. Therefore, there is no way to profit from "economies of scale," the advantage a factory has in producing a million widgets more cheaply per item than a thousand can be produced.

The value-added concept, then, is more appropriate for a single-item production or maintenance shop. Here we measure productivity by the value that the product adds to the customer's activities. Value is added by speed, by efficiency in performance, and by reliability. It is decreased by errors, by inefficiency in repair, by difficulty in training, and by discomfort in use.

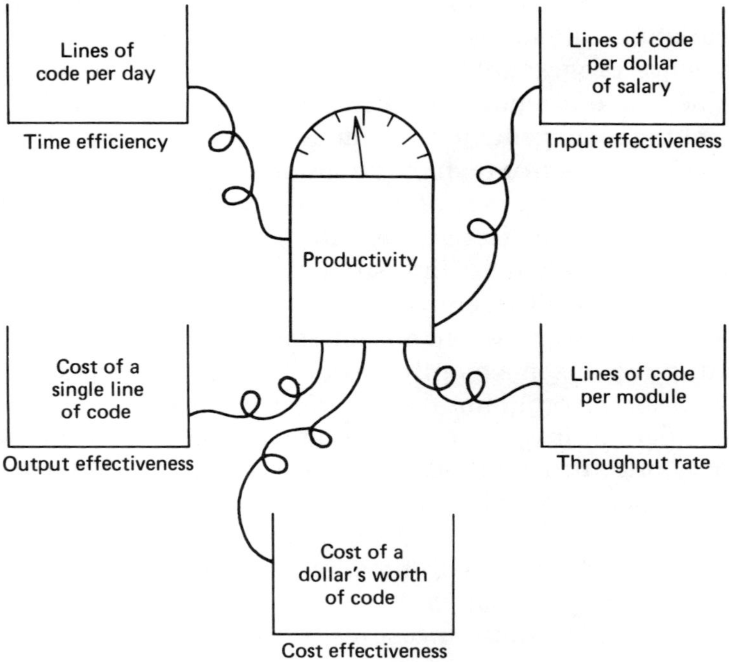


**FIGURE 3.3** Applying industrial productivity measures to programmers.

The problems of the industrial measures of productivity underscore the advantages of a value-added measure. First, the contribution of the program itself to the product is not always clear. Is a well-running program that is difficult to use as valuable as a poorly running and poorly documented program that anyone can use without training? Since many large-scale systems are sold to firms with an untrained user group, the friendliness of the user interface may more than compensate for slow transaction processing speed. In these cases, skillfully written code that is invisible to the user may be less valuable than quick-and-dirty coding that makes the user interface more learnable.

Second, the level at which a programmer codes (line, function, module, system) and the organizational environment within which the program operates (management, supervision, worker) as well as the type of program greatly influence the contribution an individual's programming activities can make to the product. User interfaces are easy to write poorly. Operating system interfaces are always difficult to write and debug. Much mathematical calculation is very straightforward and of a routine nature. How efficient must a programmer be in this variety of situations to be called "efficient"?

Third, since programmers work in a team setting but practically work alone, the efficiency and intrusiveness of the team is a direct function of the management capabilities of the MOP and the quality of the specifications from which programmers work.

Fourth, most of the common measures make an assumption that the thing created is in fact a unit with a well-known contribution (value added) to the whole. Industrial measures of productivity are the dinosaurs of the nineteenth century, third generation of work, an era of relatively uncomplicated machinery. To say that a programmer wrote four programs in a month or coded three functions says nothing. Any one of the programs may be trivial or important, complex or simple. It might be invoked every minute or once a year. It may be a supervisory or control module, and hence critical to the operation of other modules, or it may be a work module, "reporting" to a single module already checked out with dummy data. Few other factory workers toil in such fluid environments (see the section on organization of work teams in Chapter 4).

Attempts to apply these measures of productivity in analogous vocations have generally not been successful. Managerial work, as Henry Mintzberg (1974) points out, can best be characterized by a lack of characterization. Professional performance has few aspects that relate to a product. Power typing, on the other hand, has been easily demonstrated to raise productivity of the typing pool dramatically, simply because ready measures of production (i.e., keystroke or documents) were handy.

But this difference is important: the typists are not asked to understand the words they type and produce something else based on those words. Managers and professionals are expected to peruse and then cascade work to others based on information. Programming can be considered to have aspects of this cascading function, and therefore an individual's contribution vis-à-vis a line of code or a module cannot be considered out of context.

If we cannot measure contribution based upon the readily observed line of code or module, what can we use? Researchers are agreed that *amount* of production in an automated shop is less important than the value added to the customer by that production. In other words, effectiveness as well as efficiency are the major components of productivity.

This is, however, as much a function of *management* skill on the part of the MOP as it is of *programmer* skill. Management makes project assignments and provides resources. It is hard to say that one programmer is more or less "productive" than another when a manager fails to match skills and project demands correctly.

Several kinds of value are added by programmers.

Crossman (1982) has written about *functions,* which correspond in his research to well-designed COBOL PARAGRAPHS. If a shop has good standards for functional design, then to say a programmer "adds functional value" to a system will have meaning. Of course, without such standards, the phrase is empty.

Lehman (1979) believes that maintenance is inevitable. One value added by programmers is *correct* processing of information. Hence measurement of correct functionality per invocation (roughly proportional to time) is a reflection of effective production. In brief, we can measure the decay curve for discovered bugs and produce a characterization—the more bugs found more quickly the more maintainable is the program.

When budgets were growing rapidly but CPU cycles were still expensive, programmers had a great deal of concern for elegance and little for the amount of system resource used in development. Since the true value of a program is its subsequent *processing efficiency,* a third measure of effectiveness is cost of running a program per unit cost of producing it. This would be comparable to measuring the productivity of an automobile worker by evaluating the cost of running the automobile. Sadly, for autos, this efficiency ratio seems to fall as the production price increases.

Points ought to be awarded, too, for less tangible measures such as learnability, burn-in time (the amount of time it takes the user group to become comfortable with a function), documentability, maintainability, and general satisfaction on the part of the user group. A quick programmer may produce a program that is difficult to use and with which users never feel comfortable. A less efficient but more "productive" programmer may attend more to details that make the program easy to teach, learn, and document. Since there are tools to increase documentability and to an extent learnability (through program generators and architecture-based development, especially for the user interface), programmers who use the appropriate tools should be rewarded.

Figure 3.4 illustrates the older industrial measures with these proposed automation value-added measures. The management of work should aim at increased value added (effectiveness) as well as effi-

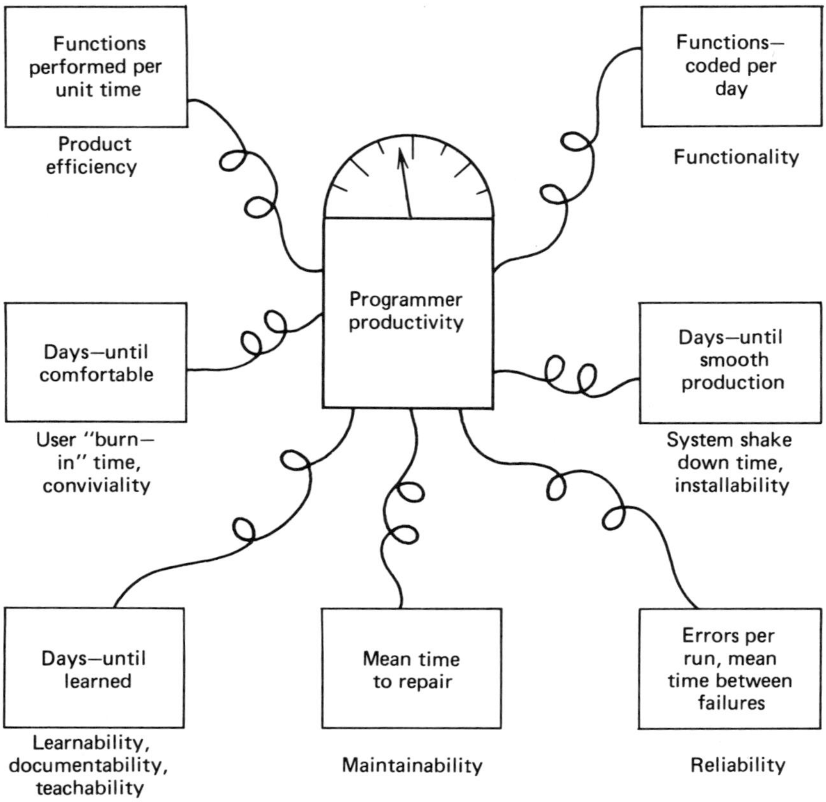


**FIGURE 3.4** Alternative measures of programmer productivity.

ciency. A management program to stress value-added measures would include the development of benchmarks and standards of functionality, maintainability, processing efficiency, and user-friendliness. Since database processing and office automation will increasingly remove much of the nitty-gritty programming from the software desk, the MOP who wishes to make statements about the productivity of the software shop should start looking at value-added aspects of programming.

## 3.4. TOOLS FOR PRODUCTIVITY

As mentioned previously, a great deal of effort is going into development of tools either to aid programmers in becoming more productive or to eliminate the programming aspects of software development. Yourdon (1982) termed the first aspect "programmer productivity techniques" or PPTs. The eldest of these techniques are structured programming, chief programmer team, code inspections and walk-throughs, and team-building. While these techniques may account for some degree of increased productivity measured grossly as "time to completion of project," it is clear that dramatic increases in productivity are not possible with such gross techniques.

Instead, there has been a movement to provide programmers with "power tools" to create software. Generally these tools may be considered to fall in the following classes (see Figure 3.5):

**1.** Environments.
   a. Program library maintenance tools and indexers.
   b. Debuggers, either at source or object level.
   c. Data control systems, such as data dictionaries.

**2.** Generators.
   a. Database managers.
   b. Code generators, including macro compilers, precompilers, and cross compilers.
   c. Very high level languages, including so-called fourth-generation languages.

**3.** Testing aids.
   a. Certified software components.
   b. Test data generators.
   c. Performance monitors (hardware and software).
   d. Simulation languages, emulators.
   e. Data flow analyzers, test harnesses, test coverage analyzers, and other, similar program analyzers.

**4.** Documentation tools.
   a. Flowcharters, cross-reference compilers, and other source code analyzers.
   b. Formatters to make code neater and more readable.
   c. Self-documenting compilers (in English-like languages).
   d. Text processors, interactive documents.

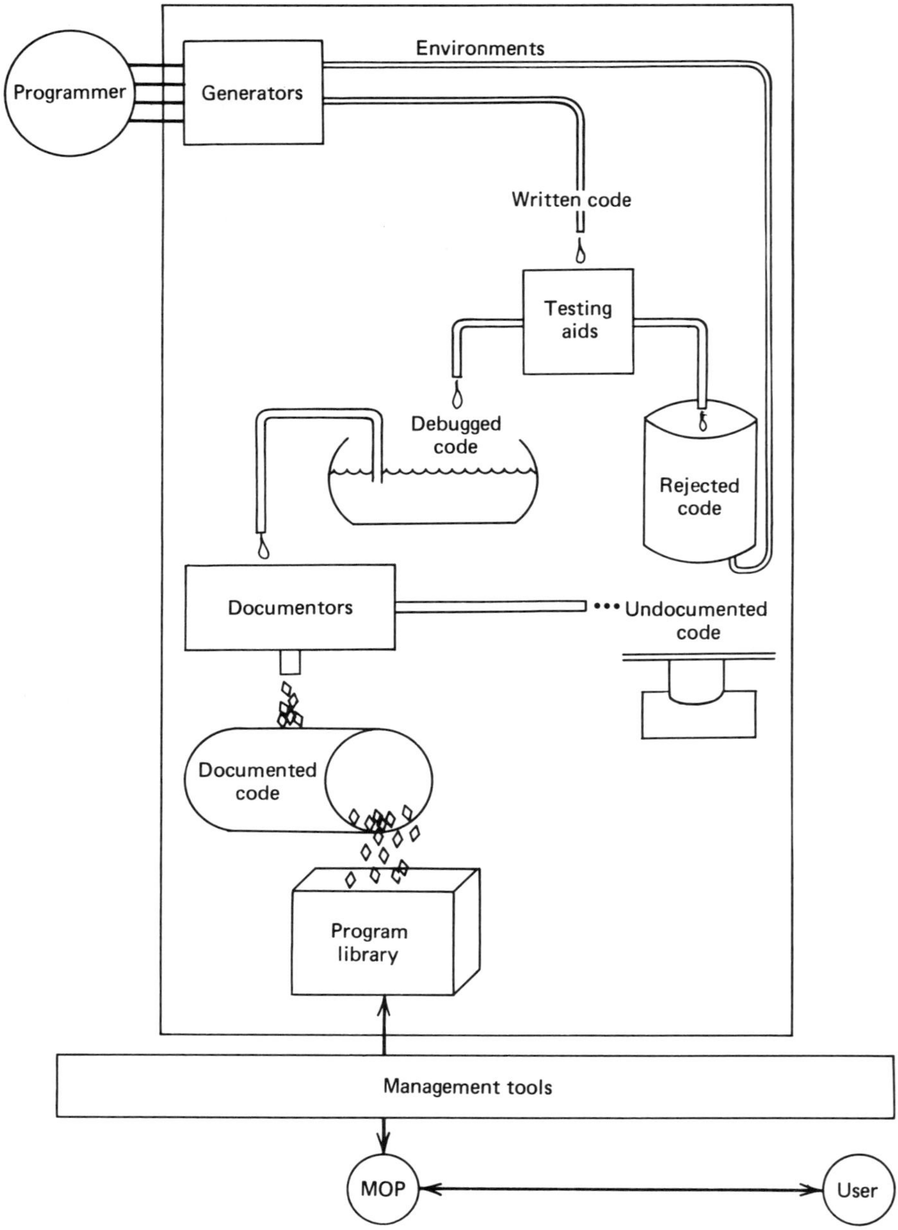


FIGURE 3.5 Program development tools.

5. Management tools.
   a. Automated project control systems for reducing the overhead involved in documenting progress.
   b. Requirements specifications languages and techniques that more closely resemble computer languages (such as PSL/PSA, SADT, SREM).
   c. Electronic mail, personal filing systems, teleconferencing available through the electronic office.

These productivity tools assist programmers in understanding requirements, building and maintaining libraries of code, testing, documenting, and coping with the rest of the software organization. Note that although the emphasis is upon increasing the *volume* of code produced, the benefits of these tools also include increased funtionality, maintainability, processing efficiency, and conviviality.

Wasserman and Gutz (1982) point out in a recent article that the future of programming over the short term is to include increased emphasis upon these tools, but they warn of several problems. Most tools exist in isolation and are not integrated with a software development methodology. They do not support the complete software development life cycle. For instance a debugging compiler is not available during testing of object code and cannot debug specifications or operating system interfaces.

These authors also warn that most tools are mutually incompatible in terms of both usage and processing of files, that they differ from machine to machine and among versions of operating systems, and that they are relatively inflexible. These points should be kept in mind by MOPs considering purchase of any of these tools. In summary, Wasserman and Gutz offer us these words of advice:

1. A tool should have a single, well-defined purpose.
2. A tool must be easy to use.
3. A tool should be adaptable for the novice as well as the expert.
4. A tool must be consistent with the other tools and have appropriate interfaces (those diagnostics shouldn't have to be copied out by hand).
5. Tools should be adaptable to specific requirements.
6. Tools should be able to document their own usage so that management may judge their value based on real usage data.

7. Tools should assist the MOP in configuration management and software personnel development.

On this last point, the tool should assist the MOP in understanding the development process, and that implies knowledge of how well work is proceeding toward goals and how well individuals are proceeding toward career goals and completion of assignments. Statements such as "I've noticed that you've been taking longer to complete assignments lately" need to be supported by data, data that doesn't just point fingers at malefactors but that helps the MOP and the programmer understand where the problem lies. This, in turn, helps the programmer develop as a technician, and also provides the MOP with the information needed to become a better manager of work.

## 3.5. CONTROLLING WORK

Controlling work means monitoring progress toward goals and correcting plans and workers when it appears that progress will not occur as desired. Chapter 4 presents details on how to create and follow a work plan with respect to individual programmers. Here we are concerned with creating and scheduling work activities over the course of the development cycle for a unit.

Essential in controlling work are these aspects:

1. Creating a work plan with milestones and deliverables.
2. Assigning individuals to work on particular aspects of these deliverables.
3. Meeting with individuals and groups to determine whether these assignments will be delivered on time.
4. Changing work schedules and resource allocations to bring the plan back into line.

Communication is the basic element in control of work. There are two components: (1) verbal interaction in meetings and interviews and (2) formal written reports.

In the former, the MOP will meet regularly with staff to go over goals and activities. Work assignments are made verbally and followed through with documentation, which forms part of the permanent record of the project and the individual. Verbal status reports provide an informal check on work progress, but they must be backed up with adequate documentation.

Two formats for verbal interaction are the team meeting and the two-person interview. Team meetings are an essential element in any project schedule. Table 3.1 illustrates the wide variety of meetings in which the MOP becomes involved during the course of a project.

*Project status meetings* are typically scheduled on a regular basis in advance. Many shops try to avoid these meetings and schedule only one or two during a lengthy project. Others subject their staff to weekly meetings. Neither extreme is valuable because the goal of status meetings cannot be accomplished merely by sprinkling them

**TABLE 3.1 PROJECT MEETINGS FOR THE MOP**

| Meeting Type | Frequency | Attendees | Purpose |
|---|---|---|---|
| Project status | Related to milestones | Project team | Prepare for milestones |
| Customer project status | Ad hoc | Customer, MOP | Reassure customer |
| Milestone | Each milestone | Project team | Concluding phases |
| Demonstrations | | | |
| Deliverables | Each major module | Worker, MOP | Certification correction |
| Observables | Each major user function | Worker, MOP | Certification correction |
| Systems | Subsystem delivery | Customer, MOP, worker | Certification |
| Operations | System delivery | Customer, DP management, MOP (maybe) | Sign-off |
| Sign-off | System delivery | Customer, DP management | Release of obligations |
| Training | As needed, near end of project | Programmers, users, maybe systems staff | Education, shake down |
| Technical review | As technical issues arise | MOP, staff | Dissemination |

in small or large quantities through the schedule. Status meetings provide distant early warnings to the MOP of impending problems and reassurances that discovered problems have been controlled. Therefore, status meetings are integral to progress and should be built around the milestones.

Let us consider the scheduling of status meetings for a medium-sized project to automate an order-entry section in a wholesale firm. The project involves 11 programmers and the MOP for an 18 month period. Status meetings are preplanned (1) to judge the effectiveness of the work assignments themselves, (2) to prepare for the first milestone meeting, (3) to prepare for the first general review, (4) to redeploy staff after the first major design review, (5) to prepare for the second milestone, which will be a test of the higher-level deliverable (i.e., a run through the system with program stubs to demonstrate the user interface), (6)–(8)—similar to (5)—to prepare for milestones three through five, (9) to account for the entire system in anticipation of the level 3 systems test, (10) in anticipation of the first operational test at level 4, and (11) to gather documentation. The twelfth and last status meeting is a project debriefing session, in which the MOP reports on the acceptance test and provides feedback to individuals and the group on their strengths during the project. One major complaint by programmers is that they receive too much negative (error-correcting) feedback and not enough positive (reinforcing) feedback (i.e., praise) from their supervisors. Making a last status meeting an integral part of the project helps reinforce the feeling that management cares about programmers' opinions and skills beyond their ability to turn bits into bucks.

*Customer project status meetings* (CPSM) are of two types. The MOP may plan for several during the project lifetime in order to maintain liaison with the customer or user group, although recent research has demonstrated that the continuous involvement of one or more users in the actual development is superior to the occasional status meeting in terms of both contributions to the project and relationships with the user group. The CPSM is too often a panicky *ad hoc* complaint session, usually because the customer is dissatisfied, insecure, or unsure of project status. Most CPSMs may be avoidable unless the project is lengthy, complex, and requires coordination of customer resources (such as those necessary for installation, training, auditing, and end-user-oriented development). Otherwise, these meetings should be integrated with the demonstrations discussed below.

*Milestone meetings* may include demonstrations. They are simple affairs with staff to conclude phases of the project. They serve two purposes. For resource accounting, they aid the MOP in allocating costs to development functions such as specification writing, file development, interfacing, and so forth. For staff, they provide another opportunity to "get strokes" for a job well done and to be relieved of responsibilities. Workaholism among programmers will probably never be eliminated, but programmers can certainly be told officially that the job is over and it's time to move to something else. Project status meetings prepare for the milestones by providing the MOP with performance data, documentation, and the like, and with some indication of whether or not the milestone will be met.

*Technical reviews* are small meetings held often in the absence of the MOP and include structured walk-throughs, code reviews, technical design reviews, and training sessions. This last may occur when a new item of equipment has been brought in or a new piece of software is to be installed for development purposes. Technical reviews may also be called by the MOP when there is suspicion that performance of products is not going to be "up to spec." However, such meetings should not be called in lieu of spadework done by the MOP with individual programmers. These meetings can quickly deteriorate into blaming and grandstanding, which structured walk-throughs and interviews are designed to avoid.

*Demonstrations* are the most important meetings. There are four sorts of demonstrations:

1. *Deliverables (level 1).* Items of software are individually demonstrated with well controlled test data. Customers are not invited to these meetings. An item that passes this demonstration is considered ready for level 2 demonstration. Faults may be noted and tolerated (and then well documented), but they usually are considered sufficient reason to reject the item and send it back for reprogramming.

2. *Observables (level 2).* Functions to be made available to the customer are demonstrated with copies of live data that conform to test data specifications. A function passing this level is ready for level 3 demonstration. Faults may be noted and tolerated at this level, but rarely are, since customers have already agreed upon the specifications of functions.

3. *Systems (level 3).* Sometimes called an integration test, the system demonstration puts all the functions together in the presence of the user, who is allowed to carry out "typical" operations in a controlled environment. System tests are informal because specifications rarely

mention how a whole system should function but rather concentrate upon specific aspects (functions) or operational qualities (transactions per hour, files so big, response time within such a range). The primary judge of the systems level demonstration is therefore the MOP and the software contractor (usually the manager of data processing or a delegate). Systems passing this level are ready for operational testing. Systems not passing this level may be documented as partially dysfunctional (if that is allowed in the contract) or sent back for reprogramming. Systems level testing is sometimes performed in a simulated environment, particularly when other, adjoining, systems are unavailable or when hardware is on order.

4. *Operations (level 4).* This is the ultimate test. The integrated system is subjected to actual or parallel operations on real, uncontrolled data in the intended environment. Operations level demonstrations are part of the customer sign-off procedure. Faults in operations may be complex to determine, and consequently this meeting must be attended by DP management as well as customer and user management. Since operations may proceed over a period of time, the actual meeting may take place "off line" and examine documentation collected over days or weeks.

*Sign-off meetings* may not involve the MOP unless there are technical questions that dictate acceptance of the software. Sign-off meetings should be followed with the final project status meeting.

*Training sessions* are also meetings in a sense. In small shops, programmers or MOPs may be called upon to provide training to users either in a classroom or on a one-to-one basis. In larger shops, analysis staff or trained trainers may provide this service. If programmer-written documentation is involved in the training, it may be necessary for the MOP to review the documentation with the trainers prior to use.

The diagram below illustrates the 12 project status meetings (P1–P12), 5 milestone meetings (M1–M5), 4 reviews involving demonstrations (R1–R4), and the sign-off meetings, which the MOP will attend. Over the 18-month span, technical reviews may occur as often as biweekly. If customer personnel are not integrated with the project, then CPSMs should be held no less frequently than bimonthly, especially if customer funds are made available before delivery. Altogether, for a single 18-month project, the MOP can count on attending at least 31 meetings!

In addition to meetings, the MOP can expect regularly to inter-

Month from project start

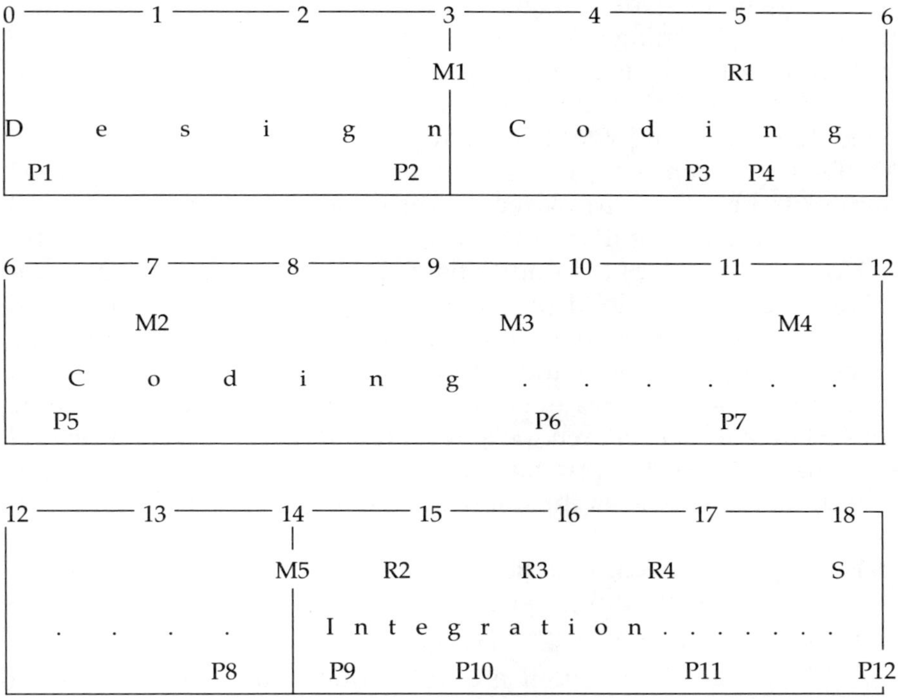


view staff concerning progress toward goals. Few managers do this well. Managers of programmers, too, must not appear to be monitoring work with a microscope. On the other hand, it is important to find out how well work is progressing and duck the famous "90%" complete syndrome (when an untestable claim of "nearly complete" is made).

The work of monitoring progress is made easier if work goals are in terms of observable progress. Typically this will be on paper in the form of documentation and listings. Where a test harness is used, either automated or semimanual, output from this environment automatically documents "completeness."

Other aspects of the work progress interview have to do with less objective qualities such as job satisfaction, comfort, understanding of the assignment, frustration with resource availability and limitations, and interpersonal relations between worker and MOP, much of which is covered in Chapters 4 and 5.

Meetings and interviews are the verbal aspects of work control, but the term usually evokes images of mountains of paperwork. Traditionally programming has avoided this (or in extreme cases overdone it) because of resistance to forms and documentation by programmers who do not see this as productive work. In a phrase, programmers don't get their jollies from filling out forms. On the other hand, MOPs don't keep their jobs if the work doesn't get done and done demonstrably. The narrow region between what programmers will tolerate and what MOPs see as necessary requires tact and creativity.

However, much of the traditional paperwork can be at least semiautomated using a good project management and documentation system. Forms can be filled out on the terminal; schedules can be accessed through commands; status reports can be boiler-plated through a word-processing system. The software shop may well be the last area to use its own tools in production, but there are several systems available for purchase or jury-rigging to specific requirements. At the very least the following are necessary (see Figure 3.6):

1. A project documentation filing system, preferably accessible through operating system commands.
2. A project database management system with a query language, either built around commercial systems such as ADABAS or NOMAD or integrated with an automated project management system.
3. A word-processing system thoroughly integrated with electronic mail to create forms for electronic transmission from worker to manager.
4. Automated project scheduling systems for performing network calculations in a PERT or CPM fashion and for maintaining Gantt charts, which are explained below.
5. A graphics interface for display of this information.

Happily, any database management system worth owning has a query language for a front end and can easily be integrated with automated scheduling systems. Integrating word processing, electronic mail, and the database manager may prove tougher and more expensive, but in the end it may more than pay off. Programmers will then see documentation and communication as computer-based activities, worthy of their attention. Narratives of experience with electronic mail in the software shop show that the bulk of the messages

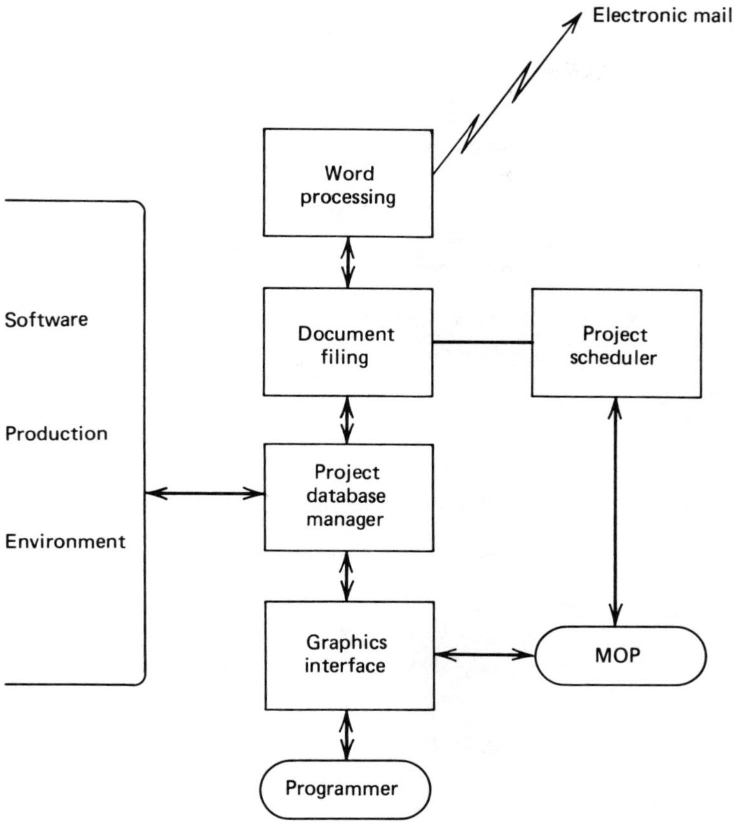


**FIGURE 3.6** Employing computers in work management.

are work-oriented without being exclusively so—hence electronic mail can perform an important integrating function on an interpersonal level and be fun, too.

The basic form of a work schedule is the *Gantt chart*. This diagram, illustrated below, is a two-dimensional representation of the allocation of time to individuals or projects. Along the horizontal axis are units of time, commonly weeks or months. Along the vertical axis are projects, module-names, or the names of individuals. A tick mark in the horizontal/vertical intersection indicates an assignment of that person, module, or project for the indicated period of time. In effect, a Gantt chart consists of a series of horizontal bars.

Expansions of this format provide for multiple parallel bars dividing work assignments into classes (programmer vs. analyst vs. coder)

```
          Jan Feb Mar Apr  May Jun Jul Aug  Sep Oct Nov  Dec
        | .   .   .   .    .   .   .   .    .   .   .    .   .
--------+-------------------------------------------------------
        |
Alfred  |      XXXXXXXXXXXXXX           XXXXXXXXXXXXXXXX
        |
Mary    |      XXXXXXXXXXXXXX
        |
Peter   |                       XXXXXXXXXXXXXXXXXXXXXXXX
        |
Stokely |      XXXXXXXXXXXXXXXXXXXXXXXXXXXXXXXXXXXXXXXXXX
        |
Ulla    |      XXXXXXXXXXXXXXXXXX
        |
Simon   |                          XXXXXXXXXXXXXXXXXXXX
        |
```

```
              Jan Feb Mar Apr  May Jun Jul Aug  Sep Oct Nov  Dec
Project     | .   .   .   .    .   .   .   .    .   .   .    .   .
------------+-------------------------------------------------------
            |
Inventory   |   AAAAAAAAA
            |             CCCCCCCCCCCCCCCC
            |             T T T T T T T T T T T T T T T T T T T T T T T T
            |
Order-      |
  entry     | AAAAAAAAAAAAAAA
            |                PPPPPPPPPPPPPP
            |                      CCCCCCCCCCCCCC
            |                                        TTTT
            |
Accounting  |                              PPPPPPPPPPPPPPPPPPPPP
  front end |
            |
DBase III   |
  install   |         SSSS
            |
System      |
  change    |  SSSSSSS
            |
```

S = Systems programming
C = Applications programming
A = Analysis and design
P = Procurement and customizing
T = Testing

or individuals (John, Mary, Ralph). Symbols placed along the bars indicate milestones or deliverables. The X's along the bars below indicate milestones.

The Gantt chart indicates a static view of work assignment in the future. The network diagram (PERT or CPM) indicates how aspects of the project interrelate over time. Figure 3.7 depicts a CPM diagram. The arrows indicate logical necessity; where two arrows converge, this indicates that a specified activity cannot begin until two others have completed. Otherwise activities can be concurrent. A network diagram for projects may not have any loops. Otherwise it has similarities to data flow diagrams. Values may be placed along the arrows indicating time or cost or both, and techniques exist to determine what is termed the "critical path" from project inception to completion, the path along which no slack is allowed and toward which MOPs should direct their efforts.

When slack or slippage occurs, the MOP may be tempted to fall into a panic mode of problem solving. Indeed, some slippage is worthy of panic, particularly when it is discovered that the hardware specs are out-of-date and terminal upgrades make your telecommunications interface nonoperational. Others may be less disastrous.

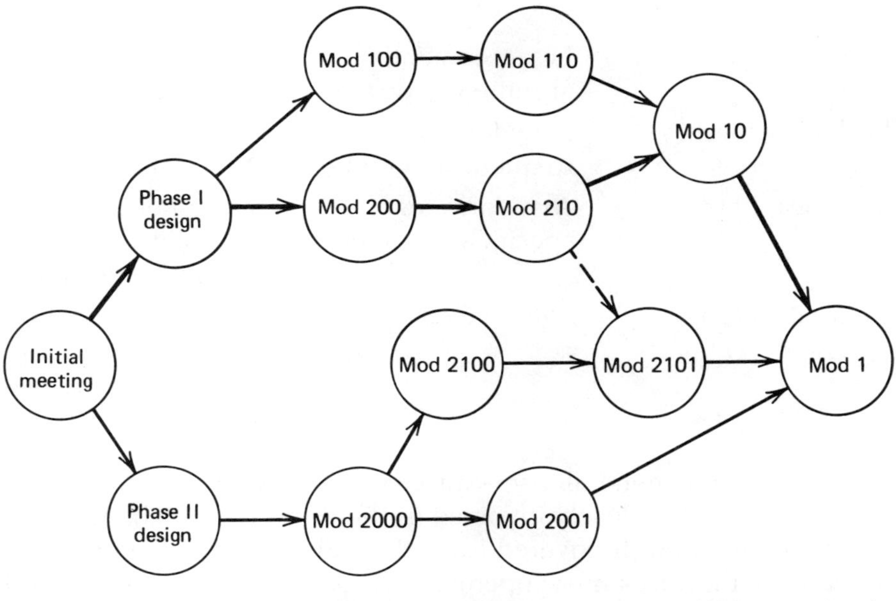


**FIGURE 3.7** A simple CPM chart, showing activity dependencies and the critical path.

Wooldridge (1976) detailed nine "project crises" and discussed how to handle them. Since these crises are best avoided, the MOP should remain attuned to warning signs of each of them. The chart below illustrates these crises, warning signs, and Wooldridge's suggestion for handling them:

| Project Crisis | Signs and Portents | Counteractions |
|---|---|---|
| Spec changes | Slower user response, sudden interest | Add staff, change deadlines |
| User delays | None | Negotiate, pass the buck |
| Lost documentation | Programmer behind on documentation | Redocument, redeploy staff |
| Key staff lost | Dissatisfaction | Add staff, change milestones |
| Poor quality work | Late delivery, many bugs | Document, boost morale, add staff |
| Personality clashes | Disagreement, arguments, delays | Conciliate, transfer staff |
| Lack of resources | Slowdowns, frequent downtime | Contract out, add staff |
| Technical barrier | Avoidance of specific assignments | Document, add staff, retrain, redesign |
| General slippage | Late delivery | Add staff, redefine system scope, freeze system, change milestones |

Note that, in general, user-caused crises may be quite surprising unless user staff is closely involved in the project. Staff changes can be anticipated and discovered early through a policy of staff development that induces more openness about employee concerns and plans. Program design problems should be caught early. General slippage seems the bane of the software shop (but not exclusive to the software shop, as any government auditor knows) and is best anticipated by frequent milestones and a good project control system. The following illustrates techniques for avoiding these delays:

| Project delay or project crisis | Avoidance counteractions |
|---|---|
| User changes | User education and involvement |
| Delays in authorization | User checkpoints and involvement |
| Staff turnover | Contingency planning |
| Staff fatigue | Prioritizing work assignments |
| Computer downtime | Contingency planning and good liaison with operations |
| Operator errors | Detailed test instructions |
| Bugs and poor quality software | Software engineering, contingency planning |
| System complexity | Pass the buck to analysis group, accept only complete specifications |
| Company politics | Good DP management practice, contingency planning |
| Project politics | Silence, tact, good relations with staff, frequent feedback |
| Overoptimism in estimating | Learn how to estimate! |

## 3.6. MANAGING FOR MAINTAINABILITY

Since the bulk of a project's useful lifetime is spent in the company of nonprogrammers (i.e., users) who had no involvement in spawning the beast, to avoid preparing a program for maintenance is akin to ignoring I/O errors. Good work management rewards efforts to make programs maintainable. A policy of quality control includes maintainability as a criterion.

A program is considered maintainable if someone other than the original programmer or project team can locate and correct errors or provide enhancements within a reasonable cost objective, that is, at a cost less than or equal to the original development cost module by module. Three principles are important.

First, documentation of bugs and deviations from specs must be complete. Automated and semiautomated documentation systems go a long way toward relieving the programmer of the guilt of having forgotten to document the minor change that became a time bomb. Second, the MOP should develop a philosophy of quality control that includes maintainability. Programmers can be made aware of the importance of maintenance in a number of ways. Individuals can be shown how maintainability assists in debugging and testing. Groups can be shown the value of adequate documentation in structured walk-throughs and design reviews. The maintenance group itself is important. It should not be treated as the personnel garbage can of the software shop. There are several documented experiences with employing experts as system maintainers. Physicians, after all, have a great role to play in health maintenance and are seldom confused with street maintenance workers. It's all a matter of spirit and philosophy. Since maintenance is expensive and certain, it pays the MOP to employ skilled maintainers.

*Staff can be trained in maintainability techniques.* Self-documentation, appropriate use of documentation tools, and the use of automated testing environments are some of the techniques that can be taught. Even in a thoroughly manual shop, standards can be developed and checked upon to insure maintainability.

Another technique is the employment of computer services representatives, or, as an extension, the Information Center concept. Computer services representatives are users who are trained in computers and data processing well enough to act as technical liaison personnel. Computer services reps (or CSRs) have the role of being alert to user needs and problems. Over a period of time, the CSRs will come to understand the limitations of software applications in general, and therefore they provide a good source of information about quality of product delivered. They can also be used to train users in being alert to the situation around a program error so that the maintenance programmer has more complete information.

The Information Center concept embraces all of data processing and is largely concerned with moving some software development and maintenance of a detailed end-user-related nature out of the software shop into the user groups. It is likely, moreover, that the Information Center can assist in the development of a philosophy of user-maintainability in software. Tools for user maintenance of user-created software are not unlike similar tools required for programmers.

Several existing techniques for quality assurance include structured walk-throughs, design and code reviews, and testing, but what about errors that haven't been successfully avoided? One meeting-based technique for this kind of quality assurance is the *quality circle* idea. Quality circles tap employee experience and expertise in focusing upon problems in delivery of quality. In a recent *Datamation* article, Couger (1983) details techniques for creating and running quality circles. Essentially a task force focusing upon a documented problem, the quality circle can develop maintainability criteria and techniques for a particular shop. In fact, the idea of quality, as in "quality circle," implies maintainability as a given. Nothing that cannot be maintained should ever be produced unless it is supposed to be consumed.

Another concept worthy of exploring is the idea of "contracting for maintainability." Since errors are expected (one pundit, John Gall, notes with some humor in his book *Systemantics* that systems always operate in failure mode), an aspect that should receive more attention is what kinds of maintainability are expected for a given delivered software product. Included are characteristics such as mean time between failures, mean time to react to failure, mean to correct, penalties for nonperformance of the software, and techniques for demonstrating nonperformance. By contracting for maintainability, the software shop implicitly recognizes the importance of managing work to keep the product going long after it's left the shop.

## 3.7. MANAGING SOFTWARE MAINTENANCE

Thus far our discussion of technical management has been limited to an artificial situation emphasizing new development work and a split between programmer and analyst functions. In practical fact, of course, these functions are often mixed. Most studies of software groups indicate that over 60% of software work is purely maintenance of existing code. In many shops this proportion reaches 100%. Furthermore, the MOP may find him- or herself managing not only programmers but also analysts and programmer analysts. This section concerns technical questions of managing software maintenance in a shop of a mixed group of workers.

The goals of maintenance include the following:

1. *Clean Up.* Redocumentation, standardization of code, removal of extraneous code and drivers.
2. *Fix Up.* Repair of software bugs, repair or restoration of files, conversion of files to new or more efficient formats, copying of new data into old files.
3. *Spruce Up.* Adding enhancements or features to existing software, creating new screens or dialogues, speeding up or decreasing the size of programs, interfacing new peripheral devices, introducing new operating environments, installing new equipment or operating systems.
4. *Wash Up.* Shifting to a new program, package, or system.
5. *Do Up.* One-time runs of programs, data extraction, reformatting of reports, tailoring packages to run within a shop or for a specific user.

Obviously the range of this work is enormous, requiring a wide variety of skills of both a technical and an interpersonal nature. Some are essentially research or investigatory in nature, requiring hours of manual reading and phone conversations with vendors. Others are purely technical puzzle-solving of the classical needle-in-a-haystack variety. Choosing the appropriate individual to work on given tasks is difficult.

Maintenance tasks can be broken down into the following classes (usually in the order shown).

1. Find the problem/define the opportunity/specify the scope.
2. Find the bug/locate the information/locate the program(s) or package(s).
3. Fix the bug/add the code/write the conversion utility.
4. Debug the fix/debug the code/debug the utility/debug the adapted package.
5. Prove the fix works/prove the enhancement works/prove the tailoring works.
6. Document the work for programmers/document the work for management/document the work for users.
7. Release the work.

The cycle may best be summarized as one of orientation, discovery, construction, testing, proving, documentation, and publication. While simple bug-fixing may be left to an individual, it is obvious that no one person can possess all the skills necessary to be a good maintenance programmer across all situations.

The life cycle of software is easily characterized in terms of the quantity and quality of maintenance required. In the early stages of operation, many, easy maintenance problems surface. The repairability of these problems is high, maintenance work is impeded only by lack of time and familiarity with the code, and the general lack of user cooperation due to the users' own lack of familiarity with the program's function.

The middle stages are characterized by decreasingly prevalent "simple" bugs and increasingly complex difficulties. Mean time to repair (MTTR) grows, as does mean time between failures (MTBF). During this phase, users discover new applications, some of which may be expensive to implement, but most of which are suggested either by limitations or opportunities provided by the existing software ("Can you get me this report, can it be broken down by regions, can you make the messages easier to understand, can you make it run faster, can you make it more secure?"). This phase is characteristic of what Gibson and Nolan (1974) have termed the "contagion" and "control" phases of EDP evolution. As users become enthusiastic or apprehensive about a system's usage, the MOP is called upon increasingly to decide which applications to include.

The final, late stage of software life cycle consists mainly of difficult enhancements, the documentation of potentially fatal bugs (and development of software patches to get around them), and very difficult file reorganizations (where attempted) to accommodate either very large databases or very wide applications involving many different data elements. As the workload for maintenance increases in this stage, the pressure mounts on the MOP to terminate maintenance and "wash up" the system—when it's *all* patches, merely reading the documentation is a chore.

MOPs have to manage the complex interaction between maintenance programmers and programmer analysts and a wide variety of nonprogrammers, as well as that necessary between programmers. In the early stages of software development and operation, users and programmers may interact personally, because it is the *code* with which they are having problems. As the difficulty of bugs increases and the frequency decreases, interaction is moved to others in the organization. DP management and the analysts, as well as user management, come on the scene into the software shop. It is likely, too, that "foreign" programmers will be using or adapting mature software for their own uses, and these individuals—often from other divisions of the same firm or from supplier and vendor firms—need to be accommodated. Documentation becomes critical as the mass of fixes and enhancements catches up to the original coding. The rule of thumb that coding only costs 20% of a project budget but maintenance is 50% shows how voluminous that documentation becomes. Merely maintaining the documentation becomes a task.

Programmers may also need access to nontechnical staff, including typists, clerks, and librarians. Maintenance work, by its abbreviated (hopefully!) nature, does not allow long waiting times for transcription, location of manuals and previous documentation, and meetings. MOPs have primary responsibility for seeing that maintenance programmers receive priority attention in these regards.

The nature of debugging and redebugging released software makes it more urgent and less plannable than development work. Because a certain bug may preclude operation of an important system, normal debugging procedures may prove inoperable. Programmers may need more access to more system resources more quickly than operations staff may feel comfortable supplying. MOPs need to be prepared with arguments for higher job queue priorities, more solo system time, and, in some cases, complete dress rehearsals of systems long released in order to debug fixes properly. Some enhancements, especially those involving new peripherals, may require similar upgrades in priority. Again, the MOP is the primary agent here.

A number of special considerations pervade management of maintenance. *The* primary question is always "with whom do I staff the maintenance group?" Others may question the propriety of such a question—in small shops *everyone* is in the maintenance group. The principles for staffing maintenance dictate two approaches:

1. The maintenance group should consist, at least in part, of the programming shop's *best* and most reliable programmers, and certainly some of the most senior and experienced people.
2. Maintenance of a product properly belongs to those who develop the package, given that they are still around.

Practical considerations, however, force many MOPs merely to assign novice programmers to maintenance in order to pick up these skills on the job. There is almost no evidence that this approach works without mentoring (see Chapter 4) or an organization such as the chief programmer team or a software task force (also discussed in Chapter 4). The costs in terms of wasted time and the learning of bad habits, as well as the damage that such assignments do both to the novices and to others assigned to maintenance, outweigh the savings in terms of salary. Maintenance programmers should be the *most* skilled workers, not the least. Skill, however, may, on the one hand, be accumulated experience with the software to be maintained (dictating the second approach) or cleverness or general experience with the behavior of software under stress. Given the high turnover characteristic of normal economic times, the staffing of a maintenance group or the appointment of individuals as maintenance experts (or software life-cycle consultants, which would be more appropriate as a title) would be most appropriate.

In addition to staffing, MOPs need to remain alert to technical developments in software engineering, testing disciplines, software quality assurance, and maintenance tools. Rammamoorthy discusses maintenance aids in Yeh's book, volume II of *Current Trends in Programming Methodology*. There are very few such aids currently available, and these are mostly documentation aids. It is certain, however, that software engineering techniques for program generation, testing, and proving will increasingly make their way into the maintenance repertoire. At least most operating systems on large mainframes take extensive status checks frequently enough to provide *systems* programmers with debugging information. Where analysts have taken care (often with the prodding of MOPs) to include sufficient checkpointing and status documentation in applications packages, maintenance, when it has to be done, becomes simpler.

In summary, the MOP who manages a significant maintenance load (and estimates range upwards from 50% across all shops) will have to be aware of and plan for the specific kinds of work, tasks, interactions, and needs for resources of maintenance work. Planning for maintenance (referred to earlier as "Managing for Maintenance") is a crucial component of this. When all the shouting is over, the champagne drunk and new software launched, maintenance work begins, and the "real" programming gets under way!

## 3.8. PUTTING IT ALL TOGETHER

Managing programming work is, of course, not independent of managing the persons who do the work. In this chapter so far we've treated the two as independent, primarily because the next two chapters look at the human relations and organizational aspects of managing people. However, some words are appropriate here concerning how to marry work with the worker, so to speak.

There are three general programming "styles" among the many variations of activities that programmers engage in. The *systematic* style is compulsive, documenting everything, and proceeding according to some set of rules or standards, either personal or taken from the shop. The *individualistic* style is impulsive, idiosyncratic, bending to no will other than the programmer's own, and documenting where it suits momentary purpose. Of course few programmers sit at either extreme. The style of most programmers is perhaps best termed *semisystematic,* using many shop and personal rules, but bending them sometimes, documenting usually but not always.

Semisystematic styles, like poorly running watches, are almost always out of synch with requirements in some degree. At least the nonrunning watch is right twice a day. The semisystematic style arises at least partly because the MOP sees merit in encouraging programmers to be individuals while asking for the very least in conformance to work standards. Thus problems arise in every aspect of programming work, and this chapter has detailed the tools of work management needed to anticipate and cope with these problems. Getting correct specs, creating and enforcing program design standards, coping with resource availability, creating and enforcing coding standards, measuring productivity, adhering to a testing discipline, obtaining appropriate and timely documentation, and evaluating programmer work and products are problems that are not going to go away in the short term. Techniques for dealing with these problems include organizational, environmental, and managerial ones. Both technical innovation (through languages such as ISDOS, programmer's toolboxes, project management automation, and database management) and management action (developing standards, structured techniques, project control activities, and managing for maintainability) are appropriate coping strategies. In the long run, however, the relationship between MOP and programmer is paramount, and personnel management is the topic of the next chapter.

CHAPTER FOUR

# HUMAN RESOURCE MANAGEMENT
## Organizing Resources

Previous chapters have laid the foundations for a discussion of the most difficult problems facing the MOP, the direction of human resources. The title of an article by Rita Shoor in *ComputerWorld* sums it up: "Supervisor Job Called Toughest in World." One reason why is reflected in another 1980 article in *ComputerWorld*, this one by Bruce Hoard: "Manager Ignorance Blamed for Staff Blues, Turnover." In the same issue, Mr. Hoard titled another article "Management Found Top Source of Discontent."

In this and the next chapter we look at some of the reasons for this ignorance and some of the impediments to good personnel management practice in the software shop. Among the topics to be covered are staffing and training, motivation, organizing work units, and controlling work activities. The focus is upon the management of people and the establishment and maintenance of good human relations between a supervisor and workers. There are few factors as important as this in maintaining high productivity and morale.

## 4.1. MANAGING PEOPLE IN A TECHNICAL ENVIRONMENT

Managing people in a technical environment such as a software shop differs somewhat from similar activities in a general business environment. Particularly important are the need that technological workers have to remain on top of their rapidly changing technology and the need that management has to provide that technology at the best cost and for the best use possible despite that change. This creates three interesting problems.

1. Managing technical people who are attracted to their profession by technical challenge and the thrill of learning and who may not be motivated by the traditional spurs to work.
2. Managing in an organization dedicated to using the best technology in the best way at the least cost to further aims not directly related to those of the technical workers.
3. Developing personnel in a rapidly changing field without limiting them or overly specializing them.

Thus, there are particular challenges facing the MOP in terms of relating to programmers personally. Finding programmers with the right technical and "people" skills for each job is a difficult task. Programmers can present reams of output demonstrating their language skills in COBOL, but rare indeed is the programmer who can or wishes to impress a prospective manager with oratory, writing, or listening skills, that is *natural* language skills. Since programming education is overwhelmingly technological, the MOP has to look for latent interpersonal skills, often unpracticed for years. Yet many MOPs haven't the slightest idea how to interview candidates for programming jobs.

It's important to note that the opposite of Phillip Kraft's touted trend toward "deskilling" is the oppressive movement toward overspecialization and pigeonholing that DP management practice favors. Not merely more detailed knowledge, but a broader view of data processing, both in the DP Department and within the firm, is required to succeed today. The challenge presented to the personnel manager is to "know the user and the user's problems" rather than "know COBOL."

People problems predominate in a programming shop. One personnel director reports that the DP Department is a source of constant catastrophe. Interpersonal relations are not always the best, and many commentators have pointed out the lack of motivation to improve those relations. A recent note on quality circles by Couger (1983) points out that, even when DP managers begin using quality circles, they often leave the scene as soon as they can and don't participate. DP managers often avoid interpersonal problems, preferring either to put them off or locate a management technique allowing programmers to work independently.

It's also likely that DP in general and programming in particular will not continue meeting the personal needs of those holding DP jobs. In the past, DP attracted persons who liked what the *work* had to offer people who were symbolic, analytic, relatively ungregarious, and growth-oriented. As we move from the third to the fourth generation of programmers, those qualities are ones very likely to disappear. Already a number of systems work in English or user terms (consider the Apple Lisa(TM) machine, IBM's Query-By-Example(TM) and Office-By-Example(TM), and VisiCalc(TM) and its imitators). The division of labor becoming increasingly apparent in DP shops isolates the analytic aspects in the analysis team rather than in programming. Programmers are increasingly being asked to work in teams and with users.

In other words, the trend is toward a situation in the software shop in which the type of person attracted to the job will be dissimilar to those who have been attracted there before. Instead of infatuation with the technology and intellectual growth, the new breed of programmers will be interested in security, high initial salaries, and good working conditions. When, as often happens, these expectations are not met, conflict will develop between the DP managers—who are still motivated by the technical environment—and the new hirees—who are in it because it's good employment.

The final challenge facing the MOP is to develop management skills and supervisory attitudes in employees. The design of the work, the form of the organization, and the style of the management have been less than conducive to a climate of skill-building in supervision. Even now, the typical programmer in-house training consists of advanced language and package seminars, systems analysis basics, and some project management.

How can these challenges be met?

The *environmentalist* view is that an increase in the power of tools used by programmers will lower the need for bodies to do the programming. This school is best exemplified by the software engineers. The *human relations* approach responds to this by pointing out that workers themselves respond quickly to improved organizational and managerial relations without the need for engineered production environments. Little of the human relations approach has born fruit *yet* in the software shop.

A third approach has not been tried in programmer shops but intrigues Western industrialists. This is the Japanese management technique referred to by Ouchi (1982 a, b) as "Theory Z." A Theory Z organization nurtures company goals, rather than technical skills. A programmer in a Theory Z firm learns about the firm, its products and plans, and most of all about its *ethos* or characteristic habits, activities, and values. In other words, Theory Z begins with the assumption that an employee is hired for life and works back to the skills necessary to do a particular job over a long period. This directly conflicts with the environmentalist and human-relations views, which begin with the assumption of technical excellence and try to append loyalty through perks and motivators.

Motivation is the fourth challenge of managing in a technical environment. Couger and Zawacki's book *Motivating and Managing Computer Personnel* (1980) is the first systematic study of what motivates DP employees on a large basis (although there have been dozens of smaller and less systematic studies). Their results are clear: thus far, programmers are motivated by the job and its potentials rather than by the organization and its goals.

Soon, however, many if not most programmers will be working for the money. Managers brought up on the golly-gee-whiz aspects of programming may find themselves unable to rouse the troops into action. Later in this chapter, we examine ways of building motivation into the programming job.

The challenge of interpersonal and organizational conflict on the job will be met only with increased skill on the part of the MOP. Few MOPs receive formal training in these areas. Most of us have some idea of how to get along with other people. However, MOPs find themselves in that department within the firm least likely to have daily interaction with others, and hence more likely to experience isolation leading to stereotyping and conflict.

Several attempts to remedy this situation have appeared in recent years. Chief programmer teams and walk-throughs and inspections have forced programmers to communicate with one another. More programmers are being exposed to customers in newer modes of software development such as prototyping. These attempts have been piecemeal, relatively infrequent, and thus far of little general impact on programmers in general. So long as development projects need to tap specialized technical skills and so long as work pressure motivates design of "efficient" work structures, programmers will never experience the organization.

This challenge will be met slowly and indirectly through less formal programs such as mentoring, learning-by-example, and by the response some user organizations have shown in developing "computer services representatives." These last are users who become quasi-analysts, representatives of the user organization to the DP Department. Other responses by the DP Department to the outcry of glacial response to service requests and poor service include IBM's concept of the Information Center and end-user software, discussed elsewhere in this volume.

The final challenge is that of developing new MOPs with supervisory and managerial skills appropriate to the changing conception of DP management. Such skills are typically acquired by poor example. Recently there has been a recognition on the part of upper management that technology is not the only answer. DP supervisors are being sent to courses in management, although not as frequently as non-DP managers are being sent to courses in "how to live with the computer" and BASIC. This volume is a response to this challenge.

## 4.2. ANALYZING PERSONNEL MANAGEMENT

Management is less science than art, even now. There is much disagreement about what a manager really does and why. The list of references at the end of this book attests to the controversy. Here we take a traditional view of management, pioneered almost a century ago and reflected in job descriptions given general managers.

Personnel management activities fall into five broad classes (see Figure 4.1):

1. *Planning.* Forecasting, costing, selling, and modeling. These are not discussed in detail since the most important considerations have been covered in Chapters 2 and 3.
2. *Organizing.* Laying out, allocating, budgeting, explaining, and subdividing work and activities.

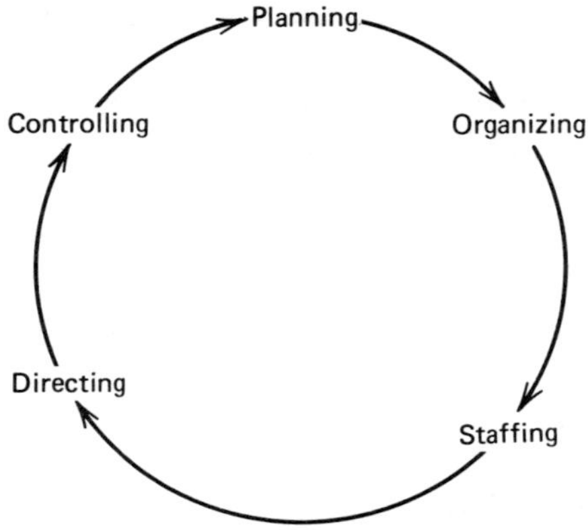


**FIGURE 4.1** The cycle of management responsibility.

3. *Staffing.* Locating, interviewing, recruiting, training, and career-counseling of staff.
4. *Directing.* Actuating, informing, communicating with, delegating to, and describing work to programmers.
5. *Controlling.* Reporting, collecting data, correcting, counseling, motivating, negotiating work, negotiating work results, and critiquing employees during work.

Because staffing and organizing relate to activities that often precede work, they are handled in this chapter. Directing and controlling are the focus of work performance, treated in the next chapter.

## 4.3. STAFFING ACTIVITIES OF THE MOP

MOPs face a number of challenges in staffing. Primary are the selection and development of programmers. Key to this is a *workforce plan*. Few firms engage in workforce planning for programmers. This is mainly due to the shortage of programmers, which has made picking and choosing quite difficult. In addition, it's quite difficult to predict skill and resource needs over a long period when the technology is rapidly changing.

This section discusses the following:

1. Creating a workforce plan.
2. Recruiting, hiring, and orientation of programmers.

3. Following a staff development plan.
4. Coping with specific staffing problems.

### 4.3.1. Workforce Planning in the Software Shop

Workforce planning is the staffing activity that creates a program for hiring, training, and deploying human resources. It is carried out in conjunction with human resource specialists on a regular, often yearly, basis. The result is a report that displays existing and forecasted needs for skill profiles.

Workforce planning begins with data collection: numbers of employees in particular positions, career paths followed, average tenure in position in firm, average number of years in position to promotion, job definitions, and performance and skill profiles of existing staff.

Next, a model is developed to state the effects of various factors on this portfolio. The diagram in Figure 4.2 is typical of these, showing how an increase in workload might result in an increase in workforce levels required in junior programmers and supervisors.

The plan is rounded out by descriptions of skills needed for levels of competence in each position, salaries forecast for each position, economic inflators and deflators, and descriptions of competence level and staffing level targets.

While the workforce plan is a company-wide effort, the MOP is one primary source of information concerning software staffing needs. Data for the workforce plan that the MOP is responsible for collecting include the following:

1. Current staffing level.
2. Short-term anticipated human resource needs.
3. Availability of staff in specific categories.
4. Success of previous workforce planning model in predicting current needs.
5. Degree of conformance now with workforce plan and reasons for the deviance if any.

Workforce planning is not an isolated staffing activity. Figure 4.3 is a data flow diagram (DFD) showing how ongoing processes of workforce planning, performance appraisal, recruiting, and hiring contribute to the overall staffing picture.

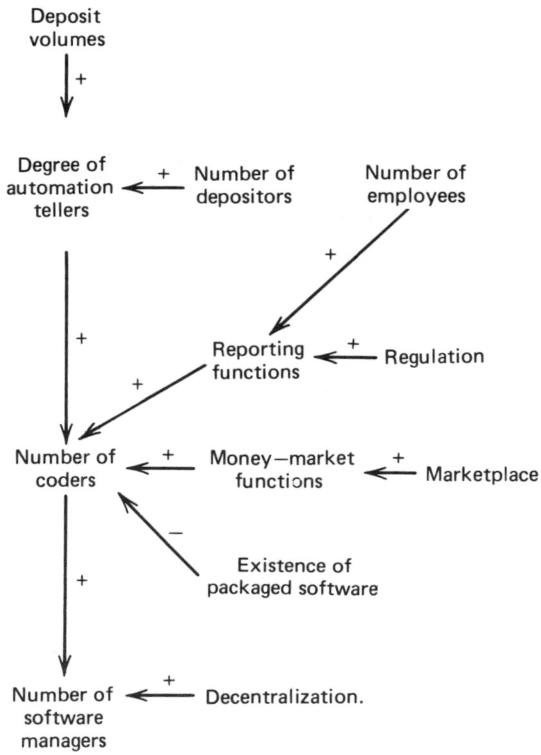


FIGURE 4.2 A workforce planning model.

## 4.3.2. Recruiting

Figure 4.4 illustrates the recruiting process. Again, this function is usually assigned to a specialized area in the Human Resources Department (i.e., Personnel), but the MOP is the primary source of information, and usually participates in the hiring process, particularly in recruiting interviews.

The recruiting interview is especially difficult for MOPs for two reasons. First, neither MOP nor applicant is trained in interviewing. Second, shortages of programmers have left most firms begging for employees and far too willing to give the cursory nod to almost anyone.

Guidelines for the interview are listed below in lieu of a course on interviewing. Remember, you are trying to determine whether or not one or two years ahead this person can lead projects, speak with users, and continue to learn:

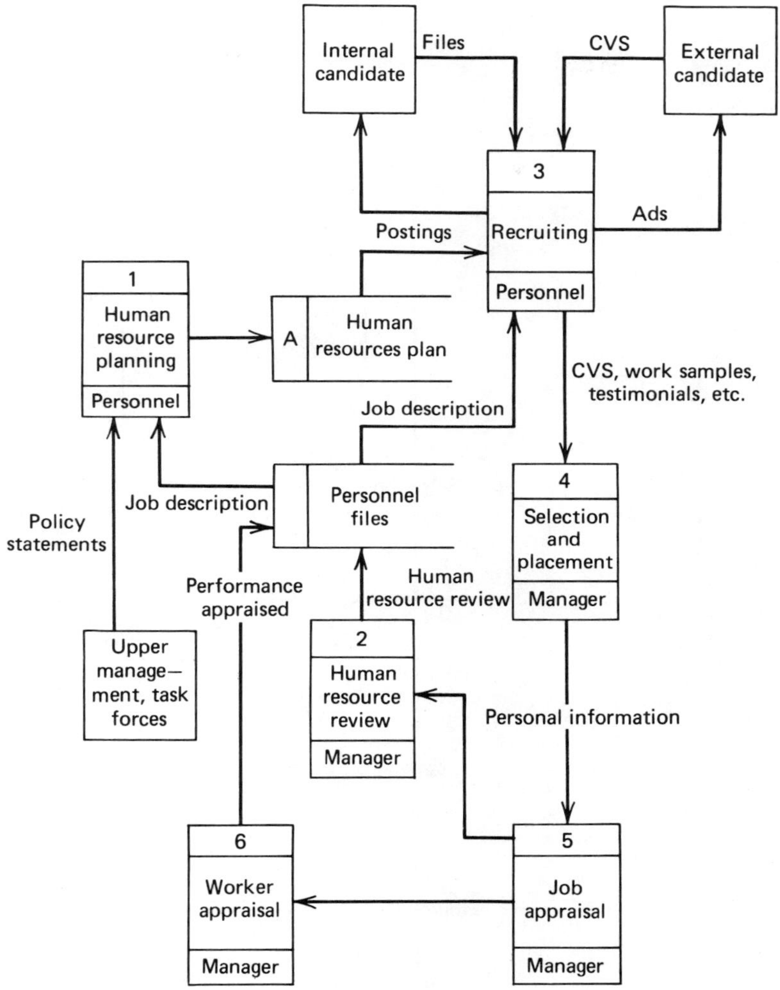


**FIGURE 4.3** Data flow in and around the staffing process.

1. Have the applicant speak with your expert employees, those who know the applicant's areas of expertise.
2. Do not ignore latent skills and knowledge picked up along the line; explore interests and aptitudes in other specializations.
3. Note the leadership and followership qualities of the applicant; can the applicant sell him or herself to your staff? Does the applicant seem to listen openly?

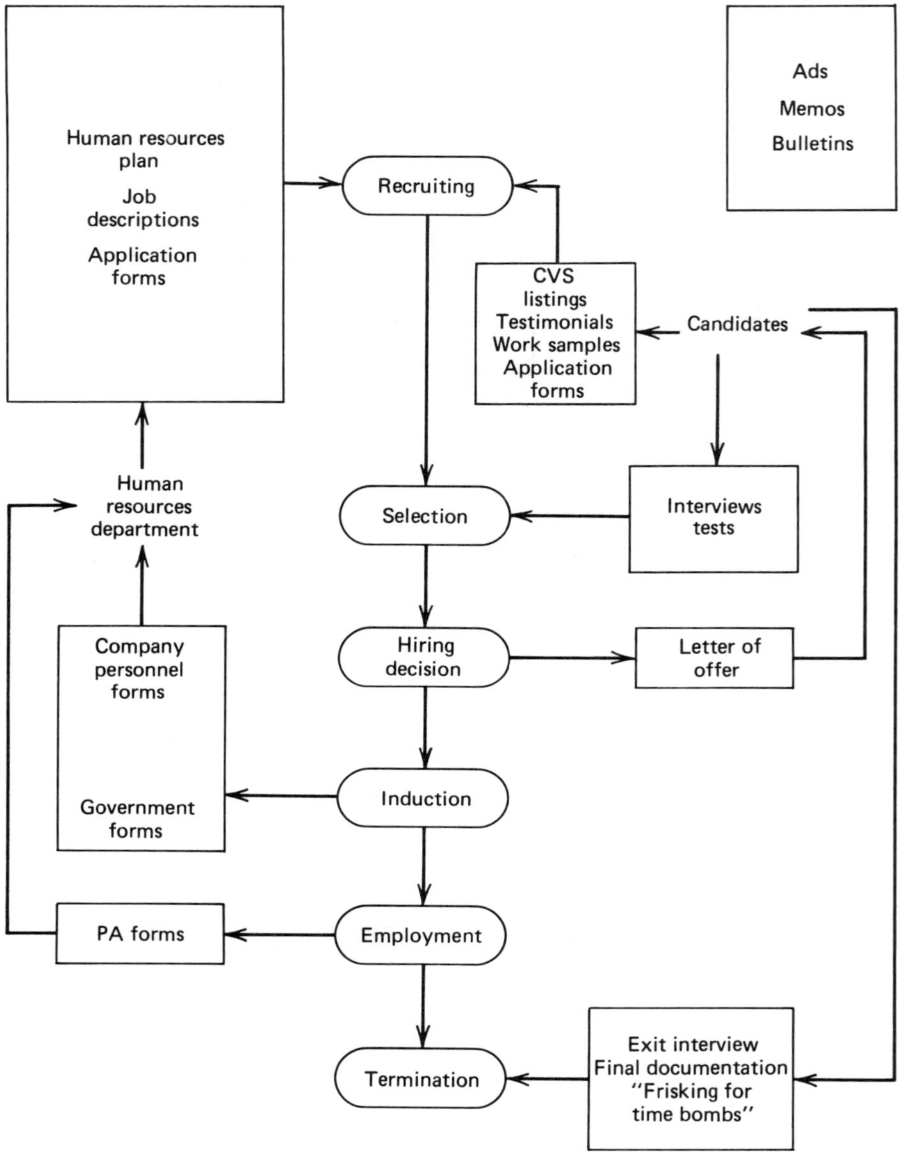


**FIGURE 4.4** Managerial paperwork in the staffing process.

4. It is not unfair to ask the applicant to produce something for you during the second interview: a program can be designed and coded, a bug can be traced, an inspection participated in.
5. No matter how strong your current needs, do not lose sight of your workforce plan; if you've planned right, you will not have an urgent current need; if you do, you can also borrow or buy the skills temporarily.

The recruiting process is not complete when a decision to hire has been made. Figure 4.5 illustrates the process following the hiring decision.

The new hiree must be *inducted, oriented,* and *supported* in order to become a full contributor to the shop. The MOP locates work space, obtains the necessary supplies, and familiarizes the new hiree with the physical area. Proper induction can decrease adjustment time by days and weeks; otherwise confusion can cost the firm and the department dearly.

Orientation to the job, the environment, and the social situation occurs next. Orientation consists of a meeting, tours, initial training, and periodic follow-up. Good planning for orientation includes obtaining samples of work to be done; a review of the new hiree's resumé; lining up organizational resources from the human resources department, the new hiree's supervisor (if it is not you), and operations; and making certain someone is around when the new employee shows up. A typed agenda is essential.

The initial meeting handles problems that have arisen since acceptance: relocation difficulties such as lost furniture or a problem in family adjustment are not untypical. Details on company and shop rules, attendance and behavior policies, the role of performance appraisal, grievance procedures, and other issues should be checked out. You should go over the job description in detail.

For programmers, the tour is important, for it familiarizes the programmer with the locations of the computer and the rest rooms, but more important it introduces the employee to the routine of work in your shop and enables you to begin a registration process for computer use. This last includes obtaining account codes and passwords, manuals, and memoranda on systems operation.

Relevant support organizations include the program library and librarian, the mail system, secretarial and clerical support, and the company library—these, as well as the cafeteria, lounge, and security station can be visited on the tour.

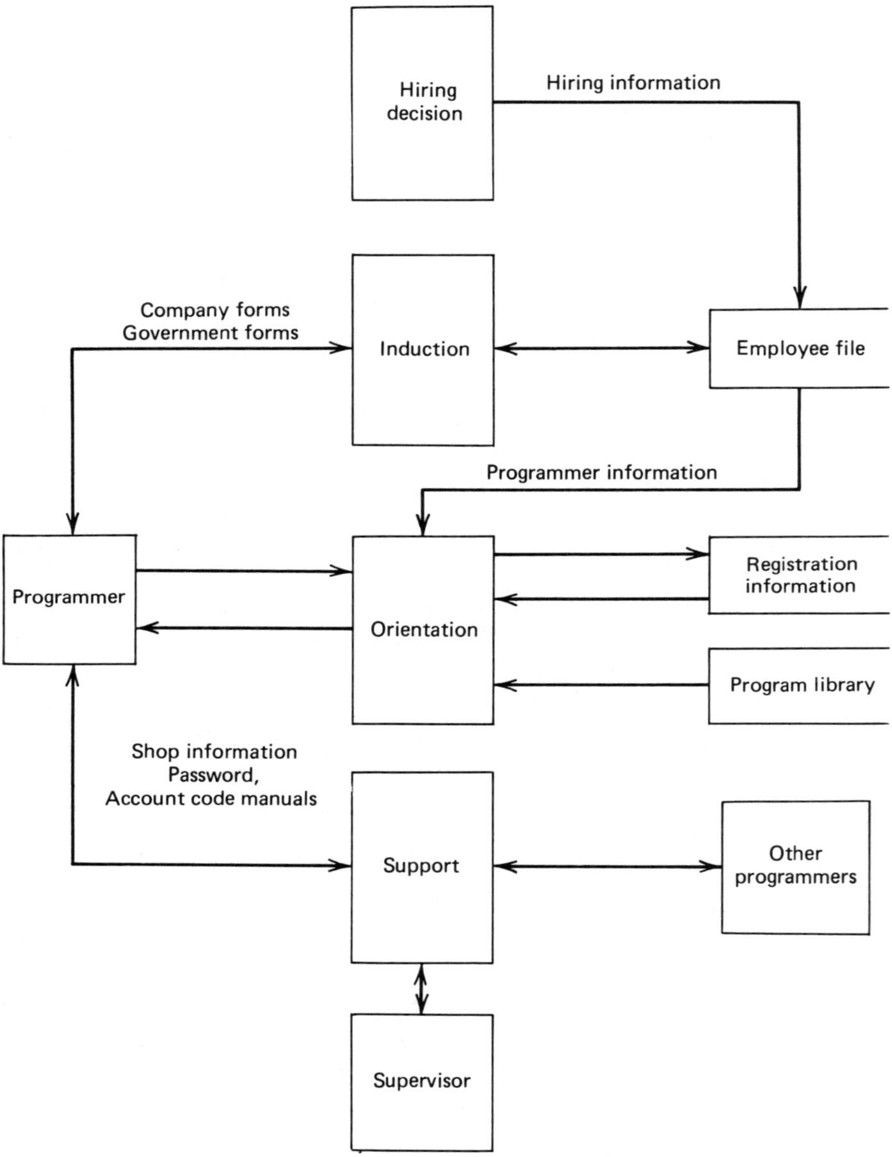


**FIGURE 4.5** The end of the recruiting process.

Support is typically available either from you (or the programmer's supervisor) or from other programmers. It's important to schedule periodic follow-up with the new hiree and to make sure that the new hiree has sources of information and help during the crucial first two weeks of employment. Since programmers are likely to be swamped with work and less likely to be skillful at supporting new hirees, this task is the most crucial of all the elements of recruiting for the MOP. *Attitudes formed during the initial orientation and support period may persist for months—you should work to insure that attitudes are positive.*

### 4.3.3. Staff Development

*Staff development* includes training, coaching, counseling, and career planning for programming staff. Each should proceed from the workforce plan and blend with performance appraisal procedures in order to insure coordination of efforts.

The workforce plan indicates which skills are going to be important at various times in the future. The task the MOP has is to anticipate those needs through the workforce plan and to develop existing staff to meet those needs. Skill needs fall into two major areas:

1. *Technical Knowledge and Expertise.* Knowledge of programming languages, database technology, hardware, packages, systems, applications and program development aids, and the expertise to construct software in these areas.
2. *Managerial Expertise, Confidence, and Knowledge.* Experience in project management techniques, understanding of analysis techniques, general management skills, competence with the organization, and content-specific knowledge relevant to the organization's mission.

In each area, skills can be acquired either through formal, classroom training or in an apprenticeship mode. Formal training is typically purchased out-of-house through educational institutions or consulting firms for detailed, state-of-the-art expertise. The common knowledge base required in the shop is typically supplied in-house. The terms "course," "seminar," and "workshop" imply the same thing: an intensive session or series of sessions conducted by one or more experts in order to impart specific knowledge.

The mentoring relationship is another part of staff development. A mentor is literally an "older friend" who provides advice and informal counseling. Commonly mentoring is valuable in stressful situations, for few of us are capable of coping with all difficult situations without some help and inside information. The mentor-novice relationship is less formal than that of apprentice. There is no pressure on the mentor to respond either favorably or unfavorably to requests to help the novice, whether the request comes from the organization or from the novice. However the relationship is helpful, usually, from several standpoints.

First, where mentoring is fostered, individuals do not feel alone. There is always someone to turn to for advice who will not report this "weakness" to management. Second, mentoring is a social skill that, like others, may help break down the artificial barriers that divide programmers from others. Third, mentoring provides a number of things that research has shown programmers like to have: recognition, an opportunity for growth and learning, and a lot of feedback quickly.

Mentoring is one aspect of the informal social structure of work of which the MOP should be aware. This topic is discussed again later. Since it is apparent that the formal structure of work is not a very satisfying aspect for programmers, MOPs should take note of any positive force that will make the workplace more harmonious.

In addition to formal and informal training, programmers acquire needed skills through coaching and counseling. The first term is applied in those situations in which a programmer requires specific skills in the short term for a specific task, such as proficiency with a software package or development tool. Coaching is really on-the-job tutoring. A skilled practitioner provides close supervision during the learning phase. The programmer learns not with artificial exercises in a classroom environment but through employment of the skills being developed on the job. Although it may be difficult for a programmer to admit to the need to be coached, it is important for the MOP to be aware of opportunities for coaching. Coaching, like mentoring and apprenticeship, provides the accomplished programmer with the chance to impart a skill to a co-worker in a cooperative rather than competitive mode.

A concept closely linked to individual coaching is that of *practique*. Practique (taken from "practice" plus "critique") is a learning mode found in many of the social services. In practique, one or more practitioners act out their newly discovered or newly developed technique for the benefit of others on staff. The staff in turn critiques the technique from the point of view of actually applying it to their own situations. While social service professionals have caseloads and programmers have modules, the analogy is valuable. Every programmer discovers new techniques almost daily (who is the veteran programmer who does not claim to have "invented" database management 15 years ago?); practique provides a forum for sharing those ideas. Two important practique forms are the *structured walk-through* and *code inspections*. These apply to specific cases of particular modules. Practique is a more general term and can apply to sharing knowledge about how to get around a specific hardware problem, how to handle user complaints and suggestions, and how to maintain nomenclature conventions in the absense of a database management system.

Practique is a group technique. Several other group techniques have become fashionable in the past several years. It is not yet completely clear that they are going to prove profitable in the sense of increasing productivity in a direct fashion. Kathryn Bartol recently reviewed the scientific basis for claims concerning chief programmer teams and structured walk-throughs. Little evidence of greatly increased productivity exists from laboratory studies. Where benefits do seem to arise they can be attributed to learning, rather than cooperation. In fact, the theme of learning pervades programming, and it is not surprising that any group technique that stresses the necessity and provides the opportunity for growth will result in decreased friction as attention shifts to the acquisition of knowledge. In other words, any time cooperation can be disguised as learning (as in the CPT, mentoring, apprenticeship, and practique), in general, productivity will rise.

Counseling provides the troubled programmer an opportunity to discuss a difficult personal or job-related problem with the MOP before the problem becomes so difficult that the programmer's work deteriorates. There are a number of approaches to counseling. The "let's be pals" approach requires the manager to be genuinely interested in the personal life of staffers. Not only is this approach basically unprofessional, but also it is unnecessary and inherently dishonest. The employer-employee relationship is contractual in nature. That is, there is an implicit (sometimes explicit) agreement that power is to be shared in particular ways. Any attempt to patch over this contract with clauses that contradict the spirit leads to problems. The only true professional relationship between an employer and the employee is one based on the nature of the product and the methods used to produce the product as spelled out in this contract. Anything else is ad hoc and prone to disagreement and fraud.

### 4.3.4. Performance Appraisal

Because we have traditionally been poor judges of programmer performance, we've tended to apply global rather than specific judgments, preferring to state how well a programmer "seems to be doing" rather than to describe specific behaviors. Later in this chapter, some redress for this unfortunate habit is given.

The overwhelming use of performance appraisal (PA) is in setting salary levels and judging readiness for promotion. Practitioners and researchers point out that this is counterproductive. Because programmers and their managers tend not to be analytic about the programmer's work, there is little real opportunity to talk about the programmer's progress toward career or work goals. Thus PA usually leads to discussion of attitudes and expectations as well as projects.

Problems arise because of the following:

1. PA is done yearly in most firms. *This is far too infrequent* and is unrelated to the usual *project* orientation of most shops.
2. PA is a poor substitute for feedback, a quality that shows up lacking in all programmer job satisfaction studies.
3. Most MOPs need more information on how to conduct a meaningful, profitable, and comfortable interview of any sort. Since the use of PA to make salary judgments adds more pressure, the interviews tend to be short, tense and pretentious.

In fact, PA is an important aspect of personnel development. It provides a formal way to review a period of work. It is an ideal chance to shift the focus of observation from tasks to the job itself and the worker. Some preparation for the PA interview, if it must be done yearly, is to focus upon the worker and the worker's skill profile rather than upon deeds and misdeeds of the past year, most of which are either forgotten or blown up out of all proportion.

#### *Case 1. The Obsolete Employee*

Quincy Mandelbaum is a headache for everyone. Five years out of technical college, three years on the job, and one year into a new system, Quincy is having difficulty getting the hang of it. In walk-through after walk-through, Quincy is unable to explain, defend, correct, or improve his designs. He doesn't understand

> structured techniques. He is fairly competent as a COBOL coder, a passable user of several obsolete packages, and a disaster everywhere else. Terrie Tanner, his supervisor, knows that Quincy should be encouraged to get work as a bricklayer, but she and her management agree that they couldn't afford to replace him for the price: 40% more in salary and half a year's training. In the six months Terrie's been supervisor, she's tried moving him from the center to the periphery. Bit by bit, his assignments have been simpler and less critical. Quincy has responded by quietly doing his job; he appreciates the decrease in pressure. But the cost, of course, has been increased work for the others on staff. Maybe Terrie will have to let Quincy go after all and start recruiting. □

Here is a typical obsolescence profile: skills sufficient to survive in a previous era are no longer valuable. Quincy and his cohort are too expensive, however, merely to let go. The firm has quite a lot invested in Quincy's knowledge, obsolete as it is. Following a vocational domino theory, firms throw good time after bad and retain workers whose replacement would disrupt work. The short-term pain of either firing or retraining these workers seems not worth the effort.

Terrie's courses of action are severely limited without good planning. Implicit in the contract with Quincy is that the company "owes" him a job if he tries hard and doesn't actively subvert it. In fact, of course, Quincy's value added is negligible, as he is. However, there are a number of things Terrie can do.

First, she can try coaching. Programmers need to learn, although they rarely can admit an inability to learn. Coaching allows Quincy to catch up, albeit at a high price. A veteran programmer should coach Quincy through structured programming and walk-throughs in a nonthreatening way. Quincy is obviously not going to respond well under the pressure of the real thing. Such a coaching program could be expected to last at least one project cycle and probably longer. Quincy can be given a shape-up-or-ship-out ultimatum, in the form of a contract-for-performance. Of course, the ability that Terrie has to carry out clauses of such a contract depends greatly upon her ability to measure certain performance aspects of programming. Again, a workforce plan and a behavioral job description come in handy.

Another method would be counseling. Every firm has skilled employees who become obsolete for a variety of reasons. Quincy can have physical, emotional, or financial problems that interfere with his ability to learn the technology. Often a little bit of failure can lead to a self-defeating cycle of lowered self-esteem, lowered performance, and more failure. The natural, and tragic, response to this is simply to stop trying at all. An employee assistance program counselor could intervene in order to provide referral to a community- or company-based program for Quincy.

A final course of action would be to trade Quincy to a user group for someone interested in a posting to software development. Most firms have the facility to provide intrafirm transfers, although transfers into and out of data processing are rare at the technical levels. Nonetheless, a progressive firm may well have a policy that allows one to *fail* gracefully in the DP Department without the stigma of being drummed out of the firm. After all, Quincy does know something of the firm's applications (he's coded some) and how the firm functions (he's received paychecks for three years). It is not unlikely that he, too, could act in a mentoring fashion outside the DP Department. In response, a user department may wish to second an individual to learn programming in order to return and act outside, in the user department, as a computer services representative (see Section 3.6). Such individuals have been employed in some firms, notably banks, to provide computer-versed employees who understand the user side because they are users themselves.

Since obsolescence is the stalking horse of data processing, it would prove profitable for any firm employing programmers to plan for obsolescence through the workforce plan. Although we cannot accurately picture the future course of technological development, we can say for sure that any data processing employee has a good chance of being obsolete some time during a DP career. The rule of thumb is that computer-science concepts have a half-life of four years. A staff that is not learning should therefore experience a turnover of about 20% per annum based on this alone (assuming that the MOPs actually fire obsolete employees).

## 4.4. ORGANIZING ACTIVITIES OF THE MOP

Organizing activities are those directed toward structuring work and resources. There are many aspects of work and project management discussed in Chapters 2 and 3 that entail organization, too. This section is concerned with organizing human resources to perform work: creating and maintaining work units involving people.

The organization of human resources may take many forms, including the task force, the production team, the chief programmer team, and the quality circle. Each organization is a response to a particular set of needs the MOP has to accomplish work. It is shaped by the available resources and greatly by the nature of the problems addressed.

Some symptoms of organizational problems include:

1. Unclear lines of authority.
2. Lack of trust.
3. Inability to delegate responsibilities.
4. Failure by programmers to accept delegation.
5. Fear of failure.
6. Interdepartmental conflict.

Figure 4.6 illustrates graphically the relationships between the dimensions of (1) degree of organization and (2) emphasis upon skill and size for a variety of different organizations of programmers.

In this section, four aspects of organization are discussed:

1. Creating work teams.
2. Building team spirit.
3. Maintaining a group of workers.
4. Exercising and delegating authority.

### 4.4.1. Creating Work Teams

A work team exists by virtue of its focus on the work and its motivation to maintain that focus. There are two extremes in doing this. A team of galley slaves is a work group that remains together because of the negative motivation against leaving. A volunteer chorus sings together because the members like hearing their voices blend. Programmer teams lie in the middle: there are elements of both coercion and pride in membership.

Most programming teams are focused upon a structure of programs to be produced or maintained. In many shops, this is further

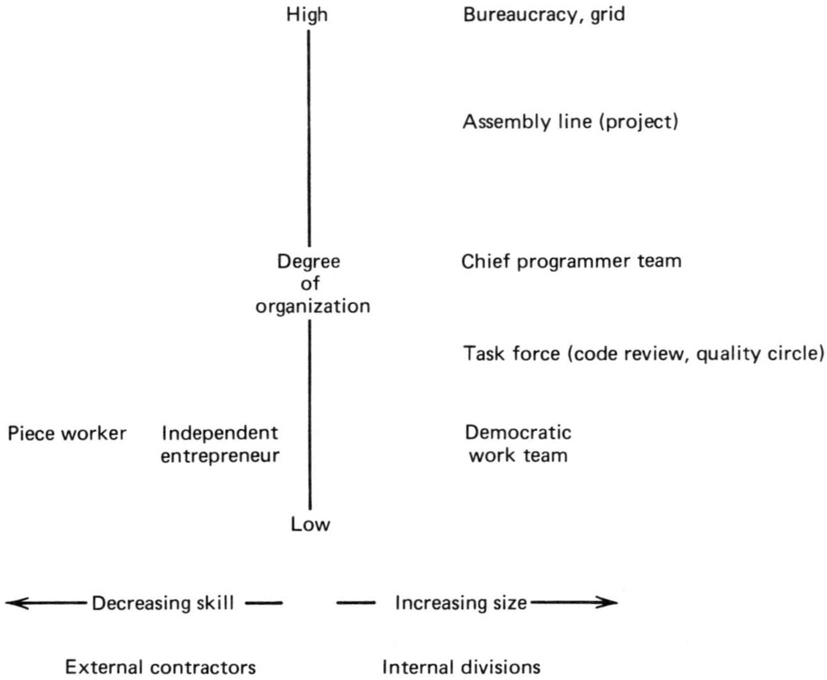


**FIGURE 4.6** Organizations of programmers.

organized into projects. This section discusses a number of ways a programming work team can be organized.

One way is by *grid*, or *matrix*, management. From a human resource development point of view, there are really few advantages to this system. This management technique has programmers working on a variety of projects, each individually supervised by a senior programmer or systems analyst. MOPs, who often have little training in administration and a great deal of motivation to work on technical undertakings, are called upon to be "discipline directors" or paper pushers. On the other hand, the "technical director," or project leader, has little time or motivation to train programmers in project management techniques except through harried example. Each of these players is an incomplete source of information and leadership. Neither integrates the structure well alone.

On the other hand, grid management does help force cooperation among DP groups, cooperation that wouldn't normally appear spontaneously. Such work teams may function smoothly by themselves.

Given the programmer's need for clarity, challenge, and learning, it is doubtful that working in grids will satisfy all programmers over a period of time, although as the profession grows by adding those from outside the science/engineering/mathematics tradition, grid management may prove more attractive to workers. Currently grid management solves a number of organizational problems superfically while introducing other, deeper problems in training, motivation, and loyalty. This classical project management technique is depicted in Figure 4.7.

An alternative is the chief programmer team (CPT) depicted in Figure 4.8. This is essentially a hierarchical task force. The CPT is, however, not multidisciplinary; it aims exclusively at software production. Team focus is also directed to a structure of programs or modules. The Chief Programmer writes all the detailed specifications and may code higher-level modules. The assistant programmer bird-

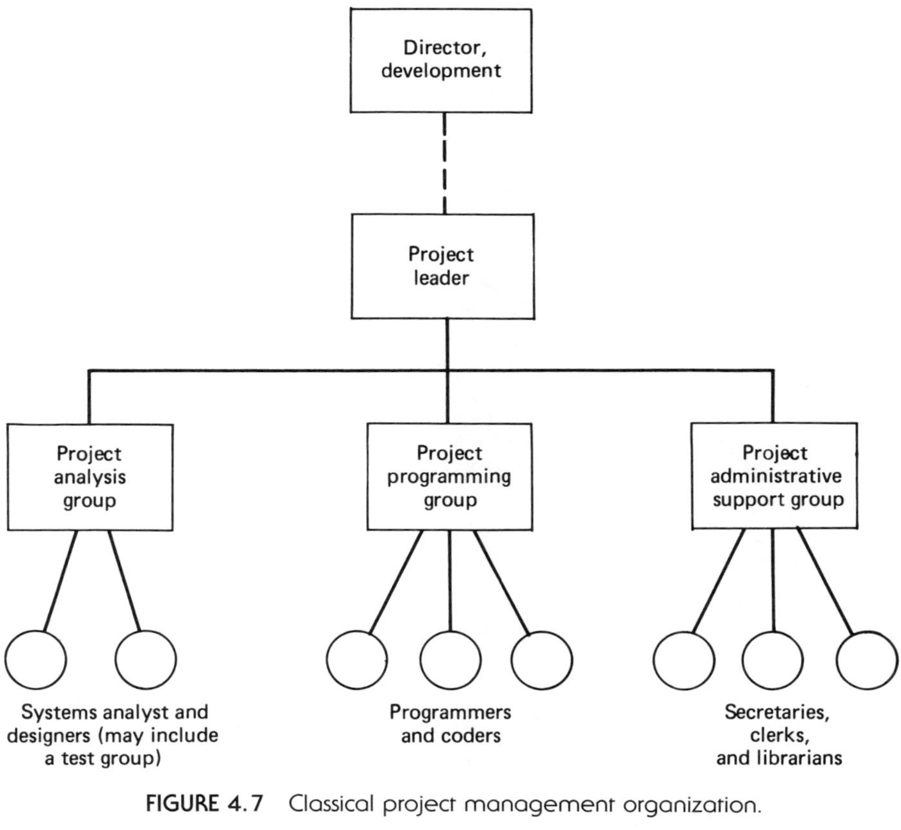


FIGURE 4.7 Classical project management organization.

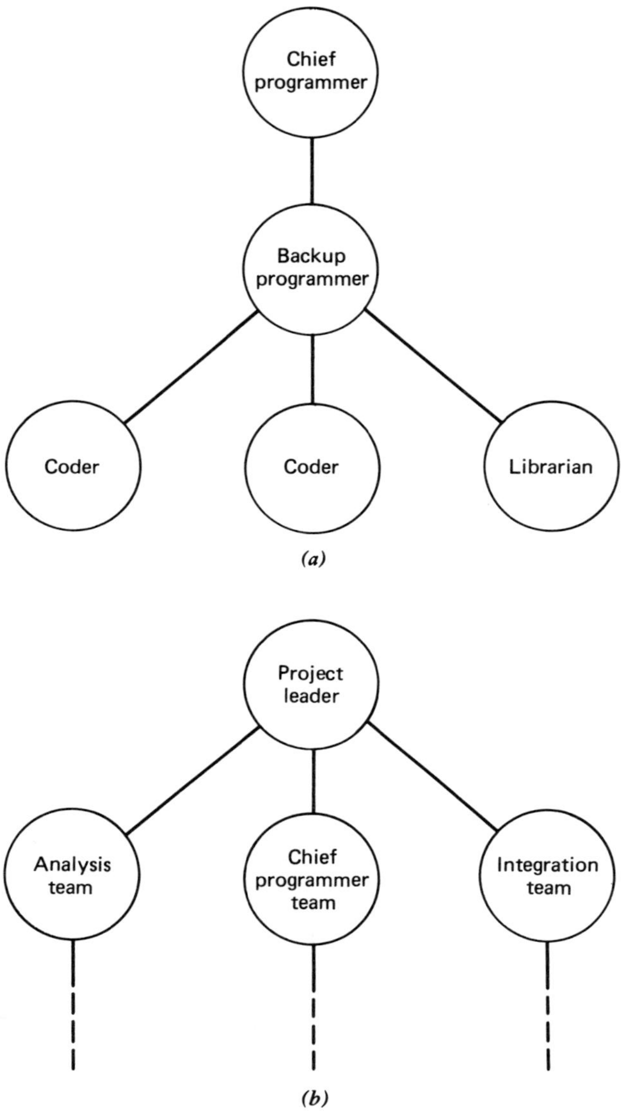


**FIGURE 4.8** Two chief programmer team organizations. (*a*) Simple chief programmer team. (*b*) Chief programmer team embedded in a project environment.

dogs the work and codes intermediate modules; coders produce the rest. Learning is by example and through apprenticeship. Although great productivity gains have been claimed, it is doubtful that these gains have resulted from group efforts as much as from clever assignment of work of appropriate difficulty to the appropriate individuals (which has been discussed in Chapter 3). Most likely it is the extreme and relevant clarity of the specifications produced by the experienced Chief Programmer that increases code quality. Nevertheless, the CPT organization does recognize the value of close supervision and stronger interaction between project leader and project member. The implications are many. Clear specifications, experienced judgment, appropriate work assignments, and skilled coding produce quality work generally.

The CPT is a miniature *bureaucracy*, the typical organization of the firm. Authority in a bureaucracy flows downward, delegated into progressively smaller and more specialized responsibilities as it goes. At the lowest levels there is little autonomy, responsibilities are finely spelled out, and information on how to work is highly proceduralized.

Sometimes bureaucracies actually work, but often they don't. A MOP may be considered an operational manager, putting work plans into action. But much of what a MOP does is also higher-level in nature, tactical or strategic. Since programming is a highly technical skill, few others in the firm understand the needs of the programming group or the opportunities that software provide to the firm. The MOP is the person who determines the needed tools and either directs the building or orders the buying of the tools. This is a tactical decision. Often the MOP is the person from whom information about future trends in software development is obtained. The MOP is perhaps one individual in the firm who can (or should) understand the costs of building and buying software and can assist in coming to conclusions about the marketability of software. That this is seldom true now merely underscores the anomalous position of the MOP, who needs to know these things but rarely has the time to find out about them.

The *assembly line* may seem an unlikely organization for programmers. It is true that structured programming makes sequential production of software rather difficult, if not uneconomical. However, many aspects of programming work *are* sequential. In particular, project management is nothing more than an assembly line that moves software very slowly through a number of parallel production lines into testing and integration "stations."

That MOPs have historically been poor timekeepers attests to the inappropriateness of the assembly line to the production of software. However, project organization is still popular. The idea that a large unit of software can be "spec-ed out" in advance and then "assembled" in a project fashion has always intrigued DP managers. Two opposing trends in technology will determine the future of the software assembly line. The movement toward prototyping is one away from deterministic, element-by-element construction of software. Prototyping is heuristic, holistic, and user-driven. On the other hand, software engineering seems an attempt to reduce software production to a sequence of small blocks that can be parceled out to relatively untrained coders and then mechanically combined into a finished product.

There is nothing wrong with either trend. Certain users appreciate the prototyping technique; it is appropriate for small systems intended for a small group of relatively idiosyncratic users. And there is a need to improve the standards of software production. Programs aren't hand-painted landscapes; some, if not a lot, of our software consists of standardized code that is uneconomical unless produced *en mass*. What remains to be seen is whether or not software engineering does lead to an assembly-line organization of coders. For in managing this software production organization, a lot of skills that have hitherto been ignored may become important. It is likely, for instance, that *all* we know about mechanical production (scheduling, queuing, materials management) can be applied holus-bolus to the production of software in an assembly line. Were this the case, today's MOP would well be useless.

At the other end of the degree of organization, we find the *task force* and the *democratic work team*. The task force is reflected in the structured walk-through and code review. Individuals participate in the task force in order to *discover* something. Typically the task force has a chairperson and a number of participants. The chairperson leads meetings and directs the group toward producing an outcome. Information is collected, and often this information is in the form of testimony before the group. In the code review, the task force actually attacks (hopefully in a nonantagonistic spirit, of course) a programmer's code, trying as devil's advocates to find weak spots.

The *quality circle* works the same way, in reverse. The quality circle begins with a problem and tries, in a similar fashion, to find a solution. Both these organizations utilize a minimum of organization (i.e., a group leader and a group) with a maximum of direction to reach a conclusion. In a quality circle, a number of workers (usually 8 to 10) meet weekly in order to solve or resolve problems. Group dynamics are very important and members receive training in communication skills as well as problem-solving methods. As solutions are produced, they are tracked and prioritized. Ultimately the quality circle derives a best solution, presents it to management, and begins implementation. Couger (1983) outlines the process in his article "Circular Solutions." Despite the productivity gains inherent in solving difficult problems, there are other, perhaps more important gains. Couger stated:

> It is the opportunity for low-social-need supervisors to learn to interact more effectively with subordinates. Improving the mutual problem-solving capability of supervisors and subordinates through the vehicle of the quality circle may be the most important return on investment.

Quality circles, like CPT, apprenticing, and practique, provide an opportunity to learn. If interaction skills are also picked up along the way, so much the better. Couger (1983) and Bartol (1977) also point out, however, that DP supervisors have relatively poor social skills and would require additional training in group dynamics in order to facilitate these learning situations. It is unlikely that the MOP will acquire these skills without some additional motivation.

The democratic work team functions in a different fashion with a minimum of structure. Here there is no unique leader, and no particular direction provided from within the group. Instead, group identification is built first, so that trust is quite high. Second, the structure of the work to be done is learned, typically in a classroom setting, so that every work team member possesses sufficient knowledge to perform any task. Third, appropriate tools are made available to the work team. In this way, each individual can work to the worker's best level without interference or assistance from outside the group. Of all the techniques of organization, the democratic work team is the most expensive to implement. There are mixed feelings about its productivity. Certainly it is most appropriate where the task to be performed requires both a high degree of knowledge and a high level of cooperation from the group as a whole. It is inappropriate for sequential activities (since there is no need for interchange except in sequence). Where the task is poorly understood, the work team may, under certain circumstances, determine an efficient solution by redesigning the work. Because most DP shops take a shortsighted view of skills and tools in the programming shop, it is unlikely that the democratic work group structure arises spontaneously without the motivation of someone who is determined to see such groups succeed.

These organizations are ways of dividing labor internally within the software development group. Alternatively, some shops are finding it economical to *contract* rather than divide.

Two kinds of contractors can be used in software development. The *independent entrepreneur*, or free-lancer, sometimes called a consultant, may be brought in to work on a specific item for a specific, limited, timespan. There may be a unit price or a per diem offered.

Working with a contract programmer has aspects of gambling. Since the work depends partly on the MOP's skill at writing contracts, an element of faith cannot be discounted. Using consultants in conjunction with staff programmers might introduce dissension and jealousy, since the consultant obviously has even more freedom than staffers vis-à-vis company rules. Often, however, the consultant brings needed skills in at reasonable prices and, more important, is willing and able to share that experience with programmers. This can increase morale significantly, since the programmer's first need is to learn and most consultants can do a bit of teaching.

The other kind of contractor is the *pieceworker* who codes from specs and is expected to produce modules on a time-limited basis conforming closely to closely written specifications. Pieceworkers aren't often employed in DP. Historically, programmers have demanded—and received—a high degree of control over their work and a great deal of freedom in how they choose to get programs to work. The lengthy apprenticeship and the large amount of practice necessary to achieve proficiency in languages has simply not yet created a pool of piecework talent willing to be paid on a per-module basis without reward for elegance, efficiency, or charm. This trend will be reversed with the democratization of access to programming through "kiddy computing" and the proliferation of computer "literacy" courses. Within 10 years a large number of passable, if uncreative, BASIC programmers will be ready for employment, ready to work on a piece basis.

The decision to employ any contractor may be moot, of course, if the trend toward end-user software development continues. In another scenario, MOPs may have to learn how to define, cost, and test "pieceware" fairly and accurately.

In summary, a work team may exist as a division within the software development group, within DP as a whole (or may even include users). It may also be a "cloud" of consultants and pieceworkers. Divisions range from the diffuse democratic work team through the rigid assembly line and the bureaucracy. Divisions may be unidimensional, such as task forces and assembly lines, or multidimensional in grids, bureaucracies, or CPTs.

Each such organization has particular forms appropriate to software development. The CPT is a micro-bureaucracy. Code reviews, structured walk-throughs, and quality circles are styled on task force organization. Projects may look like assembly lines. Some shops consist of a MOP and six contractors.

Time will tell whether or not democratic work teams and extensive contracting to pieceworkers will become important in software development organization. The definition of the work team is determined by the skills of the workers, the demands of the job to be done, and the available resources.

### 4.4.2. Building Team Spirit

Three sets of factors, according to Kathryn Bartol (1977), influence what she terms the "synergistic" team: those relating to the environment of work, to the team itself, and those relating to the activities the team performs (see Figure 4.9). The composition of the team is important, for if it lacks the user's viewpoint the value of the software produced may be small. A number of important points in building team spirit in the software shop have emerged, as reported on by Bartol and by Unger and Walker (1977):

1. The size is important; all work teams should have from five to seven workers.
2. The group needs to feel responsible; individuals should feel some responsibility for group functioning.
3. The adequacy of resources affects group performance.
4. The group needs to communicate; someone in the group should know how to present the group's viewpoint.

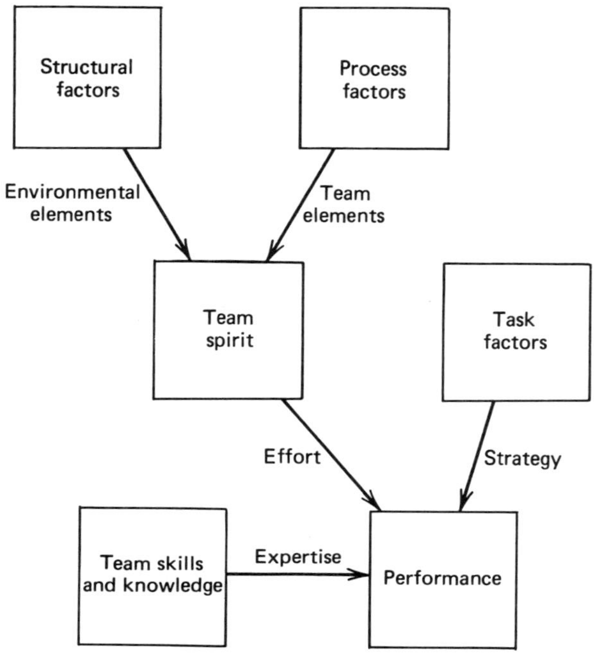


FIGURE 4.9 Contributions of task, structural, and process factors to programmer performance.

5. Conflict is inevitable; a procedure for resolving conflict is necessary—expect to use it.

A programming group, like any group, has a natural life cycle, illustrated in Figure 4.10.

The phases have been termed "forming," "storming," "norming," and "performing," reflecting the maturation of the group in facing internal and external conflict. Communication skills are important in the forming stage when programmers are orienting themselves to the work and each other. Conflict, disagreement, and hostility naturally arise from a clash of wills and a difference among individuals. These conflicts are normal. In the storming phase, conflict resolution procedures will have to be invoked by the MOP, openly and productively for the benefit of the group.

In the storming phase, too, programmers will react with characteristic tactics, including avoiding one another, smoothing or ignoring difficulties, forcing potentially inappropriate compromise, and open

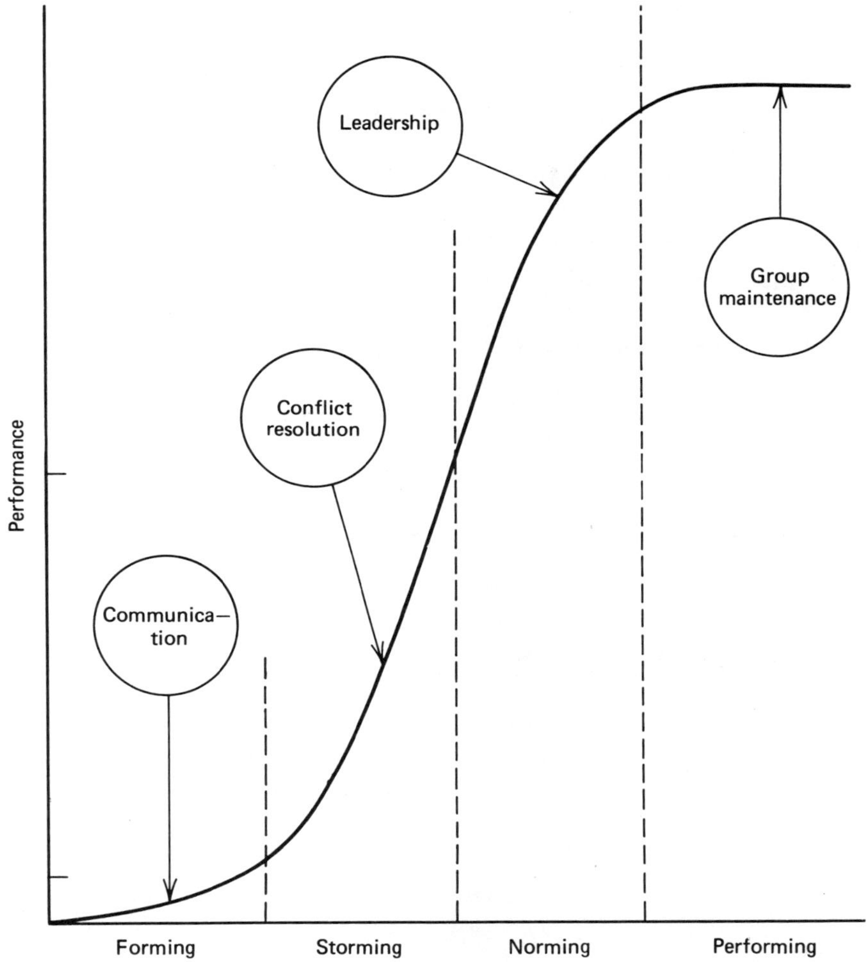


**FIGURE 4.10** Four phases of team development.

argument. The MOP will have to confront individuals and these tactics to avoid the problems the tactics themselves bring.

The norming phase builds team identification through the development of norms, or informal rules about expected behavior and attitudes. Leadership counts here. The MOP as leader has to exemplify these required norms for behavior and attitude. If not, someone else may set the group tone, usually a veteran programmer. This can reintroduce conflict.

A group that has successfully passed through the first three stages is ready for performing harmoniously. Team spirit arises naturally out of the feeling of identification and responsibility within the group. However, as facilitators point out, putting five people together in a room with a set of specifications doesn't naturally *perform* anything.

Instead, the MOP has responsibility for making sure the appropriate skills and resources are available, that the atmosphere is right for developing team spirit. The MOP is the primary teacher of communication and listening skills necessary to survive forming and storming.

### 4.4.3. Maintaining the Software Group

A performing group is only over the hump; it needs to be maintained much like any item of software. Four factors greatly influence how well the group is maintained:

1. Similarity, shared characteristics.
2. Common goals.
3. Proximity.
4. Identification with the group.

In the software shop, similarity has usually been guaranteed by the rigor of training in languages and packages. If nothing else, everyone in a COBOL shop can GOTO one another, CALL on their colleagues for help, and PERFORM according to that advice IF so desired. On the other hand, it is the MOP who creates and guides efforts toward common goals. Technical management, discussed in Chapters 2 and 3, provides guidelines for creating and maintaining common goals in the group.

In addition, there is a sort of programming credo that if somewhat mythological provides a true—sometimes embarrassingly true—basis for the maintenance of common goals. Common beliefs are these:

1. Users don't understand computers and never will.
2. Management doesn't reward programmers well enough.
3. All programs naturally have minor bugs.
4. All bugs can be caught.
5. All caught bugs can be fixed.
6. All caught bugs must be fixed, no matter how minor.

And so on. These beliefs come as part of a package for programmers. MOPs need to understand them, even if they form part of a mythology.

Proximity is seldom a problem in programming groups, but achieving visibility when everyone is hiding in cubicles or is wrapped in a cathode-ray force-field isn't easy. Some firms are finding that electronic mail is most heavily used by programmers who can't be bothered to write or talk. Certainly the MOP should pay attention to keeping these appropriate channels open to insure that, in being "near," programmers can actually "reach out and touch" one another.

Finally, a number of techniques can insure that individuals identify with the group. First, programming is still an elite profession; pride in knowing something almost no one else knows or can learn is important in establishing group identification (and, unfortunately, arrogance too). Programmers *can* feel pride at having mastered COBOL or assembler. Knowledge, too, that everyone else in the group suffered through this learning period is akin to fraternity initiations. MOPs can capitalize on this by rewarding expertise and encouraging its development among the entire group.

Finally, groups identify with the powers of their products. A company-wide accounting system is a powerful contribution from a small group. The power to maintain a large system, the "finger in the dike" syndrome, enlarges group spirit. Programmers get to talk to VPs about their work; other employees don't. This feeling is important for all technical employees and doubly important for programmers, who rarely see their products outside their workshops. MOPs also play a part in helping programmers understand this power and its limitations.

Through their ability to set goals, define work, and teach and motivate group members, MOPs exercise strong influence on the maintenance of groups.

### 4.4.4. Exercising and Delegating Authority

Our emphasis now shifts from the group to the force that drives the engine: authority. In this section we are concerned with how a MOP delegates responsibilities and the requisite authority to carry them out.

Consider the following conversation between Joe and his manager, Tom:

Tom: Joe, I'm sure you've noticed that lately I've been too busy to check with you often on the TACS system.

Joe: Sure. I've just carried on, anyway.

Tom: Well, that's fine. But some problems have come up because of decisions you've made in the last design review. You know what I mean, don't you?

Joe: No, I'm not sure I do, Tom.

Tom: Well, I never gave you authority to change those specs. If you were going to change them, you should have come to me first, not announced them in a *review*!

Joe: But Tom, you told me I could do the work my way!

Tom: Yeah, but not over my dead body. Now I've got the whole Finance Department breathing down my neck. We've got to put that system back the way it was.

What's wrong here? Tom has given Joe certain *responsibilities* in no uncertain terms: get the system going "any way you can." Joe's taken Tom at his word, and where necessary has changed specs and correctly informed the client. But Joe never had *authority* to change those specs. In other words, Joe's responsibilities exceed his authority.

Now consider these people. Marcie is Ellen's manager. Ellen speaks first:

Ellen: Wow, what a meeting! Did you see the look on old Titchner's face when we told him the marketing package was going to be ready a month early? He almost smiled, the old crow!

Marcie: Yeah, it's sure great to see those old guys perk up when you show them you can deliver.

Ellen: Yeah, uh. . . hey Marcie, that's what I want to talk to you about. You see . . . uh . . . there's no way we can give him that package next week.

Marcie: *What*? But you promised him. When I told you you were in charge, I assumed that you could schedule jobs well. What are you telling me, that you promised the VP of Marketing you'd deliver something you have no intention of delivering? (Voice getting a bit hysterical here.)

Ellen: Well, not exactly. I'd like it delivered next week, but y'see, Taylor's doing the integration testing and you know how they are. He'll probably take two weeks at least. I thought maybe you could bring a little pressure to bear on him to speed it up, no?

Marcie: (Reaching for her resumé) I don't know about you, but I'm updating my resumé right now.

What's wrong here? Marcie's given Ellen a lot of authority for the marketing package project. Ellen's in a position to negotiate delivery times with the client, the VP of Marketing. But unfortunately Ellen doesn't have overall responsibility for the project. An analyst named Taylor is doing the integration testing, and this work is out of Ellen's hands. In other words, Ellen's authority exceeds her responsibilities.

In each case, there is a mismatch between authority and responsibility. Authority means the power to command, but the word stems from a Latin root meaning "to increase." The authority controls growth and is the source of strength for the work. Responsibility, on the other hand, means literally the ability to respond, to be answerable for, and ultimately to carry out obligations. The two, authority and responsibility, are two sides of the same coin: commanding and responding, controlling and being obliged. A look at the typical organization of authority (see Figure 4.11) illustrates why these two concepts are often confused and mismatched.

In a bureaucracy, a manager has authority (i.e., control) over certain things simply because that authority is inherited through the hierarchy. Authority is passed down the management hierarchy and subdivided at each level. Passing up the management chain are responses to that authority. These responses may be products, reports, or pledges of allegience. *Every authority granted carries with it the implicit assumption that an appropriate response will be returned.* This is not merely an abstract statement. It is the way of life in an organization. When Bill says to Mary, "Where's that report I asked you for on the progress of the XYZ system?" Bill isn't just complaining or wishing. He is demanding his due: the response (report) in return for the authority (to get the work done) he has given.

Most MOPs and programmers forget this simple arithmetic, which is easily stated in the BASIC language:

```
LET RESPONSIBILITY = AUTHORITY
```

Without the authority to get the work done, the appropriate response cannot be given. Authority means the ability to gather resources and

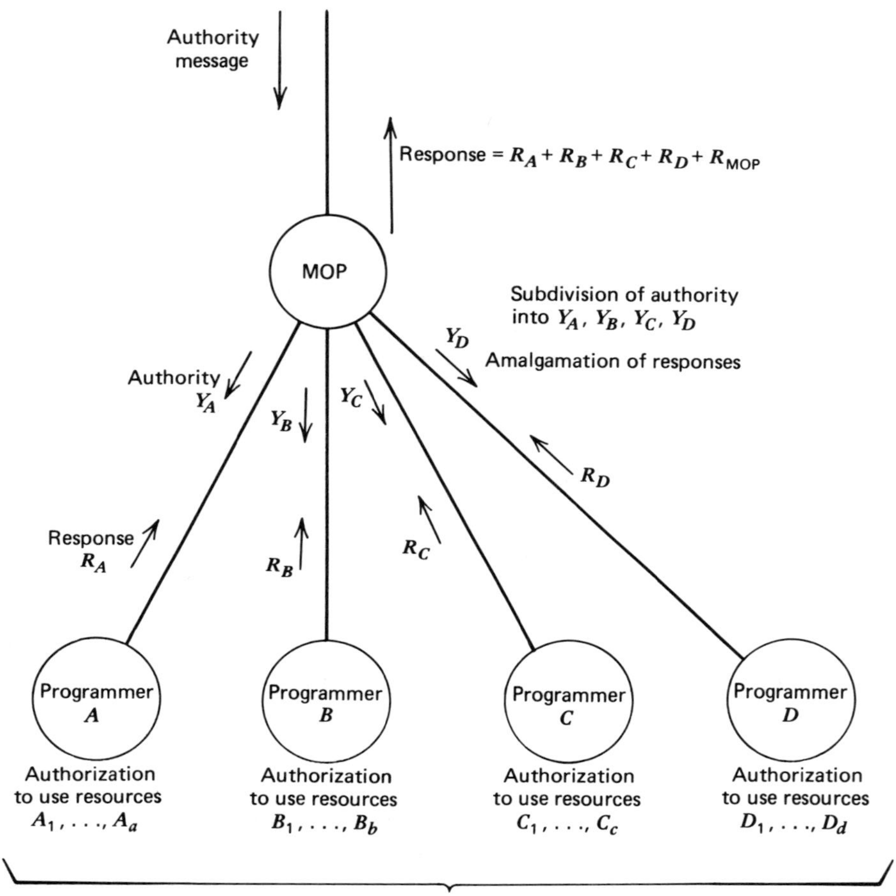


**FIGURE 4.11** Delegation as subdivision of authority and amalgamation of responses.

expend them. A typical example is the manager who tells a team, "Harry is in charge." By this, the manager means that Harry has the authority to direct the efforts (a scarce resource, sometimes very scarce) of the team members toward specific goals Harry will announce. Without this authority, those resources will not be directed in any particular fashion, and the work probably will not get done.

Without the responsibility of doing the work, authority is an empty shout into the void. Harry may be in charge, but if there is simply no time to do the work (i.e., the resource, time, is unavailable), no amount of proclaiming, no large number of memos or edicts, no shouting or screaming is going to help. The work will not get done.

In our previous examples, Tom has demanded responses (i.e., the TACS system) from Joe, but has not delegated the authority to command the resources needed (i.e., the authority to change the specs) to him. Joe is bound hand and foot by demands from Tom that cannot be met. In the other example, Ellen has exercised authority given her to control the schedule of the project, but unfortunately does not have responsibility over the whole project. She cannot respond, either, in an appropriate fashion.

What Joe needs, of course, is the authority that goes with the assignment; Ellen needs to have her area of responsibility expanded to include testing. Otherwise neither will get the job done.

The term "delegation" has noble roots. It means the act of appointing a representative, and also the act of entrusting authority to others. The representative acts for the delegator. Delegation connotes both meanings of authority (trust) and responsibility (acting for). We speak carelessly of delegating responsibility or delegating authority as though we could in fact separate the two. It is the separation that causes problems. Strictly speaking we should only be delegating. That way, the authority and responsibility should match well.

Barriers to that match include the following:

1. The organization may not be responsive enough.
2. People do not always use all their authority.
3. No one is perfect; we all fail to carry out responsibilities sometimes.
4. The informal organization may be working to counter the message of the formal organization.
5. Delegation is difficult with a large number of subordinates.

The organization chosen through which to delegate may not be responsive enough or may be inappropriate to the task to be carried out. It is one thing to entrust code reviews to a chief programmer team, but the organization, which is basically hierarchical, works against the ultimate aim of the review, which is to look at the code, not the coder. A quality circle is a good way to generate ideas and a poor way to create software. Choosing the right organization for the job so that delegation can be done correctly is important.

Although people say they want power, few know what to do with it when they get it. The saying that power corrupts bears a bit of the human spirit: we let power drive us and not the other way around. Giving a programmer authority over program development schedules cannot be done by saying so. A great deal of skill is needed to manipulate schedules and to test them. Given the skills, one needs also to jolly people into keeping to the schedule. Programmers may find it easier to avoid confrontations over schedule difficulties and attempt to alter the schedule rather than face other programmers' ire. Knowing how to command is the lesson kings learn as princes, generals learn as colonels, and head chefs learn as pastry chefs. The irony is that programmers, who exercise almost total authority over the machines they program, are almost never trained to exercise authority over their colleagues until the morning they arrive at work to find they've been promoted.

Little need be said about the imperfectness of the human being. The able manager understands and plans for delays, frustrations, and losses because it is human to err, if somewhat less than divine to manage.

Since group identification as elites is quite strong in the programming area, programmers often develop an informal organization built around skills and experiences, which sometimes makes it difficult to exercise delegated authority. "You can tell Chuck to tell me what to code, but there's no way that turkey's going to tell me what to code" is a common enough response, if not always spoken. The informal organization is built upon relationships that programmers form with one another over task-related, but not necessarily job-related matters. For instance, Agnes may be seen as an expert on JCL—everyone will go to Agnes for help on difficult JCL problems. This is great, so long as Agnes doesn't accept any responsibility for what goes on. Unfortunately, if she does, the formal lines of responsibility are changed. Suppose, however that *you*, the MOP, appoint Tod as "Chief JCL Consultant" at a meeting. Granted, you may be half-kidding by the title, but you want to be sure that everyone knows that Tod is going to be the expert on JCL. That's fine, so long as Tod really knows JCL; otherwise everyone will continue going to Agnes. In fact, chances are large everyone will continue going to Agnes anyway. After all, what do *you* know about JCL to delegate that to Tod?

The final barrier is known as "excessive span of control." A manager who has to delegate to a few people can usually have a good mental image of what is going on. With only a few delegated responsibilities, there are only a few responses. If work is well organized, those responses are handleable. But a MOP who has seven employees, each working on a different package, will find little time during the day to reflect on the horror of managing seven employees. Instead the day will be spent in interminable meetings patching over squabbles between the employees arguing over responsibilities and in reading or demanding reports on those responsibilities. Since each programmer is working on 2 to 20 modules simultaneously, with a span of control of seven employees, our beleaguered MOP can have to judge responses involving up to 140 modules. Why he or she would require a computer to do that! This situation, of course, sells project monitoring systems and grows managerial ulcers rapidly.

Delegation, especially in a software shop, is not a difficult task, but it is hard to do well. There are eight steps to follow:

1. Specify the job to be done.
2. Determine what the performance standards will be.
3. Set deadlines and resource limitations.
4. Choose the person to whom you will delegate and communicate 1 through 3 above.
5. Ask that person for feedback, checking to see what the understanding of your communication is, and make sure you understand his or her viewpoint.
6. Rework 1 through 3 if there are any disagreements.
7. Use the checkpoints for control and check back exactly as often as you have promised.
8. Follow through by rewarding or not as performance merits.

The reason why this is easy in a software shop is that what you are doing is essentially programming: delegation itself is easy to understand. What makes the job difficult is that most MOPs and seemingly all programmers lack an idea of what appropriate standards are for performance. Deadline estimation is such a black art that one recent article cited almost two dozen different ways of doing it.

Working in a project mode, which requires estimates several weeks or months in advance, makes estimation of resource requirements almost witchcraft.

Recognition of achievement is number one or two on a list of motivators programmers appreciate, according to research. Programmers can provide their own rewards only so long—after a while the MOP should applaud, too.

### *Case 2. "Work with Garth? No Way!"*

Garth and Patty have always argued, day in and day out. They can't stand each other. Patty thinks Garth is a sexist boor. Garth thinks Patty's B.A. in English is a poor credential for programming. Patty criticizes Garth's code in reviews; Garth points out every flaw he can in Patty's pseudocode. Steve Randolph supervises them, them and eight others. Most of the workers have university degrees or advanced technical training, and Steve thinks of them as a bit high-strung and overly motivated. But only Garth and Patty give him the kind of pain that brings him to organizational tears. Steve *thinks* that the trouble is that Garth is jealous of "The English Teacher's" progress, since Patty got promoted faster than Garth did. Garth is good, but Patty's better. On the other hand, Patty's very insecure about being the only woman in the group and thinks that Garth is harassing her because of her gender, not her pseudocode. So far Steve's been able to avoid World War III. But today he's got to put a team together and so far as he can tell, only Garth, Patty and a third programmer have the time. Anyway, it's time Steve stopped avoiding the problem and met it head on. Patty's already pronounced her verdict: "Work with Garth? No way." □

Steve really can't avoid the problem and things look hopeless. But he can try team-building techniques. First, both Garth and Patty are good, but each has a low opinion of the other. A structure within which they *cannot* work is the task force—structured walk-throughs have been a disaster. Each has had a chance to shout the other down.

Instead, Steve may opt for a more structured organization such as the chief programmer team. There are relatively quick benefits here. The relatively rigid formal pattern of communication in the CPT may facilitate their communication, especially if the chief programmer (who could be Steve) helps them see that it is their communication, not their coding skills, they need to work on. As chief programmer, Steve can control exactly which issues arise and can force (and hopefully guide) confrontation on the true problems (jealousy and insecurity) that keep two fairly capable people from cooperating profitably. Since the success of the CPT depends greatly upon how well individuals work together, Garth and Patty can be shown that their fortunes as individuals depend upon how well they work together. By working together they will see that they *can* work together. That alone may start them talking.

Outside this temporary organization, Steve can work for group identification through creation of shop standards, promotion of professional standards, and by reinforcing the feeling that the programming group Steve manages is an elite, possessing some superior knowledge and skills. Patty and Garth cannot fail to be hooked by this, since it appeals to their needs to be recognized by others and to feel that they are achieving.

Not everyone loves everyone else. To be sure, Patty and Garth are not going to fall into each other's arms just because Steve sets them up to work together. But if Steve is going to ask them to work together, he will have to work, too, to establish a climate in which Patty and Garth's disagreements can be worked out rather than buried any longer. Steve can't afford to discount 20% of his staff at every meeting.

CHAPTER FIVE

# HUMAN RESOURCE MANAGEMENT
## Working with Programmers

The previous chapter has discussed ways of obtaining and organizing the human resource in the software shop. Now we zero in on techniques for helping programmers get work done, that is, *actuating* the human resource. Hiring and organizing good people is only the beginning of any job. Creating a climate of trust, assistance, loyalty, and cooperation is crucial to allowing the human resource—the programming staff—to work at its full potential.

Directing and controlling are the major day-to-day functions of supervisors. Programmers, by the nature of the work and some specific vocational traits, need special assistance in getting work done. That is the focus of this chapter.

## 5.1. THE DIRECTING ACTIVITIES OF THE MOP

Organizing is to directing as laying cards on the table is to playing the game. Four activities stand out as important:

1. Motivating programmers to work.
2. Leading programmers and the group.
3. Supervising programmers' daily activities.
4. Communicating with programmers about the work.

Directing is the process of guiding others toward the achievement of work goals enabled by staffing and organizing activities. Now that labor, rather than hardware, is the major component of system development (as it has *always* been in maintenance work), a great deal more attention is being focused upon computer personnel research, especially in the area of motivation. The values of strong and effective leadership and careful supervision are rapidly achieving great importance, too. This contrasts sharply with the earlier years of programming, in which technical excellence was stressed almost exclusively.

### 5.1.1. Motivation and the Programmer

The term "motivation" brings to mind the idea of putting something into motion. In work terms, it means getting someone to do work. While we'd like to assume that motivation is a positive aspect of work, motivation, sadly, is often treated in a "do-it-or-else" fashion.

Traditionally, motivation has been studied and pursued in two ways. First, researchers have concentrated on the tendencies workers show: their attitudes, opinions, and feelings. On the other hand, others have examined environmental forces that cause workers to exert themselves. Research into tendencies is a part of personality research. In recent years a number of studies have appeared on the "programmer personality," of which the most notable has been Couger and Zawacki's (1980). Little that we haven't suspected for years has come from this school of investigation. But the benefit has been a series of terms by which to describe programmers in a statistical fashion. It is doubtful, however, that a clear-cut, unique "programmer personality" will ever emerge from this work. The vocation is moving toward an ever-increasing variety of individuals, away from the mathematically oriented group of the first two decades of programming.

The other research path has looked into the effects that various environmental factors have on productivity and the desire to work. This research, too, suffers from oversimplifications, but there have been some intriguing findings here.

Figure 5.1 summarizes the current thought in how tendencies and forces work together to influence performance and job satisfaction in the programming workplace. Consider a programmer trying to get a clean compile of a complex PL/I program. The programmer's *ability* to get a clean compile depends upon native abilities to code, the existence of tools and aids (such as good diagnostics in a compiler), and the lack of barriers and distractions (such as downtime, errors, or

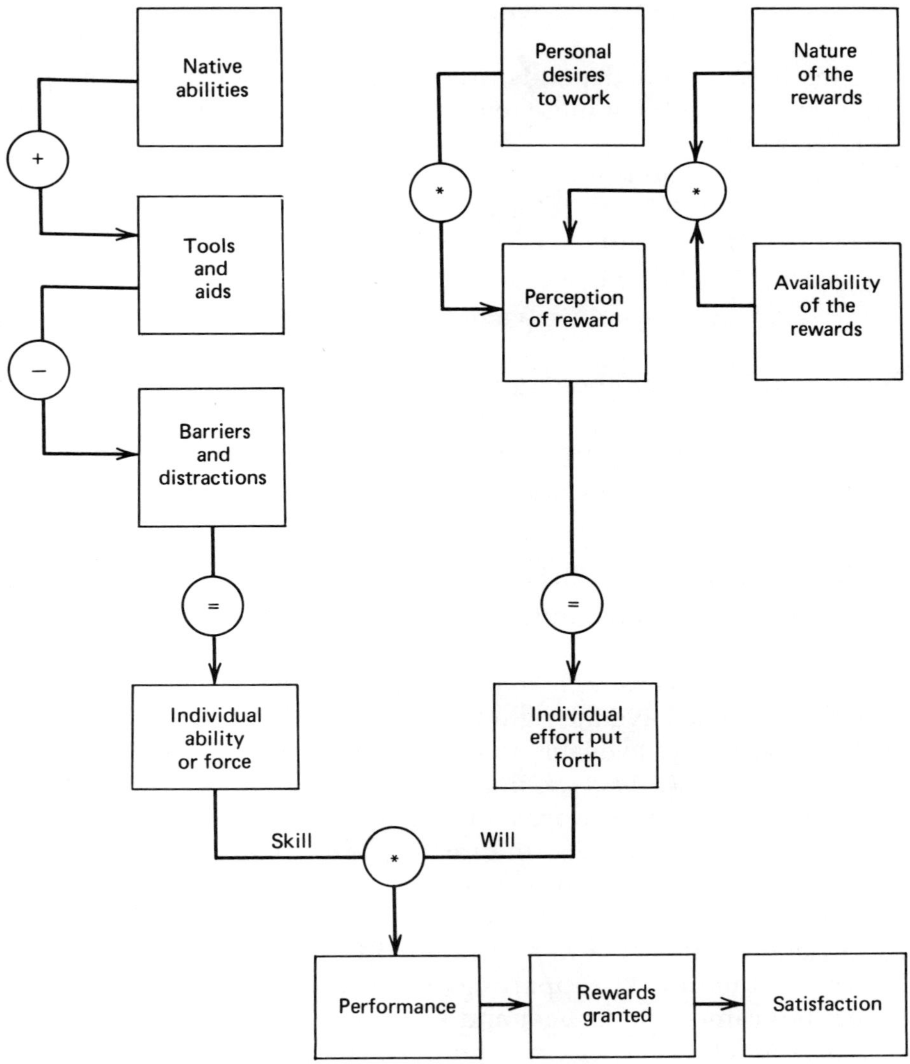


**FIGURE 5.1** Motivation in the psychology of work.

undocumented syntactical features). But ability alone will not result in a clean compile. The programmer has to *try* by putting forth the effort to clean up the program and resubmit it for compilation. The level of effort put forth depends upon two factors:

1. The programmer's desire to work in general, initiative, alertness, happiness, and so on.
2. The perception that cleaning up the program will in fact be rewarding in some sense.

This latter factor depends, in turn, on whether or not the programmer knows what these rewards are and whether or not they are forthcoming.

These connections are summed up in the following equations:

$$\begin{aligned} \text{performance} &= \text{can} * \text{try} \\ \text{can} &= \text{able} + \text{assisted} - \text{prevented} \\ \text{try} &= \text{wants} * (\text{value} * \text{availability}) \end{aligned}$$

Low motivation can therefore arise in a number of ways:

1. Lack of ability and tools.
2. Barriers or distractions that are strong.
3. Lack of rewards.
4. Low-value rewards.
5. Lack of personal initiative.

The MOP who wishes to motivate effort must therefore assure that the right people have the right tools and few distractions, that high-value rewards are available to people who like to work. *Hiring programmers who like to work is the MOP's first staffing responsibility.* Providing tools and rewards and barring distractions is part of the MOP's daily responsibility in directing work. The remainder of this section is devoted to a discussion of personality and motivational factors over which the MOP has control and how MOPs can use knowledge in this area to motivate work.

The first hard data supporting any claim about programmer personalities came from Couger and Zawacki's now-landmark study of DP personnel, including programmers, analysts, managers, and operations staff. Two important conclusions came from their data:

1. Almost all DP personnel exhibit a fairly low "social need strength," an indicator of the desire an individual has for social interaction.
2. DP personnel, and programmers in particular, showed an extremely high "growth need strength," reflecting a desire to learn and achieve through that learning.

The figures aren't even subject to the usual statistical fudging. Apparently, programmers are almost noncommittal about interaction, ranking far below all other occupations in this scale. Even more astonishing is the need programmers have to learn and grow, outstripping most managers in that regard. The interested reader can check the data and study the survey results in Couger and Zawacki's book (1980) or in a series of articles they authored in *Datamation* in 1978 and 1979. The results speak for themselves.

They say even more, though. Not precisely cave-dwelling, hairy, smelly brutes, programmers aren't country-clubbers either. And those who are promoted into management, who represent the effective cream-of-the-crop in terms of social interaction, are scarcely more sociable, at least when compared to other professionals. What does this mean?

We can learn several lessons:

1. For MOPs, it appears that there is almost a trade-off between interaction between programmer and computer and interaction between programmer and other employees, managers, and clients.
2. For programmers, it means that implicit expectations that managers will take up the slack in interpersonal relations with staffers are certainly going to remain unfulfilled.
3. For DP management and its clients, it means that for some time, at least, relations between the DP shop and the rest of the firm will remain strained as the tension between society's new perception of what computers can do and DP's continued focus on personal growth through dominance of the technology increases.
4. For organizational designers, academics, and a firm's upper management, it means that the chances for complete integration of data processing into the firm through cooperative projects, intertwined career paths, and diffusion of DP skills

> throughout the organization are going to remain slim for a while.

For the MOPs who consume research such as Couger and Zawacki's, however, there are rays of hope. First, they demonstrate that the enormous need to grow results in a high motivation to work, although this motivation is tempered by management's failure to exploit this "motivating potential." Most managers are happy that their programmers like to work—they do too, after all. But MOPs are using this intrinsic motivation to confront the technology in only the most rudimentary way: by keeping the programmers busy. It's very much like harnessing the great strength of the internal combustion engine in order to produce interesting clouds of exhaust.

More evidence is available from the Couger and Zawacki study on this. For instance, although general satisfaction with the job is high, programmers are less satisfied with their interaction with other programmers and with their managers than equivalent professionals are with their corresponding interactions. For most professionals, general satisfaction seems to depend heavily upon just this kind of interaction. This is not the case for programmers. What's the hidden factor? Obviously the work itself.

Furthermore, the evident source of dissatisfaction with management is the quality of the feedback programmers receive from the supervisors. This is apparent from diagrams relating growth need strength (GNS) and social need strength (SNS). MOPs are just not providing sufficient and appropriate information to their programmers. Structured techniques tend to limit the contribution programmers make, and thereby add to this lack of feedback. Since programmers begin with a limited window on the results of their work and since managers supply only a little more, programmers end up with a narrow and shortsighted view of their products. Where else can they learn about them? They aren't inclined to venture from the DP shop in the first place. And this leaves only complaining users to inform them.

Does this sound familiar? It should. The habitual disdain in which programmers hold users only reinforces the image each has of the other.

How does the MOP exit from this loop?

Until the programming cadre changes in ways already mentioned and until the evolution of programming progresses in the way discussed in Chapter 8, MOPs can only work with the rewards and tools of work. Couger and Zawacki speak of job redesign to suit the programmer personality, but their specific recommendations may mean more trouble than improvement considering how little we know of the future.

More benefits may accrue to programmers and MOPs who learn better communication techniques and who learn to employ the computer itself to relieve the programmer of nonmotivating features of the job, particularly documentation. Electronic mail is an exciting concept, too, to which programmers take easily. In Beau Shieil's *Datamation* article "Power Tools for Programmers," the professional work station concept, central to office automation, is put forward as an important aid. In fact, all the features of office automation are pertinent and appropriate: electronic mail, personal filing, word processing, document retrieval, scheduling, and so forth. Certainly the programmer will feel more motivated to interact with these tools than with unpredictable people. Having spelling errors automatically corrected, having "instant" access to a remote MOP, and having the ability to *command* documentation to flow off the listings into a preformed format would suit programmers just fine.

Professional work stations can also deliver programmed instruction in social skills (a kind of computerized Emily Post?), meetings via computer conferencing, maintain a datebook, and handle aspects of project management. The multiimage, windowed, active screen of SMALLTALK and INTERLISP as well as the simulated desk of the Apple Lisa(TM) and Ashton-Tate's Framework(TM) can serve as the programmer's window on the world.

MOPs can also take an active role in breaking down barriers. Feedback is crucial; avoiding feedback negates the act of delegation. The computer can be used to provide this; at least one performance appraisal system has been implemented on a microcomputer and can run *continuous* performance data and human resource development applications for MOP and programmer.

In concluding this section on programmer personality research, some words are in order about stereotypes. To say that the programmer group "tends" toward lower social need strength says nothing, of course, about individual programmers. Yet most of us nurture a number of stereotypes about programmers. Those of us who have worked as programmers easily recall the tediousness of the work and the rush of excitement at seeing something compute correctly. Nonprogrammers have visions of reams of output and hairy beasts roaming about bellowing in COBOL. The public reads about programmers' addiction to their machines and how their marriages fail in competition with electronic mistresses.

These stereotypes are rapidly changing, yet there are some enduring characteristics with which MOPs have to cope. Chadwin and Cross, in a recent article, describe DP people—and this probably holds for programmers too—as "rational," "orderly," "systematic," "methodical," resistant to external authority, strongly logical, and desirous of consistency. Yet there is really no data to back up these assertions. What *is* obvious is that these are characteristics of the computers and the working environment of programmers! It's as though a racial or national stereotype were working in which characteristics of the land were seen as rubbing off on the inhabitants.

That's the major difficulty with generalizations about programmer personality that are not based upon data: we tend to assume that the workers resemble their tools. Given the tendency of modern system development techniques to systematize, rationalize, order, proceduralize, and make consistent, we shouldn't be surprised to find the irrational, disorderly and unsystematic programmer.

MOPs need to remain alert to the needs of individual programmers more than to general traits, however. Whatever *all* programmers *might* be, a MOP will surely manage a group consisting of a wallflower, a joiner, two busybodies, one perfectionist, one who can't cope with anything, and three rock-solid family types. What is important is that the MOP not ignore the differences.

In terms of other approaches, researchers have looked at environmental factors; some work on *motivators* over the past 20 years has opened questions about what a manager can do to motivate workers. Ted Herzberg's (1959) ideas are typical of the human relations school. Figure 5.2 illustrates the concept of productivity, which shows the role of personality, environment, work, and management in affecting job satisfaction, which in turn affects productivity. In pursuing this model, Herzberg isolated two types of factors affecting job satisfaction and thus—he felt, probably incorrectly—productivity. These types are (1) motivators, factors that increased satisfaction when present and (2) hygiene factors, those that decreased satisfaction when absent. In a phrase, workers are happy to get motivators and unhappy to have hygiene factors taken away.

Motivators included achievement, recognition, the work itself, responsibility, and advancement. Hygiene factors included salary, quality of technical supervision, interpersonal relations, company

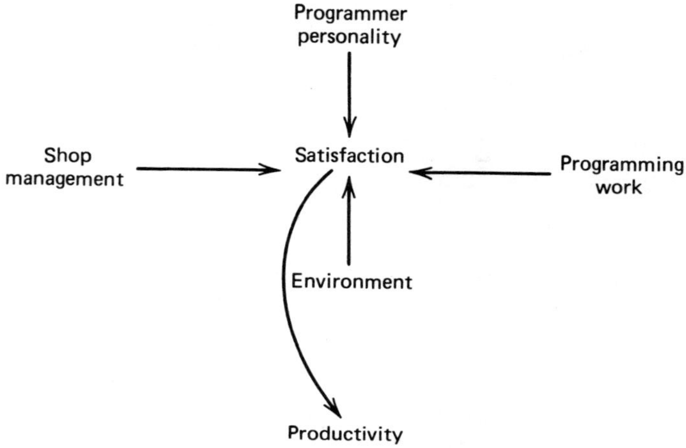


**FIGURE 5.2** The roles of personality, work, management, and environment in determining job satisfaction and productivity.

policies, working conditions, and job security. Herzberg felt that increasing salaries beyond a certain level did not motivate further, but reducing salary demotivated. Not having achievement didn't demotivate, but the possibility for achieving did, in fact, motivate.

Herzberg's 1960s research still has some relevance. Today many crave job security and money, both of which are reacquiring motivational value. But what about programmers? In a study from the late 1970s, Fitz-enz (1978) repeated Herzberg's work using computer programmers as subjects. His findings are interesting. The younger and technically minded programmers of 1978 matched the older and more general employee of the middle 1960s. If anything, motivators from 1965 motivate programmers even *more* now. Hygiene factors were even more hygienic for 1978 programmers than for workers of a decade and a half previous.

This research demonstrates that programmers are very much attuned to working for rewards. Given the low general awareness of the organization and its needs by programmers, the relatively good salaries and working conditions, the only thing programmers could ask for in terms of improvement is the quality of technical supervision. Taken at face value, Fitz-enz's study indicates that programmers want *better MOPs*! But they still don't want much in the way of interaction with superiors. "Manage me better, but leave me alone" is the plea of the 1979 programmer. Stated another way, programmers may recognize their management as simply another—slightly defective—development tool.

Underscoring this is Woodruff's (1978) work on job satisfaction among programmers, accountants, and engineers. Although his work involved only 63 programmers from Atlanta, it is typical of the kind of work we need done to determine motivational factors. Woodruff noted that the three groups differed little in terms of components similar to those of Fitz-enz's study. Where programmers found deficiencies were in possibilities for advancement, salary, and interpersonal relationships with support staff and subordinates.

Two other approaches to motivation and job satisfaction are the Theory X/Theory Y concept of McGregor (1960), and Blake and Mouton's managerial grid. These approaches attempt to describe managerial styles and their effects upon motivation.

McGregor contrasts two styles, the Theory X style, which proposes that people don't like to work and therefore have to be forced to work, and Theory Y, which reflects belief that working is natural and not necessarily disliked by workers. The chart below contrasts these two styles. Programming management has many aspects of a kind of cowed Theory X; MOPs act as though programmers hadn't any minds, but they realize that there is no way to direct the daily activities of programmers. One of the dilemmas of programming management is that a lot of MOPs feel compelled to adopt a Theory-X-like style for workers they know respond poorly to Theory X. But Theory Y requires skill and tact, political awareness, and a great deal of trust from the MOP—these are not present in abundance in the software shop.

| Theory X | Theory Y |
|---|---|
| People dislike working and will avoid it | Working is natural and not inherently disliked |
| People must be coerced, controlled, directed, and punished to motivate them to work | People are sometimes self-directing and seek rewards |
| People do not like making decisions and avoid responsibility | People can seek to have responsibility; poor experiences can make them passive |
| People have no ambition and desire security above all | People can exercise imagination, creativity, and initiative |
| Therefore authoritarian leadership is necessary | Therefore a more participative approach may be appropriate |

If Theory Y is an archetypical approach to the application of human relations in *any* workplace, Blake and Mouton's managerial grid is a graphical representation of the two opposing forces that are at work in the software shop: concern for the technology and concern for programmers.

Blake and Mouton describe combinations of proportions of such concern. The 1–9 management style is primarily concerned with employee needs and feelings, to the exclusion of concern for getting the product out. On the other hand, the 9–1 management style is the typical Simon Legree sweatshop philosophy in action: all that counts is the bottom line. The ideal blend, the 9–9 team management, is probably unattainable in reality; the 5–5 organization man compromise is what most managers work for.

In the software shop, concern for people is relatively low; concern for the technology, the computer, and software, relatively high. An 8–2 management style would fit many MOPs, who have neither training, time, nor tendency to fit concerns for programmers into their schedules.

From these four approaches to motivation (Couger and Zawacki, Herzberg, McGregor, and Blake and Mouton), four motivational principles stand out for the MOP:

1. Concern for people implies feedback, which means guidance, recognition, and appropriate criticism.
2. MOPs need to be responded to, also. Programmers need to improve their interpersonal skills and participate if only to hear the MOP out.
3. Programmers don't think any more highly of management than managers think of nontechnological factors. But MOPs will have to make it clear that management is also rewarding for programmers, keeping computer time available, making schedules mesh, keeping documentation available, making status reporting more meaningful, and ultimately giving work more meaning.
4. Responsibility is a two-way street. Programmers have to feel some responsibility for their products after they've left the shop. This doesn't mean proprietary interest; it means feeling worthy if the product works well.

These four principles will build motivation directly into the job. But to benefit from them, the MOP needs patiently to build skills in communication and group identification into the programming unit. Responsibility for products comes about through a feeling of awareness of the firm's need for those products; the MOP is the channel that communicates this. In a phrase, the MOP is the key element in motivation in the software shop.

### 5.1.2. Exercising Power in the Software Shop

Direction implies power, the ability to induce others to perform work. Part of this induction comes from within the worker: Motivation. The other part is termed "power" in its literal sense. Power in an organization takes five forms:

1. *Legitimate.* Power conferred from the organization.
2. *Expert.* Power by virtue of knowledge or skill.
3. *Reward.* Power through positive outcomes.
4. *Coercive.* Power through negative outcomes.
5. *Charismatic.* Power through force of personality.

*Legitimate* power is delegated to the MOP through the organization. Legitimate power is considered weak because it has no force of its own. "Do it because *I*, your manager, tell you to do it," is the cry of a desperate manager.

*Expert* power is derived from knowledge or skill that a manager—or a nonmanager—possesses. The programmer who knows JCL is just as powerful as the manager who commands you to use it. Expert power is quite strong. In the software shop, such powers naturally arise because of the enormous pull of the technology and the desire of programmers to learn. Expert power tends to dilute legitimate power unless the MOP is also an expert. That's why the most "commanding" and respected managers of programmers are also expert programmers themselves. That it is almost impossible to remain expert as a programmer and simultaneously respond to the crises of a programming shop is, however, axiomatic.

*Reward and coercive powers* are derived from the abilities of MOPs (and others) to provide rewards or mete out punishments to employees. While some rewards can be given out only by MOPs and some of these only upon authorization from above (such as salary increases and promotions), other rewards are available "free," so to speak. These include praise, encouragement, approval, recognition, comradeship, access to special information, and coaching. MOPs can often provide assignment to favorable projects with liked co-workers, training, and improved or high-status working conditions such as flexible hours, a desk by the window, and a personal terminal to take home on occasion.

Coercive powers are, unfortunately easier to use, because we are often under pressure and haven't the time to be polite or rewarding. Criticism, withdrawal of other rewards, assignment to difficult or frustrating projects with difficult or unattractive people, as well as more serious punishment requiring organizational approval—such as demotion, suspension, or firing—should be used rarely. Unfortunately, being a manager tempts an individual to use this source of power with insufficient justification.

Finally, *charismatic powers* are those one acquires because one is friendly, interesting, dynamic, trusthworthy, or bold. When a charismatic leader says "Do it!" the command is more forceful than when a noncharismatic leader says "Do it and I'll let you work with Sally," or "Do it or I'll move your desk away from the window," because these latter commands are part of tit-for-tat accounting of favors and misdeeds. Charismatic leaders galvanize others into action because of their strong personalities, not because of their position in the hierarchy. It's their charm, wit, piercing eyes, or some other quality that makes their requests into commandments.

In the software shop, expert power is the most effective. The work is technical and information heavy. MOPs can also use the milder rewards in larger quantities than they do now, especially praise, the opportunity for freedom from working hours restrictions and meetings, and time off for training. The following chart lists the rewards and punishments MOPs can reasonably expect to control.

| Rewards | Punishments |
|---|---|
| Praise and encouragement | Criticism |
| Approval | Withdrawal of privileges |
| Recognition | Probation |
| Comradeship | Suspension |
| Job security | Firing |

| Rewards | Punishments |
|---|---|
| Favorable performance appraisal | Demotion |
| Access to confidential information | Withholding of rewards |
| Challenging work assignments | Undesirable assignments |
| Promotion | |
| Improved working conditions | |
| Capable and congenial co-workers | |
| Status symbols | |
| Assignment to desirable or high-profile projects | |
| Project management responsibilities | |
| Courses, seminars, conferences | |

In his book *The Human Use of Human Resources*, Marvin Karlins (1981) lists 14 rewards that satisfy employee needs. Praise and public recognition top the list. Others, such as employee involvement in decision-making, leisure time, informational feedback, and what Karlins terms "pleasant forms of moderate distraction" (food, music, and interior decoration) will appeal to programmers. As the programmer workforce changes, stronger and more tangible rewards in the form of salary, promotion, and delegated responsibility will become more important.

The problem of legitimate powers is peculiar in the software shop. MOPs often have clear job descriptions spelling out responsibilities and powers. A typical list might include words such as "assigns," "recommends," "initiates," "schedules," "sees that," "is in charge of," and "enforces." These are terms that reflect traditional delegation of authority, that give the appearance of life-and-death power over the software shop. In fact, however, MOPs complain that these powers exist only on paper—they seem insufficient to get work done.

The reason for the insufficiency is that MOPs are seldom trained in the exercise of authority and provided with the necessary resources. Some of the MOP's authority requires mathematical and organizational ability to exercise. "Enforcement" is possible only if the MOP has the time to enforce and the ability to detect variance from standards. A MOP can create a schedule, but unless it works well and unless the MOP can otherwise motivate workers to stick to it, scheduling can be an empty exercise.

Legitimate power depends upon having the ability and resources to exercise it. Abilities in negotiation, interviewing, delegation, mathematical programming, listening, and persuasion head the list. This clearly underscores *control* as a critical factor in direction.

### 5.1.3. Leadership in the Software Shop

Direction requires leadership qualities. The leader most clearly and strongly embodies the ideals, attitudes, and skills of a group. If the leader is also legitimate, then productivity and effectiveness rise.

Five indicators of leadership problems are exemplified by these comments:

1. "Why don't you get off the computer and let us *programmers* work?"
2. "You don't know my program—so why criticize it?"
3. "You're telling *me* how to program? You haven't programmed in five years!"
4. "Don't ask me, ask him. It's not *my* problem."
5. "I won't work with Tom."

The first points to an *identification* problem. Historically programmers have been unconcerned with management's problems, and by extension, unconcerned with the fate of the software development group. Where this trend has become extreme, about the only thing a MOP can do to try and exercise his or her leadership is make an occasional public address to a sleeping group at a weekly staff meeting.

The second problem stems from the *narrow focus* programmers and their supervisors direct on programs as products. The complaint here owes its credence to programmers' misconceptions of the MOP's leadership role. That role is to see that the work gets accomplished. Any criticism arising from that role is not necessarily of technique. If programmers insist that code remain off-limits to management, the MOP's ability to judge and direct work will be seriously limited.

Problem three, one of *credentials*, is hard to meet head on if indeed you haven't programmed in five years. However, why meet it head on? "How" does not mean "what." The MOP rightfully leads by defining and applying standards. These can appear in a standards manual or in memos. Everyone can read them. It helps enormously if programmers can help write them, too. Then, when *they* become MOPs, they can thump the book with pride and deflect the irrelevant reference to lack of current application of programming skills.

The general *lack of responsibility* that DP has often felt for its own products is reflected in the fourth comment. This is changing. However, MOPs naturally respond still to low responsibility in their staffers with a declaration of responsibility by *fiat* ("Be responsible!"). As an alternative, MOPs may try to avoid responsibility problems by crystal-clarifying responsibilities to the bit and byte levels. The first seldom works and can bring resentment. The second is more trouble than it's worth. A quality control program brings better results. This can be built around group responsibility and team spirit, employing code walk-throughs and reviews. Weinberg's (1971) "egoless" programming can be made more positive by building "responsibility" programming—responsibility to the group. As the group leader, the MOP should exhibit that responsibility first.

Producing a *climate of responsibility* is the fifth leadership challenge facing the MOP. A leader can provide solutions here through exercise of certain powers and adoption of specific leadership styles appropriate to the situation.

Figure 5.3 illustrates the factors that influence your choice of leadership style. No single style stands out at all times, for all employees, and for all managers, however.

Four *leadership styles* are indicated by example in Figure 5.4. They are (1) participative, (2) directive, (3) supportive, and (4) achievement-oriented.

Consider a programmer who arrives at your desk at 4:45 in the afternoon with a tough bug that won't go away. Your choice of leadership style at this point is determined by *your feelings* about the *employee*, the *problem* the employee presents, *who* the employee is, the *employee's skills*, and the *resources* available in the shop at this time (see Figure 5.5).

The *participative* leadership style involves the leader with the problem and the employee. Together you sit down and figure out where the bug is. Participative leadership style is best when tasks are well defined and when the programmer wants to work on the problem but doesn't have all the skills needed to succeed.

In the *directive* style of leadership, the MOP simply tells the programmer what to do. This extends the direction originally given in more detail. The directive style is most appropriate with novice programmers or with those who are otherwise unskilled or depen-

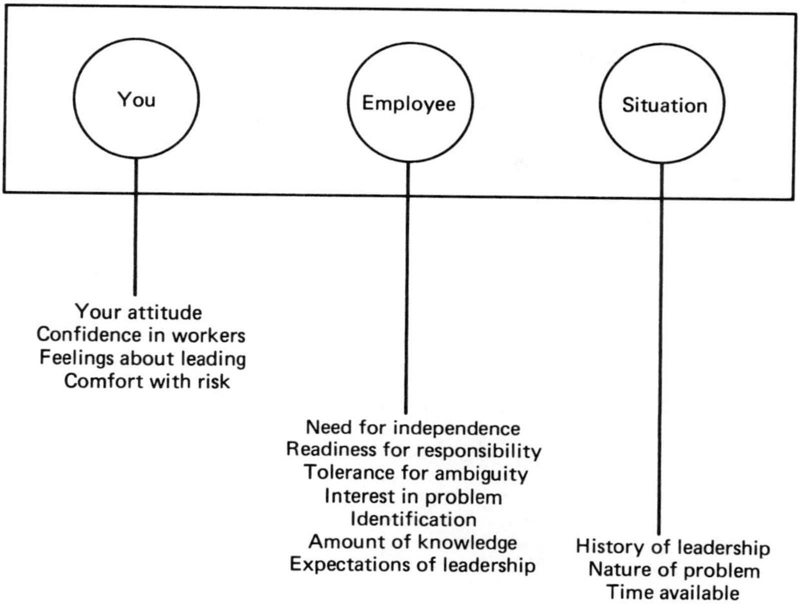


**FIGURE 5.3** General factors influencing leadership styles.

dent upon you. It is also appropriate with tasks that are still unclear in their goals or specifications—such as how to debug in a specific situation or environment. Of course, constant use of the directive style does not help programmers learn to solve their own problems.

*Supportive* leadership shifts the focus from the problem (finding the bug) to the confused or insecure employee. In stressful situations or when work is distasteful or confusing, the MOP can provide emotional support for the programmer by listening, sympathizing, and cheering. As with the directive style, the supportive style should be offered freely, but only temporarily. Programmers should be encouraged to acquire skills and resources of their own. Of course, the MOP should look carefully at the situation that is inducing stress or causing confusion, in order to make improvements.

*Achievement-oriented* leadership is, in general, the most appropriate style in the software shop. Since most programmers find work itself motivating and are technically skilled, many MOPs will find they can lead comfortably with encouraging words and sufficiently—and appropriately—high goals. Even more important, however, is following through with praise or constructive, relevant, and nonjudg-

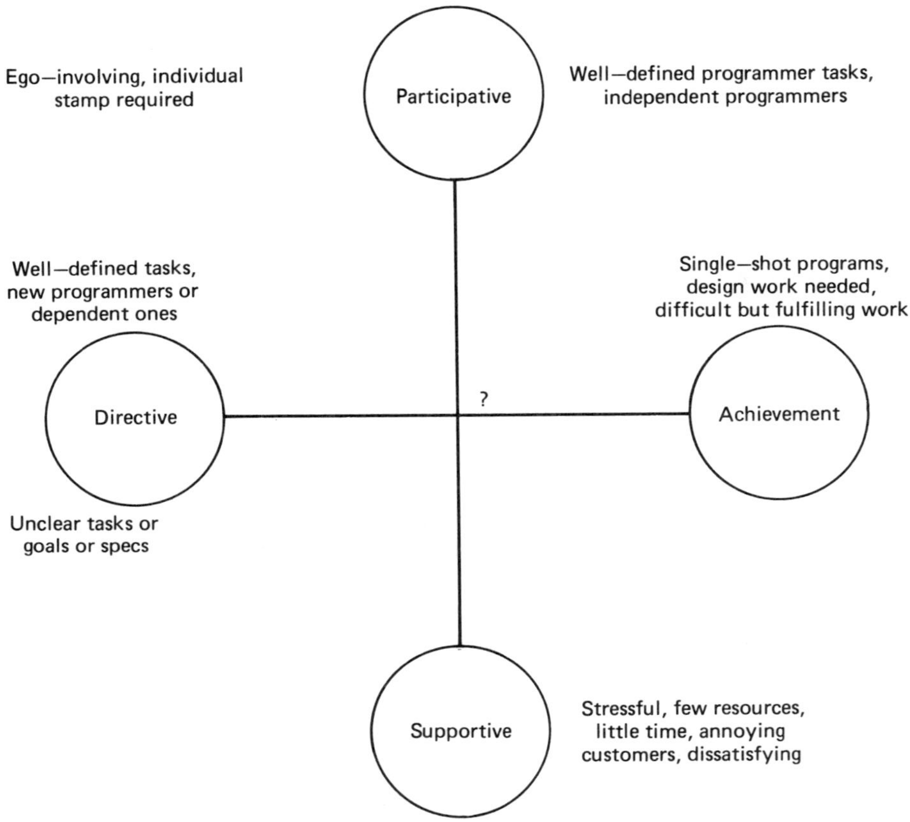


**FIGURE 5.4** Indicators for four leadership styles.

mental feedback. It doesn't suffice to inspire; the MOP has to follow through to lead.

### *Case 1. Swearing Allegiance. Where Is Loyalty?*

Alice Kerns was having a difficult time with Warren Talbot, one of her staff programmers. Warren had worked for Alice for two years, and Alice considered him a competent and valuable member of her team. But yesterday, Warren walked into Alice's office and dropped a bomb.

Warren had floated his resumé through an employment agency and had located a consulting company out West offering top dollar for programmers with two years experience at anything. Although Warren felt he'd been treated fairly by Alice and

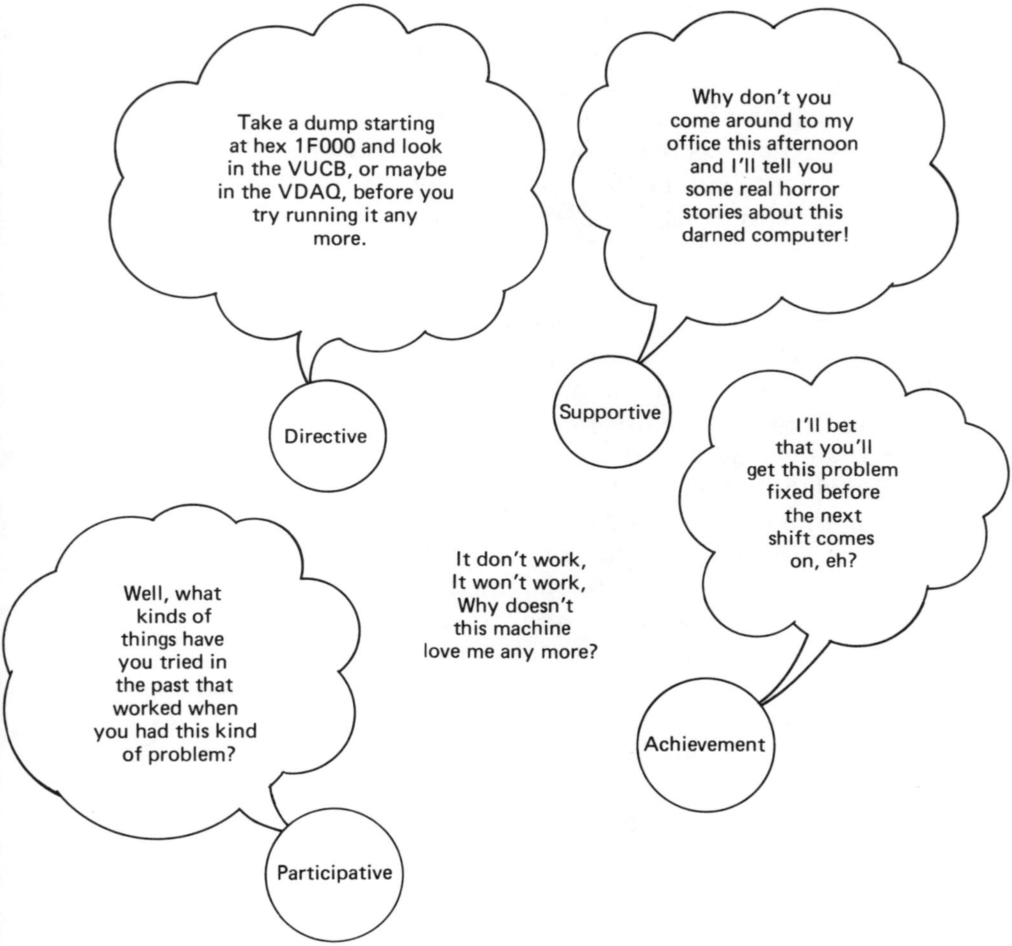


**FIGURE 5.5** Responses of four types of leaders to a programmer's problem.

saw some promotion possibilities, the temptation of higher salary was too much. Warren wanted his rewards now, not two or three years down the road. Even if things didn't work out at the consulting company, there were always other firms who'd bid well for his skills, Warren thought.

Alice was stunned. What about loyalty to a firm that had trained Warren for two years? What about the chances Alice had given Warren to work on a variety of projects, to get to work with the best users, to advance beyond coding and into analysis? What about all those courses? What about the projects Alice was working on now, including the one for which Warren had responsibility—it had almost a year left to go? Warren could be senior programmer soon if he stayed. And what made him so sure that the firm would *not* meet the consulting company's offer—what was that ridiculous amount again? Where was loyalty? Alice felt it; the firm had done well by her and she, in turn, gave it every consideration back. Why couldn't Warren be the same? What was wrong with him? □

In today's market for programmers, Warren's attitude is not unusual. Through recessions and even depressions, the need for competent programmers far exceeds the supply. Even without the obvious monetary enticements, loyalty in the software shop is abnormally low for a number of reasons. Alice's response is more typical of the traditional technical jobs such as engineering, construction, manufacturing, and the like. That is not to say that the concept of loyalty is foreign to programmers, but, as was mentioned in this chapter, programmers are alienated from the reward system that Alice feels has done well by her. Instead, programmers are loyal to immediate things they can control: programs and *paychecks*.

Alice is not correct thinking that she is being blackmailed, for Warren has nothing more evil on his mind than receiving rewards he trusts. Money is one of these. Having a program run right the first time is another. Project responsibilities, courses, variety in tasks, talking to the best users—these provide some rewards, but not long-term ones. These are *contingent*, based upon Warren's providing *quid pro quo* through working for Alice. Salary is forever, so to speak.

Of course, this line of reasoning is defective for a number of reasons. First and foremost, salary is not forever. Salaries can be reduced; others can get more. Second, project responsibilities and user relations can also be long-term benefits, but Warren probably won't see things that way unless Alice spells it out to him. For most programmers, project management and relating to users amount to nothing more than a pain in the neck. Especially if Alice is merely fobbing them off because *she* doesn't like them, Warren can never see these responsibilities as having much meaning for himself. Loyalty is built through vesting interest. Alice has to let Warren know that rewards depend upon Warren's providing rewards to the firm. It's not *merely* tit-for-tat; it's the building of a long-standing relationship of trust.

Probably Alice has not made this clear. Programmers are no less trusting of others than any other vocational group. Nor are they inherently less capable of being shown trust. But the typical management style of the MOP is to trust them as little as possible on nontechnical matters. It is, however, these nontechnical matters that reflect the *firm* as opposed to the *work*. Given this situation, it is not surprising that programmers come to trust the work and their skills at getting it done rather than the firm and their skills in the organization. This is then further amplified by the firm's untrusting response to this lack of confidence. The vicious cycle results in a lack of loyalty. "If the company doesn't trust me, why should I trust it?" asks the programmer. Of course the company trusts the programmer. It trusts the programmer to write specs, code, and document. But it seldom makes clear that the rewards the programmer gets, both monetary and technical, depend greatly upon working to help the firm achieve its primary goals. Since only the MOP can provide that message, the burden falls on the programmer's manager to interpret the firm to the worker.

Alice should begin by providing achievement-oriented leadership to Warren. But the goal should be organizational, not technical. The following conversation should take place if Alice is to retain Warren.

Alice: Well, Warren, what are you looking for in this consulting firm?

Warren: Alice, it's nothing against you, but I'm really good and all I really get out of this place is a few courses and a piddling salary. At least West Coast Consultants is offering me five grand more a year.

Alice: I hear you telling me that salary and courses really aren't enough. Maybe what you need is a range to ride?

Warren: A what?

Alice: A horse, some cattle, and a range. You see, Warren, I like this company, but sometimes I wonder what I'm doing for it. After all, since all I get from it is a few bucks and some courses, too, I wonder if the company really appreciates and trusts me. At times like these, I get on my horse and drive a couple hundred head of cattle to market in Kansas City, y'know?

Warren: You mean you turn computer cowgirl?

Alice: Yeah. I like to see if anybody out there is really watching and counting the cattle. And y'know, almost every time I do that, somebody, maybe a VP for Feedlots or the Director of Slaughterhouses perks up and calls me down to the office and pins an honorary sheriff's badge on me. Then when I get the raise or the course, I know it's because they not only care, but they appreciate my caring.

Warren: So where are *my* cattle?

Alice: Now here's the tough part. There are a lot of cattle running out there. This company's bursting at the seams with work. Nothing makes those folks at the top sit up in their saddles more than a ranch-hand who single-handedly stops a stampede. There's a lot of work to be done, but unfortunately we've got to tell them where the stampedes are. I've got two projects doing nothing because I don't know how to sell them to my boss. If we sell 'em, we've got work, real work, for several years. And maybe promotions and maybe more salary. But mostly what we've got is some stake in what happens around here. Now that's something you won't get in a consulting firm, I can promise you that. How about putting your move off for a half a year and trying out some *difficult* work with me on these projects?

Warren: Well, tell me something about them. . . .

There is no guarantee that Warren will stay. But Alice has at least not fallen for the easy analysis. Warren isn't blackmailing; he's asking for reasons why he should care about staying. And only Alice can give him those at this point.

## 5.2. THE CONTROLLING ACTIVITIES OF THE MOP

After staffing, organizing, and directing programmers toward specific goals, the MOP can't sit back and watch work happen. Responsibility is completed only when the MOP *controls* programmer work activities to ensure that work goals are met. These responsibilities include the following:

**1.** Monitoring.

2. Evaluating.
3. Adjusting.
4. Reporting.

This doesn't imply a sweatshop atmosphere. What it does imply is that the MOP has to remain aware of the flow of work, its progress, developments that threaten meeting of work goals, and opportunities that may enhance performance toward those goals.

### 5.2.1. Control in the Software Shop

Figure 5.6 illustrates the control cycle in the software shop. Work goals are created from specs and knowledge of the available resources. These may change during the job, so they are included in the control cycle.

Based on goals and past performance, the MOP decides on whether or not corrective action is needed. If not, the MOP may

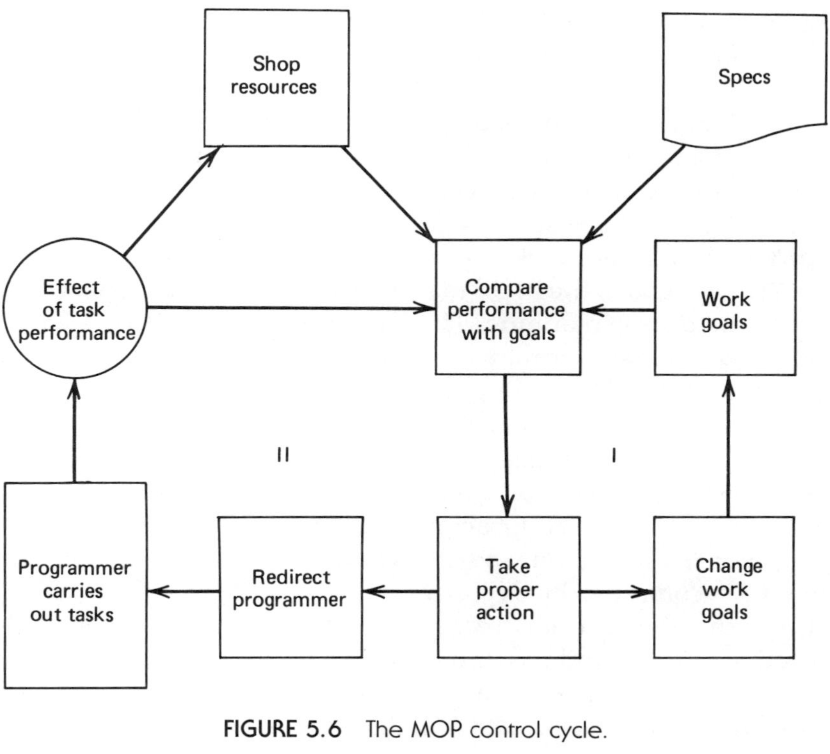


FIGURE 5.6 The MOP control cycle.

provide encouragement or small rewards—otherwise the message is that work is defective and needs to be improved. If, however, there are deficiencies, the MOP has to propose some change.

There are two kinds of correction. First, it is possible that work goals are unreasonable given available resources. A key programmer may quit, the CPU may be down for two days of unplanned maintenance. Customers may change their minds and ask for changes in the specs. In these cases it's proper to change work goals.

On the other hand, when work performance is truly not up to previously agreed-upon standards, the MOP will have to redirect the progammer in the following ways:

1. *Clarification.* Work goals are explained better.
2. *Training.* The progammer is coached or given courses.
3. *Tool Provision.* More tools are provided or resources are reallocated.
4. *Counseling.* The programmer is given help in nontechnical areas that are interfering with job performance.
5. *Reassignment.* An exchange of human resources moves the programmer to another task.

Of the five, clarification is the most cost-effective, and usually the easiest. Often work goals *are* unclear. Programmers may not be aware of which files are to be used, which testing techniques are called for, how much time is to be spent realistically on each module, and what the production schedule is and where it is flexible.

In clarifying goals, the MOP may also discover some inconsistency not apparent during planning. The programmer is not always wrong. In fact, a veteran staffer may spot problems in meeting work goals immediately upon attempting to meet them.

Sometimes training or coaching is necessary, especially for novice programmers. New languages, operating systems, and work procedures take some time to get used to. A rule of thumb is that a novice may require half a year to acquire full facility with the program development system alone; a new recruit may need several months merely to become productive.

During this time for new recruits, or for veterans who need help, both active training and coaching, as well as a substantial amount of time reading the manuals, may prove necessary. Programmers may be unwilling to admit lack of knowledge, however, and MOPs should remain sensitive to this issue. Coaching is a relatively extreme measure for programmers. If used sensitively, both MOP and programmer will profit.

Redirection may mean providing tools and resources that weren't in original plans. Extra computer time, higher priority for batch processing, a better quality terminal, and access to systems analysis personnel can often provide the little bit of help that distinguishes good software from a late, low-quality product.

In exceptional circumstances, the work deficiency is unrelated to the job. Programmers are human beings living human lives. Stress, anxiety, accidents, and life "passages," such as the birth of a child, are important factors influencing job performance, factors over which MOPs cannot assume control or feel guilt. Solutions can be as simple as a day off or referral to the company medical unit to complex and expensive regimens at centers for alcoholism and drug abuse treatment. Since the MOP isn't a trained counselor, it's important for the MOP to be aware of sudden drops in performance and to have a resource to refer the programmer to for help. Many firms employ an Employee Assistance Program counselor for this sort of referral. Often the company physician or nurse may provide this service. As the programmer group ages, non-job-related stress will become an increasingly major player in work performance.

Finally, MOPs may have to admit that the wrong person is attempting the work. In these cases, programmers may be reassigned, switched, or doubled up. Reassignment is *the* extreme move. It puts work plans in jeopardy. It may signify a lack of planning ability and tact on the MOP's part. Because programmers are people, reassignment may not be easy to carry out, especially half-way through a project. Part of good planning is planning for personnel change contingencies and the need for backup.

In addition, specs and shop resources may change regardless of tasks programmers perform. Some of these changes can be anticipated ("Accounting always has changes to specs after they see the reports"), but others cannot be predicted. Economic and political conditions in the firm and in vendor and supplier firms cause significant fluctuation in resources. Programmers quit, new ones are hired, pressures to forego or speed up planned upgrades are applied, the DP Director quits and along come new policies with the new Director. Chapter 6 points out ways in which MOPs can anticipate, plan for, and adjust to organizational imperatives and the changes they bring. Workforce planning can help anticipate staffing changes. Working closely with a technological planning group and keeping an ear and an eye open to user needs can help the MOP anticipate these sorts of changes.

This completes the control cycle. Exercising control resembles direction, and the next section discusses the whats and hows of control in the software shop.

### 5.2.2. What to Control

Below are resources a MOP should control. Only two are related to the phrase "on time and under budget." The other 15 are shop resources that are expended as programmers work. In each case, a different kind of awareness is needed by the MOP in order to judge performance:

Access to access codes.
Access to design personnel and customers.
Access to files.
Access to project control software.
Access to systems software.
Computer time.
Cost, time expended per module.
Materials and supplies (tapes, diskettes, etc.).
Module flow.
Personnel development (courses, seminars, conferences).
Quality of work and documentation.
Quantity of work and documentation.
Meeting schedules, invitations, and attendance.
Use of support software and tools.
Use of support personnel (secretaries, clerks).
Work methods and testing techniques.
Work schedules.

Other items need to be controlled because they represent scarce resources that should be shared equitably among staffers. Computer time, materials and supplies, support personnel time, meeting time, and the programmer's time are nonreusable. Again, the MOP should be aware of resources both in terms of planning long-term resource acquisition (i.e., staffing, hardware, supplies, software tools) and in terms of examining individual programmer performance.

### 5.2.3. Control Techniques

Management control techniques include four types of activities:

1. Use of planning tools during control of work.
2. Writing reports on performance.
3. Conducting meetings to obtain verbal reports.
4. Use of project control software.

Planning tools such as the project schedule, PERT and Gantt charts, work assignment charts, structure charts, and other paperwork discussed in Chapter 3 are useful during control. The technique is to compare the *current* with the *planned*. The difference is then justified or work is changed. The term for this is "management by exception," letting daily activities take care of themselves and concentrating upon variance from the plan.

Often these planning tools fail to provide much detailed information on performance. In this case, MOPs resort to written status reports on a regular basis to fill in. They have limited value, however, even when the MOP has time to read them. Programmers, like many technical workers, are not great documenters. There is little reward for writing a nice status report. The chances are large that the very act of sitting down and writing pushes important facts from the programmer's mind. Many people freeze up when they have to write such reports. The result is often fiction, poorly written with bad character development. Because programmers already have problems with documentation, it is unwise to rely on status reports unless creation of the report is relatively automatic. That's why project control software is proving popular: writing documentation at least superficially resembles writing code.

The most effective way of controlling work is through verbal reports, interviews, review meetings, and structured code walkthroughs. These are time-consuming, but very rich communication modes that MOPs should not shy away from. A well-run review meeting can provide enough information to make accurate judgments of performance. On the other hand, it is very easy to have such meetings turn into free-for-alls.

The important thing to remember about controls is that they exist not to punish poor workers but to make sure that the work is done and that the MOP can assume responsibility for getting it done. Controls work both ways. The MOP has enough information to make valid judgments about the work, and the programmer knows how that judgment is to be arrived at. In other words, the control cycle is honest. Several guidelines need to be followed in order to keep it so:

1. Controls must be meaningful: they should pertain to the work and the control responsibilities of the MOP.
2. Controls must relate to things that can actually be controlled, improved, and measured.
3. Controls are subject to negotiation—they have to be accepted by all to be effective.
4. Controls must relate to goals that can actually be met by reasonable expenditure of effort.
5. Controls must not become a major object of work—they shouldn't be a burden to programmers and they should become a major aspect of the work of the MOP.
6. Controls should be as automatable as possible, as simple as possible to carry through, and as easy as possible to report on.
7. Controls should be public knowledge.
8. Controls exercised should be of value to the worker, too, by providing useful feedback and by being an avenue of communication between MOP and programmer.

### 5.2.4. Performance Appraisal

The topic of control naturally implies performance appraisal (PA). By definition, PA examines overall job performance. Typically this is done annually or semiannually by the immediate supervisor. We are all familiar with simple but potent PA forms, such as report cards in school and the kinds of evaluations professors make of their students' work in college. In recent years, formal PA systems have become commonplace in larger firms. Figure 5.7 diagrams the usual process. Packaged systems built around computers are now available for all but the smallest firms. In these systems computers are used to maintain the data and to produce reports to employees and summaries to management.

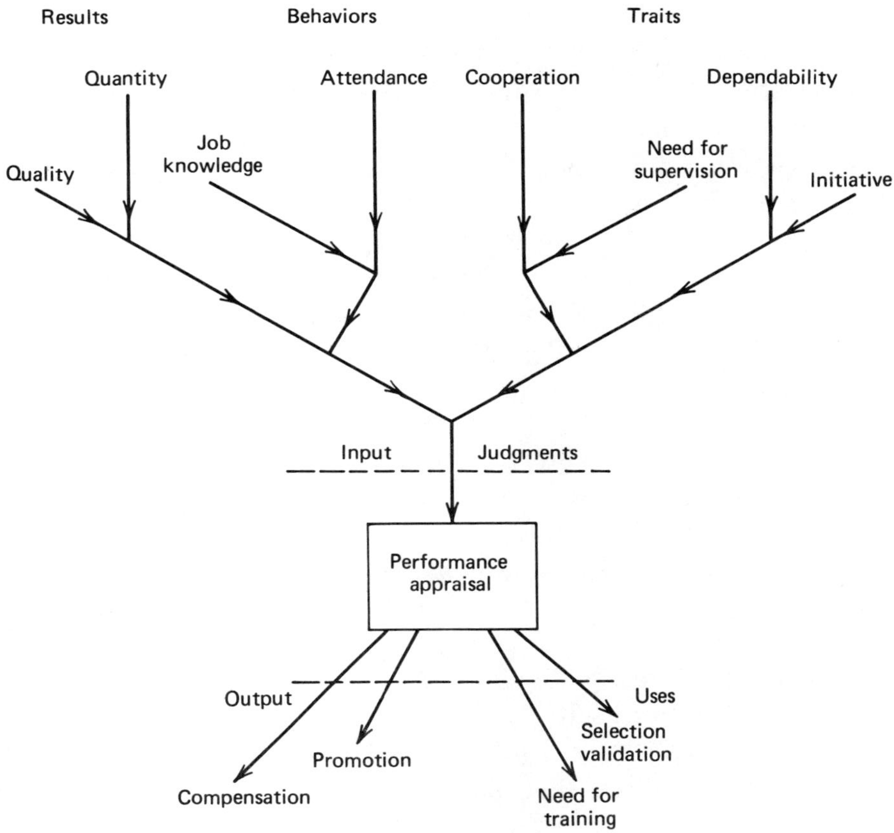


**FIGURE 5.7** The performance appraisal process.

Problems in PA occur because PA requires judgment by individual supervisors who have little to base their judgments upon. One may know when a *program* works correctly, but be confused when it comes to knowing how well a *programmer* works.

Programmers, too, cause special problems in PA. Often it's difficult to separate the individual and his or her work habits from the work accomplished. In fact, programmers identify highly with their code. So strong is this feeling of ownership that negative judgment of work is often taken personally as character judgment even when it is *not* intended so. MOPs naturally steer clear of these calls. "Egoless" programming is still not the norm. But making judgments on the quality and style of work *is* the essential core of the PA process.

Below are nine issues in performance appraisal of programmers. None is unique to this field, but together they challenge the MOP:

1. *Units.* What units can we observe? Lines of code, programs, projects, daily behavior?
2. *Periods.* When should appraisals be held? Yearly, semiannually, after every project, when problems occur?
3. *Measurement.* What is an "exception" when programmers work independently and problems may not be noted in products for months? What is "poor" performance when standards don't exist and when tools and project management techniques are exploratory or imperfect?
4. *Teams.* How can teamwork be evaluated?
5. *Responsibility.* Who takes responsibility for errors?
6. *Personalities.* How can discussion of personalities and individual traits be avoided?
7. *Technicalities.* How can work be discussed when job descriptions are often poor, project goals poorly defined or fluid, and start-up costs are high on maintenance work?
8. *Computerization.* Why can't the whole process be handled by the computer itself?
9. *Work Habits.* How can disputes over work habits be avoided in favor of discussing the *work*.

In brief, the problems of units and periods arise because of the nature of programming work: on modules in projects. Since programmers don't produce inert objects but tools for others' use, the problems of measurement, especially where specs themselves may be arguable, is quite difficult. Teamwork and the assembly-line-like atmosphere of the SDLC make assigning of responsibility and brownie points difficult. Personality problems have already been mentioned. The problem of running after not only the job but the technology is especially acute in the software shop. The PA process is unrewarding in general and even less so for MOPs and programmers; computerization of the entire process might help. Finally, the idiosyncratic nature of programmer work habits further complicates the problem. How can a MOP make valid judgments of the performance and behavior of erratic but probably effective individuals when their work habits differ so much from those of ordinary office workers?

The answer is not yet clear. Certainly the *need* to judge performance is rising as accountability becomes the single overriding issue of the 1980s. But the resources available in the software shop to make these judgments are no more sophisticated and valid now than in 1960. New techniques, such as the performance data and development system (PDD), created by Dr. Tom Janz of the University of Calgary, seem to address some of the problems and the PDD is being used currently on a number of programming units in Western Canada.

Results occupy the highest niche in making judgments, trailed by behaviors and traits. Making these judgments is, however, quite difficult. We are relatively uncertain about what constitutes a "productive" programmer, nor are we really clear about what the appropriate behaviors and traits might be. Lists have been created, most of them invalid, detailing appropriate skills but in this period of rapid change in the workforce, it's doubtful these lists apply any longer.

One way out has been to employ management by objectives. Management by objectives, or MBO, replaces judgment of a worker's products or actions with a matching of goals and production. In most cases goals are set cooperatively by manager and employee, although the distribution of power in this negotiation rarely allows for equality Once a year the manager and employee review the goals, judge meeting them, and set new goals for the coming year.

MBO has a major problem with programmers because the availability and appropriateness of tools is a great determiner of the quality and quantity of product and therefore of goal attainment. Consider the effects of unscheduled maintenance; unscheduled meetings; changes in specifications, support staff, operating systems, system configurations, compilers; and missing or incomplete documentation on goal attainment. For maintenance programming the list is even longer.

The other major problems with MBO include the lack of ability to create specific objectives that don't read like this: "Code, debug, test, and certify 100% of modules assigned." Also included are problems such as the project- rather than job-orientation of the shop, the long length of time a year is for feedback, the large volume of work expected in one year, the large number of projects a programmer may engage in, and the fact that programming work is becoming indistinguishable from analysis and operations work in some modes. In fact, the general problems with MBO are those historically facing programming in general.

Below is a representation of the format of traditional ranking scales.

| | Clearly unacceptable | | | Acceptable | | Clearly superior | |
|---|---|---|---|---|---|---|---|
| | 1 | 2 | 3 | 4 | 5 | 6 | 7 |
| Quality of work | | | | ✓ | | | |
| Quantity of work | | | ✓ | | | | |
| Reliability | | | | | ✓ | | |
| Knowledge of work | | ✓ | | | | | |
| Cooperation | | | | | ✓ | | |
| Leadership | ✓ | | | | | | |
| Total for each column | 1 | 2 | 3 | 4 | 10 | | |
| | | | | | Grand total | | 20 |

As an alternative, attention has shifted to the *activities* of workers. Termed behaviorally anchored rating scales (BARS), this technique for collecting data concentrates on comparing behaviors to those characteristic of productive and unproductive work:

Please rate your employee on the following scales, noting examples of each behaviour indicated for each value. Circle one value on each scale.

1\. 1 ——— 2 ——— 3 ——— 4 ——— 5 ——— 6 ——— 7

| 1 | 2 | 3 | 4 | 5 | 6 | 7 |
|---|---|---|---|---|---|---|
| Product is always late, typically wrong or faulty | Product is frequently late, and may be wrong or faulty | | Product is rarely late and sometimes has minor faults | | Product is always on time and in correct form and faultless | |

2\. 1 ——— 2 ——— 3 ——— 4 ——— 5 ——— 6 ——— 7

| 1 | 2 | 3 | 4 | 5 | 6 | 7 |
|---|---|---|---|---|---|---|
| Employee never assists others or does so under coercion | Programmer sometimes helps others when asked to do so | | Employee always helps others when asked | | Employee helps others without being asked | |

An extension of BARS is the PDD system previously mentioned. This system requires a great deal of paperwork, which computers can handle nicely. MOPs and programmers meet over a period of time to establish examples of productive and nonproductive work. After agreeing upon these examples, they meet regularly to document actual incidents that conform to these descriptions.

The descriptions are unique for each individual and change during each PA cycle. Thus the descriptions and the meetings constitute a kind of program for the MOP and programmer to follow. Because actual examples are given, it is easy to make judgments, or at least easy to have something to argue about. This can help make PA a common, rather than rare, occurrence. In addition, programmers will have written behavior standards against which to make their *own* judgments of themselves. This provides better feedback, and it can contribute to self-awareness and personal growth if used well.

PDD is a two-part process. One part focuses upon the collection of performance data, as discussed above. The other part concentrates on the development of staff. This is the most productive aspect of PDD. It plays an essential part in staffing, a followup at regular intervals that PA is supposed to provide but that is rarely achieved. PDD has been successfully implemented in one large Canadian firm. Since a great deal of paper is generated for employees, and since a series of meetings rather than a single yearly get-together is required, the computer is the natural medium for PDD, in conjunction with office automation software. At least one version of PDD is available on a popular microcomputer.

Regardless of the PA system used, if performance appraisal is to prove useful in control of programmer work, the following Ten Commandments of Performance Appraisal should be kept in mind:

1. *Don't* make judgments based exclusively on personality.
2. *Don't* spring surprises at the PA meeting(s).
3. *Don't* ignore programmers' ideas about job definition.
4. *Encourage* self-evaluation by the programmer.
5. *Don't* be impatient, argumentative, or pushy.
6. *Restate*, clarify, and provide feedback during the meeting.
7. *Don't* be sidetracked into irrelevancies and diversions.
8. *Don't* concentrate on a list of complaints.
9. *Feed back* performance information outside the meeting, especially if meetings are infrequent.
10. *Prepare* yourself for the meeting by being aware of your own limitations as a judge; avoid bias and stereotyping.

These are also the Ten Commandments of Control in work situations. Unless the MOP is aware of these, and lets the programmer know that these are important, there is little chance for effective control. The goal of personnel management should be *continuous performance appraisal*, both by the MOP and through programmer self-evaluation. This is possible only with well-defined goals and standards and an attitude on the part of the MOP that feedback is an integral part of controlling programming work.

### *Case 2. The Perfectionist*

Jim Johnson had just heard Laura Larkin's latest lamentations, but somehow he didn't have to listen at all. It was always the same story. Laura, a Programmer III for Jim, who was Manager of Software Development, is a perfectionist who is always late delivering code, always trying to optimize just one more line, always documenting to the *n*th degree every violation of specifications, and always late, late, late. Jim finds her work satisfactory but he really doesn't see where Laura's work is any more reliable, readable or efficient than the work produced by his other four coders. In fact, wading through all that documentation is itself a pain.

Jim has noticed, too, that Laura works long hours, coming in before the others, working later, and using a lot more CPU cycles than the others. For instance, Laura seems to need 25% more machine time than any of the other coders. That translates into almost $200 more resource time monthly. True, it's "funny money," but why does Laura need all that time? Rob Kroneberg, another Programmer III, uses one-third the resources Laura does. Maybe his code isn't as "elegant," but it works as well for less.

Also, the other programmers don't seem to like working with Laura. Laura's really intolerant of others because of her perfectionism. This in turn makes the others seem to conform to Laura's view of them, and confirm Laura's ideas that her coding is better. Laura is vicious in code reviews, criticizing others where it is unnecessary and playing dumb in reading code that is clear to others. The devil's advocate has turned into a devil herself. Jim is tired of hearing about how code has to be perfect. □

Jim's got a problem on his hands. He has started on the control cycle, but he's not carried it through. By taking a measure of the cost of producing code, Jim is beginning to understand that he's paying more for Laura's work than for others'. Yet Jim so far has not developed a standard and incorporated that into the work goals. In other words, he's got measurements, but he doesn't know how to apply them.

On the other hand, Jim doesn't have to be satisfied with code that merely works. He *can* incorporate development costs into work plans, since programmers have access to these costs, too. He *can* demand that programmers pay attention to these costs, and he can request that these costs be translated into goals.

However, Jim's problems with Laura go deeper than mere cost objectives. Laura is a perfectionist. She is intolerant of mistakes in herself and others. This intolerance shows up in her relations with others, and in her inability to see their side of any issue.

Reprogramming the perfectionist is difficult. The causes of perfectionism are many, and not all of them are related to the job. Jim can begin by discussing with Laura just why Laura feels so strongly about optimization and documentation when Jim, who has ultimate responsibility for the work, doesn't have these feelings. It is possible that Laura is afraid of being judged a poor worker. It is likely that previous managers have sprung surprises on Laura either during tasks or during performance appraisal. Another possibility is that Laura has a fear that she will be replaced by a software tool and is competing with a mythical program. Jim can help allay Laura's fears in this regard.

Another cause of perfectionism is training. Many schools train programmers with an eye toward exactitude. After all, grades, certificates, diplomas, and jobs depend greatly upon handing in assignments that conform closely to predefined specs. As *many* graduates discover—Laura has not, obviously—there is a world of difference between a school assignment and a task to be done in the real world. In school, exercises are done by dozens or hundreds of students and done semester after semester. The instructor is highly motivated to "make the answer come out right" if specs are followed. In the business world, there are a lot of loopholes, some left in intentionally and some developing simply because not everything is known. True, the *ideal* is to have error-free designs, but that ideal is typically not met. Jim knows this. Laura does not. While it is not good for Jim to teach Laura to distrust specs, he can certainly show Laura examples of specs that had to be changed. They are not the word of the gods; Laura can observe their *human source*.

This is an example of a "self-controlling" employee who is actually out of control. Many MOPs would be quite happy to have a staff of perfectionists. This is misguided desire. A true perfectionist will not put up with a MOP who is only a mortal. Perfectionists cannot work with nonperfectionists. The only value of a perfectionist is that the MOP never has to talk to one. By designing in controls on the work and actively working to measure and compare work against the controls, MOPs insure themselves that perfectionists aren't required.

## 5.3. CONCLUSION: MANAGING THE HUMAN RESOURCE

Effective personnel management in the software shop is a complex task involving staffing, organizing, directing, and controlling. MOPs acquire skills in these areas in many ways, but of the greatest importance is the support the organization provides new MOPs in adjusting to the demands that personnel management places upon them. Managing is just not "harder" programming. It's a different kind of job and taps different skills.

Staffing, organizing, directing, and controlling are not isolated activities, either. Acquiring staff may depend upon the kind of organization planned for work. Directing in a project environment is different from directing maintenance or systems efforts. Control of work is made easier when appropriate resources are available to supervise and discuss work performance.

MOPs experience a number of critical personnel management situations because of the type of work being done, the kind of person doing the work, and the kind of organization found in the DP Department. Problems with loyalty, redirection, supervision, meeting schedules, prima donnas, avoidance, workaholism, and stress abound in the software shop. This chapter has provided a number of guides for meeting the demands of these problems. The following chapter discusses the role of the organization in the MOP's daily activities and the challenges that face the MOP both inside and above the Data Processing Department.

CHAPTER SIX

# MANAGING PROGRAMMERS IN AN ORGANIZATION

## *Case 1. War in the Trenches*

"It's war!" thought Harvey Watson, "And I intend to win." These military thoughts were brought about by a conversation Harvey had had with Kate Lambert that afternoon after a user design review on one of Harvey's major projects. Harvey heads the software development group and Kate heads the analysis group within a larger DP Department of a major resource industry. Harvey has been Programmer Manager for two years now; Kate's headed the analysis group for over six years. Also, Kate's a DP veteran and has almost two decades with the firm, Great Western Energy Resources. In the past, Harvey's tended to defer to the older woman's wishes. But Harvey's had the biscuit, so to speak.

What has happened is simple to describe. Kate accused Harvey, privately, of deliberately and "illegally" encouraging his programmers to change design specs to make coding easier. Although the effect on the users is minimal, Kate angrily hissed at Harvey, "*We* design. *You* implement. *We* write specs. *You* write code. That's it."

Harvey retorted that as manager of seven programmers he had the duty and authority to assign work in packages that were most efficient to manage and that included "...redesigning, if you will, the module structures." Especially, Harvey pointed out, if the documentation were changed to agree with the changes and if there were no effects on user procedures, data, data formats, and staffing.

"Not so," claimed Kate. "Specs are specs. If everyone felt the way you do, there would be chaos." Kate warned Harvey to watch out and to quit overstepping his authority or Kate would have to complain to Sam Underhill, Director of DP. It sounded like a threat. Maybe Harvey should go to Sam first and head 'em off at the pass. Meanwhile, Harvey's going to review the specs of all of Kate's projects in recent months and see just what's going on. Maybe Harvey's been a patsy for too long. □

Does this sound familiar? Harvey and Kate are like a bad marriage that needs counseling. But their real problem isn't Harvey's relative inexperience and Kate's intransigence. Although they certainly could use help in these areas, the major obstacle to good relations here is their lack of ability to function within an organization of individuals, tasks, goals, and pressures.

This chapter looks at what working in an organization means to MOPs and how technical managers can function better, away from their terminals, in boardrooms and strategy sessions. Near the end of the chapter, we'll return to Harvey and Kate and prescribe some organizational potions for their ailments.

The plan of this chapter is first to look at some principles of organizations, particularly those organizations in which programming plays an important role. Next, we look at specific roles played by the Manager of Programmers in meeting organizational objectives. Third, we'll contrast technical management with other kinds of management within a firm to understand where a number of conflicts unique to the management of programmers arise. Fourth, we'll dissect these conflicts through a number of case studies and determine how best to avoid or to cope with the kinds of problems with organizations that MOPs seem to confront. Often this means avoidance.

Unfortunately, this merely avoids the consequences of ignoring the organization's needs while tending to one's own. The truth is that no one can afford to be sheltered from organizational life in today's working world of interlocking dependencies. Without knowledge of the organization, programmers and MOPs live in an organizational fantasyland, shattered with each change of management or policy. This chapter comes to grips with the problem of coping with the organization after coping with the computer (Chapters 2 and 3) and the programmer (Chapters 4 and 5).

## 6.1. PRINCIPLES OF ORGANIZATION

Organizations are based upon *constraint,* limitations placed on the possibilities. These constraints may come, as illustrated in Figure 6.1, from physical, logical, control, or authority relationships. MOPs will recognize these as manifested in office layouts, mail routes, procedures, and bureaucracies. Each of these has a set of rules (what ought to be) and regulations (how things get to be the way they are). Each reflects "organization" in a different way.

Organizations have "concerns," too, which reflect their operations. For instance, a business organization is "concerned" with the flow of cash, customers, supplies, and ideas inward and the flow of products or services outward. As illustrated in Figure 6.2, MOPs may not share these same concerns. A MOP may see the organization as a collection of skills, motives, feelings, and expectations from which work (i.e., usable software) is produced. These differing views may cause a great deal of conflict. The view from the software shop and the view from mahogany row have rarely been consonant. What is astonishing is that the software shop has been allowed to go its own way for so long without being directly accountable to "the organization" for its use of resources and technology. As MOPs come under increasing pressure to respond to organizational concerns, this difference is being drawn in sharp relief.

An organization "runs" on five principles, diagrammed in Figure 6.3. These are (1) self-regulation, (2) openness, (3) formal communication, (4) goal-seeking, and (5) division of labor.

An organization regulates itself through rules,called policies, that its members follow. Any organization must be open to input from outside if it is to survive. Often it is *more* open to these outside influences than to those from within, much to the frustration of workers. Much of the external and all of the internal input is formal,

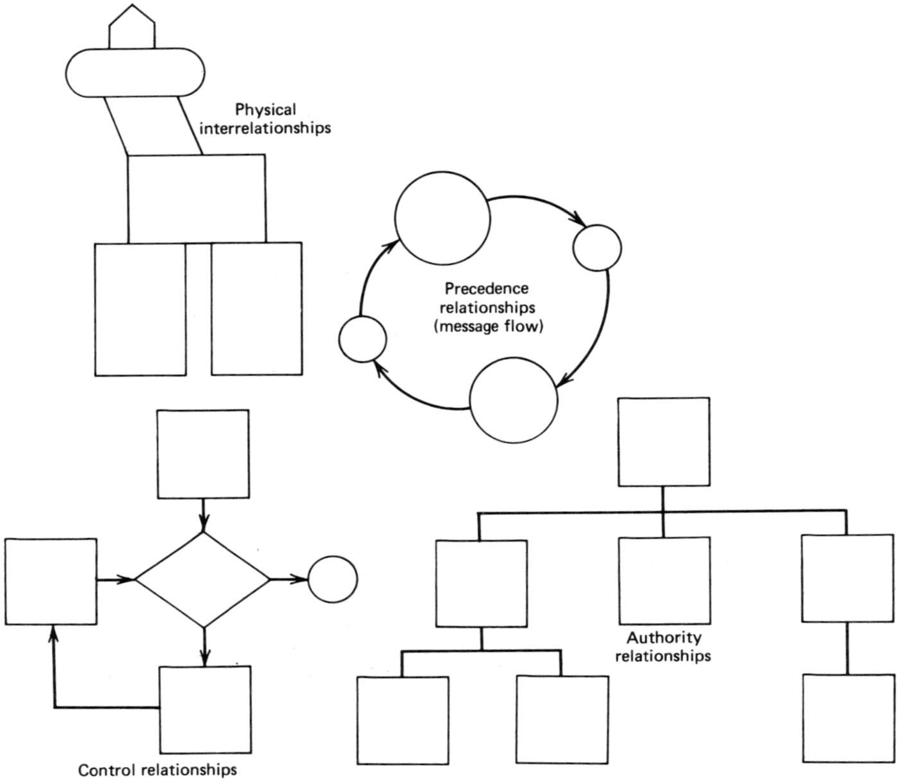


**FIGURE 6.1** Some organizations and their constraining forces.

usually written. Nonorganizational messages of a social nature are less likely to be formal and more likely to be spoken.

Organizations ruthlessly tend to seek goals: profit, influence, growth.Often this pursuit is at the expense—or more charitably, in ignorance—of goals of workers. Finally, organizations seem to survive best when work is assigned in pieces to those who are highly trained to work only on those specific pieces.

The software shop is still a relatively isolated and specialized department or division within the firm. Unless the firm exists to create and market software (there seem to be more of these daily), upper management cannot be counted upon to empathize with the problems that programmers have with software production and maintenance. That no one cheers when you have a bright idea for producing more reliable software is not surprising. No one really

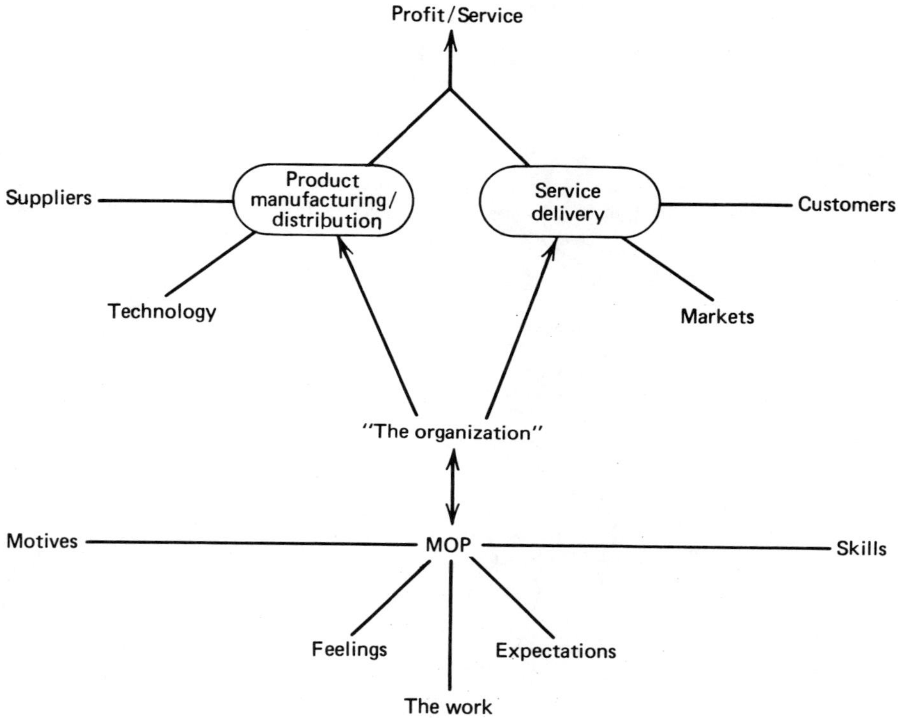


**FIGURE 6.2** Contrasting the concerns of the organization with those of the MOP.

understands what it means for a program, as opposed to a system, to fail. Since it has no moving parts, how can a program wear out? The organization will instead, and incredibly, punish you if you persist in selling ideas that are not only incomprehensible but will also cost money. Most MOPs forget that, while the software experts in the DP shop may have the *right* to talk in COBOL, they also have the *responsibility* to make their ideas relevant to the firm if they wish to move their soapboxes outside the shop.

*MOPs have trouble getting programmers to document. You shouldn't be surprised that your management might consider you recalcitrant for lack of response to memos or requests for forms.* Each suborganization has its peculiar information needs and resources and has styled its own "MIS." Some are quite inefficient and maddening to those who have long since solved their own information problems. Astonishingly, the MIS department is often the last to implement a systematic information management plan. MOPs understand instinctively the

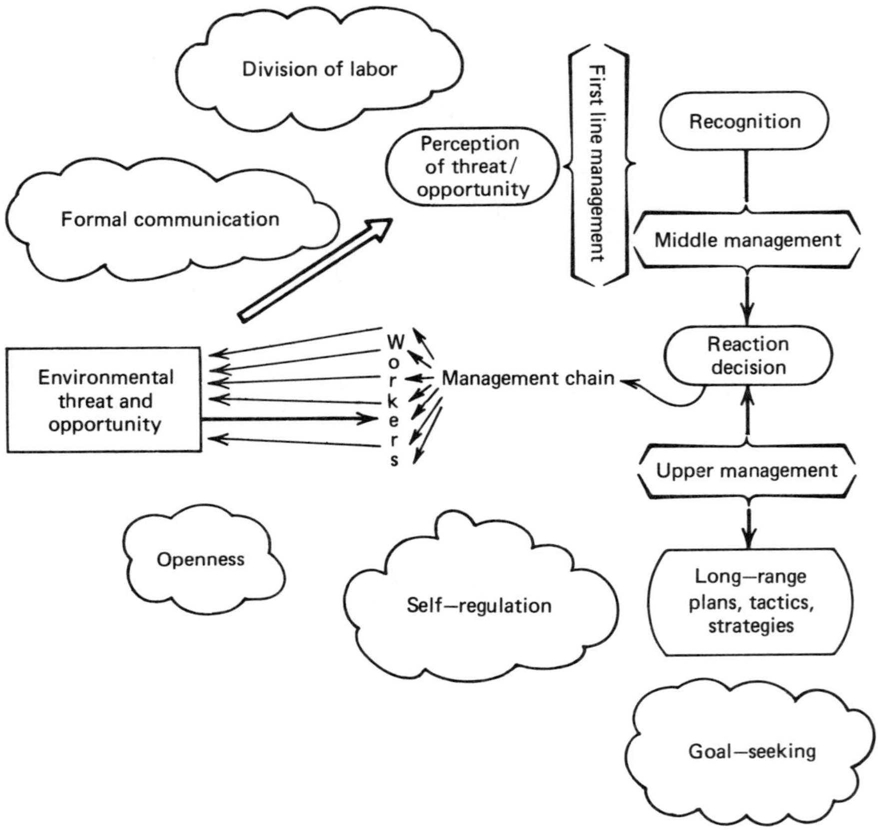


**FIGURE 6.3** Organizational principles.

need for information to run a decision process, but it doesn't impress upper management if these same experts forget to file reports on time and argue over the necessity for timesheets, status reports, and formal requests for stationery and pencils. From these other managers' viewpoints, this "informed" view is indistinguishable from arrogance.

*The MOP provides the bridge between the firm and its goals and the worker and the worker's needs.* This is so because organizations don't respond well to individuals but rather are concerned with maintaining the status quo within small confines. Many MOPs come from a tradition in which the organization's needs are purposely ignored. Possibly this arose in an era in which DP was seen as necessary, but impossible to understand. Now, however, the firm depends upon DP and expects DP staff to conform to some degree to its goals. A VP who has taken a computer seminar can, in all fairness, expect some reciprocity from staffers, who might, at least, try to comprehend the firm's goals and plans. The MOP has the job of interpreting the firm's goals into work plans and supervising these plans to execution and software production. The MOP has to respond to the worker and, at the same time, be responsible to the firm for these goals.

*The MOP who understands the organization is far more comfortable than the MOP who chooses to ignore it because he or she is afraid.* However, understanding the organization really means understanding the individuals who make up and execute the firm's plans and formulate goals. This requires a level of involvement by MOPs and other DP management that historically has not existed.

## 6.2. THE ROLE OF THE MOP

The role of the Manager of Programmers in a firm that consumes software products is to provide an interface between the firm, with its goals, and the individual workers, who pursue their vocational goals. Just as any interface must provide smooth transition, catch erroneous messages, and provide an attractive format to users, the MOP serves these interface functions in the following fashions:

1. Managing technical resources.
2. Training individuals to use the organization's resources in an efficient fashion consistent with goals.
3. Providing the organization with a finger on the pulse of the shop.
4. Advising the organization of the technological opportunities and threats.
5. Interpreting the organization's goals into work statements for shop employees.

The technical resources of the shop have been discussed at length in Chapter 2. The organization views these resources as expense items and requires both justification for their deployment (i.e., a budget) and a fair return on their use (i.e., software, exception reports, documentation). Thus in carrying out the role of technical resource manager, the MOP is expected to prepare budgets and provide periodic returns.

One popular form of budgeting outside DP is zero-based budgeting (ZBB). Simply stated, each expense item is justified at the start of each budgeting period. This contrasts with other budgeting formats in which this period's budget is made up contingent upon other, prior periods. In the past, a software development budget could usually be extrapolated by taking last year's figures (gross or individual item) and multiplying by an inflator, often 125% or more. ZBB disallows this and requires reasons for each request. Budgeting techniques are beyond the scope of this book. However, it is important to note that success at budgeting requires that the MOP have a well-tested *theory* of expenses in the software shop: what requests will require which resources for what length of time. Without this theory, it is impossible to justify any request for resources.

A second role the MOP plays with regard to managing in an organization is in training the programmers and others to use the firm's resources in a manner that is appropriate and consistent with the firm's goals. This may range from creating a spirit of managing for maintainability to teaching individual programmers how to use a new debugger efficiently. Another aspect of this role is in providing effective transfer of knowledge from the programming group to other groups within DP and elsewhere. Specifically, the organization expects the MOP to work well with peers in the DP shop and in user groups. This work should include helping others understand how to make their needs known to the software development group. Also, the MOP has a responsibility to learn how to respond appropriately to them in return. The overall objective is to enable all the players to come to a mutual understanding without unnecessary conflict.

Because the MOP directs technical people, the organization expects the person in this role to keep the organization aware of the situation within the shop. Specifically, the firm needs to know the following (See Figure 6.4):

1. Short-term and long-term personnel needs.
2. The state of knowledge within the group with respect to the technology.
3. The emotional state of the group, including morale, working conditions, understanding the organization itself, and progress toward career and personal goals.

4. Attendance, adherence to shop and company rules.
5. Short-term and long-term resource needs within the group.
6. Other information pertinent to specific company or DP department goals.

Provision of this information is seldom in formal, written format. Instead, these are topics of conversation between the MOP and DP management and others. Certain firms require this information in a formal fashion on an annual basis through workforce appraisal reports, especially where the software shop is organized around proj-

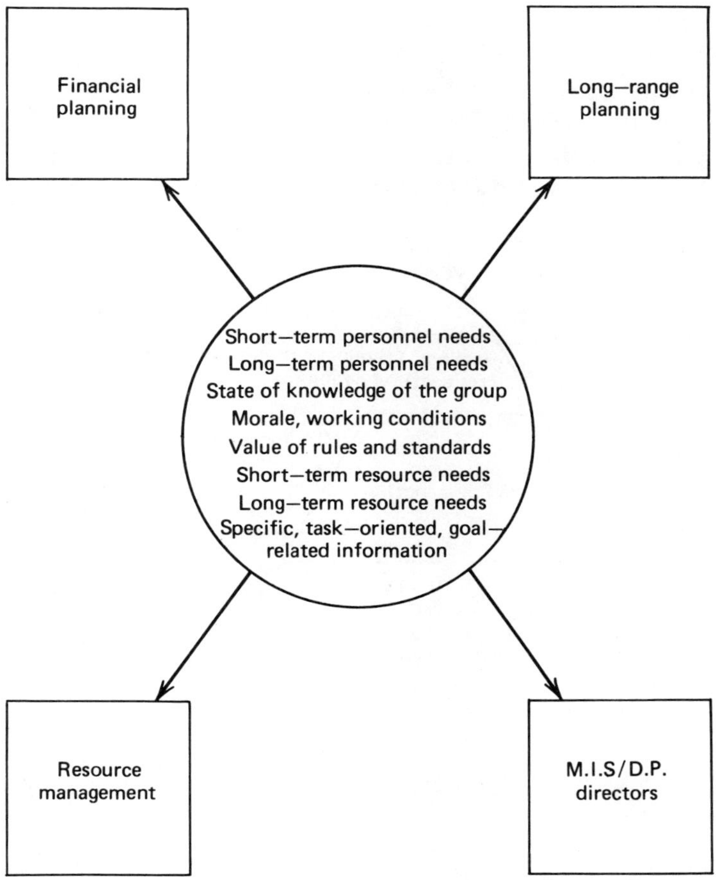


**FIGURE 6.4** What the organization's management needs to know about the software development group.

ects. In these cases there has to be some means for the organization to become informed about the shop as a whole, not merely the projects.

Equally as important as advising the firm about conditions within the shop is the role of advisor to the firm on technological opportunity and threat. The MOP is the only person in the company who can credibly tell management about advances within software development that can make an important difference to the profit-and-loss statement. If plans to develop a particular system will make little sense six months hence because of the vendor's intentions to drop a line of hardware or software, the MOP has a role to play in informing management of this threat. Purchase of software from a failing company is ill-advised, says the MOP. Try looking at microcomputer applications in process control, the MOP will advise. And the firm will reward.

Finally, the specific role the MOP plays on the organizational chart is that of interpreting the company's goals into work statements for shop employees. As Figure 6.5 illustrates, the four levels of management operate in different time ranges and vocational scope.

The MOP works at the lowest and most specific level of supervi-

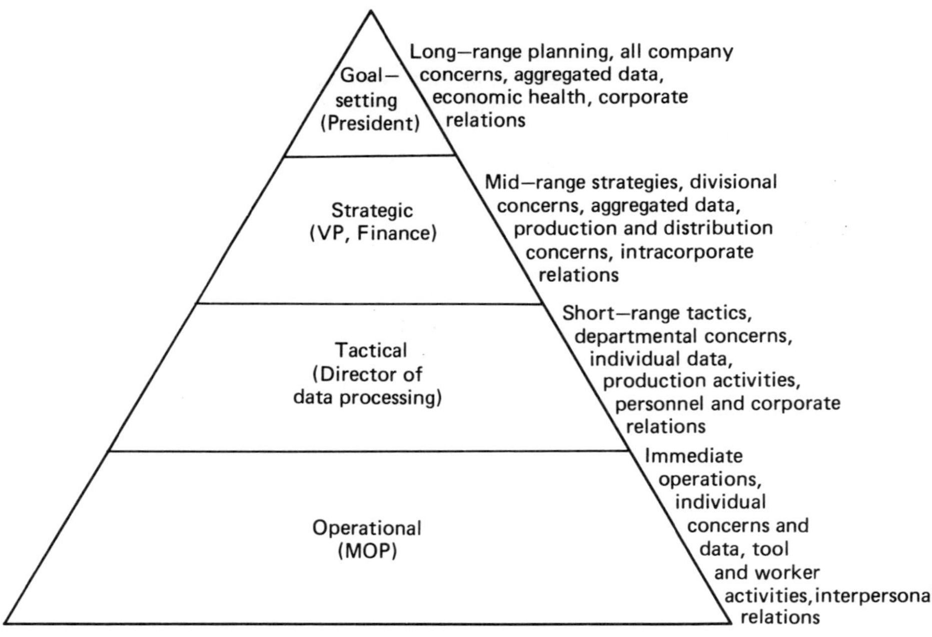


**FIGURE 6.5** Levels of management in data processing.

sion. Here, the focus is sharply upon short-term, closely specified tasks relating to coding, testing, and program design. This is the *operational* level of management.

The Director of DP, the MOP's supervisor, works at a *tactical* level, developing plans for the medium range to meet development goals. At this level, the DP Director delegates responsibilities that lead to the creation of DP products: analysis to the analysis group, operations to the operations group, software development to the MOP.

One level higher are found divisional responsibilities. At the *strategic* level, managers work to plan strategies for achieving corporate goals. Often these are stated in terms of new or improved products, higher sales, more efficient production and distribution. DP is often found in the finance division or associated with accounting and other cost control functions. In other firms, DP may be located with a specific manufacturing division.

In any case, the strategies with which DP is associated are usually cost-control rather than profit-generation. That is, DP has traditionally been seen as a way of making administration and production more efficient; few firms have sold the software products directly. This may be changing. Certainly in recent years firms such as Exxon, McDonald-Douglas, and Texas Instruments have discovered profits in integrated software-hardware or software-service systems. As this philosophy spreads, DP may become more of a profit center and ultimately a divisional unit of its own. Then, the MOP may expect to fulfill more tactical roles (i.e., discovering new means of achieving software production goals).

At the highest levels of the firm, the roles become those of goal-setting and long-range planning. The Board of Directors and the President are concerned with determining the goals toward which the firm will be directed. These include market positioning, acquisitions, diversification, financing, relationships with governmental regulators, consumers, and major corporate customers, and the like.

Here, DP is seen as a service organization that keeps the firm functioning efficiently rather than a cost (or profit) center. This, too, may change. As firms come to understand the critical role of information in today's environment of business and government, DP is starting to play a unique role in the organization, that of the corporate nerve center. The integration of word processing and communication with DP has been brought about by the trend toward the automated office. The Data Processing Department finds itself misunderstood and misunderstanding its role. Instead of responding well to this evolution of responsibility, DP has, as it has in the past, fallen back upon the wave of technological innovation in society at large to define its corporate role. Instead of defining itself as the corporate nerve center at the planning level, it has seemingly contented itself with proudly pointing to the technology. In fact, when the conflicts are faced instead of avoided, DP can achieve a number of advances.

First, those who control the corporate database control corporate direction. Those who determine the type, amount, frequency of access and update, and security levels for data entering and leaving the firm have an opportunity for greater say in corporate direction. Skeptics may point out that floors are important, too, but no one respects the janitor's opinions. However, the janitor's advice is limited to cleanup procedures and waxing. The impact the MOP has on corporate direction through the design and maintenance of software products is far greater. The firm may walk on floors, but it runs on information.

Second, jurisdictional battles between DP and WP on the one hand and between the software development group and the rest of the DP Department on the other are going to be far less important than the battle for control over the corporate information function as we move to the end of the twentieth century and an era of information centers, end-user software, and decision-support systems. The MOP who remains locked in conflict, as Harvey does with Kate, over who in the DP Department has the right to change specs is the MOP who will perish in the upheaval predicted for the DP shop within 10 years.

As company goals become more information-oriented and as data-processing applications begin to pervade the firm through decision-support systems, information will be seen as another important product of the firm. When this occurs, MOPs who have learned information processing in addition to programming will find themselves in a powerful position. Chapters 7 and 8 point out strategies for the MOP to follow in order to be correctly positioned for this eventuality.

## 6.3. HOW MOPS DIFFER FROM OTHER MANAGERS

While MOPs have specific tasks, they are similar in many ways to other managers in technical areas in a firm. However, the differences are important, because historically they have meant that MOPs do not get along well within organizations. These differences are detailed below. They matter a great deal because the image of data processing has been that of the "bad boy" of the firm, the department that gets what it wants because it kicks up a great cloud of fuss. With increasing computerization, managers in data processing can ill afford this image, whatever the truth.

MOPs can be contrasted on the one hand with general managers in functional areas and on the other with technical mangers. The important differences in the first instance are these:

1. It is rare to find a MOP who has experience outside data processing; it is rare to find a successful general manager who has not had some experience in several departments.
2. General managers in functional areas are connected with the income-producing items of the firm, that is, directly with products or services the firm offers; MOPs manage from within service groups generally committed to speeding up or weeding out inefficiencies in administration.
3. MOPs are rarely given access to management training programs, and when they are, these programs are heavily weighted toward technical, as opposed to personnel, management.
4. Entry into general management is seen (by many) as a reward for good performance—it is the start of a career of promotions; young technical managers seldom view promotions as ends in themselves.
5. While the technology of programming has been changing rapidly, that of general management has not, although there are exceptions; general managers are not expected to be technical experts.

These differences influence the image of DP greatly. MOPs have little time to spend on developing themselves as managers, and the firm has little sympathy for their shortcomings as managers. Instead, they are expected to deliver software products throughout their entire careers. The possibilities that any given MOP will advance into an executive position are practically nil (at present); any other manager can at least hope for cherished promotions and increased scope of responsibility.

Hence DP is seen as an isolated unit of very highly specialized individuals with narrow viewpoints. MOPs are often seen as narrow-minded, COBOL-speaking computerniks with long hair, because that's what others see programmers as. In some ways, the firm views

MOPs less as managers than as foremen. No doubt many MOPs share this view.

Even granting this distinction from general management, how do MOPs differ from other technical managers, say in engineering, quality control, production, and distribution?

Here the differences lie less in the degree of specialization (although MOPs are going to be treated as knowing only one thing no matter how many people they manage) but in the kinds of things MOPs are expected to make decisions about. Technical managers in other areas are aware of their strong dependence upon other departments: they have responsibility for some aspect of the firm's income: they create the product or market it or distribute it. They see the product and directly experience the firm's relationship with the marketplace. Not so the MOP, who—in extreme cases—may not even know what business the firm is in. That a COBOL programmer may move with impunity from one firm to another based only upon the tools in the firm tells a lot about what the MOP knows about the firm's business. Unless the firm is in the software business, the product of the firm is not software, and the MOP has no involvement with the product at any point in its manufacture. Where the firm delivers a service, there is a greater chance that the service is related to software, but here, too, the MOP is relatively isolated from the clientele.

Other managers, however, may share this isolation. In a communications conglomerate, many work on developing sales strategies or marketing positions. Others develop price structures. Many may do research. These people don't experience the product either. How do their managers differ from MOPs?

The second difference is not isolation, but involvement. In most of these office positions, the data utilized still concern the product or the service offered. A series of prices for options is a series of prices for the product. Research is done about factors in communications network usage. Market research concerns consumers of the firm's services. In contrast, the MOP may be unaware of facts about the firm or its products but is surely concerned about operating systems, development tools, software production schedules, and "user" interface that the firm's clientele never see. The MOP never has to respond directly to a customer, a client, or a guest of the firm. The manager of market research may interview clients; the manager of the rates department may well examine data on company sales or on sales of competitors. The manager of the engineering department will want to look at data on strengths of materials that go into the product. The manager of the construction department will be quite concerned with getting the most recent data on building sites in a remote region. The MOP needs up-to-date manuals, the latest fixes to an operating system, and access to vendors. In the firm, the MOP is the only manager who never need fear an irate customer (but of course he or she *will* fear DP clients inside the firm).

Thus, while the MOP may have many things in common with other managers, and more in common with other technical managers, ultimately, the MOP remains isolated from the firm and its products and customers. This creates a barrier betweeen the MOP and the organization, a barrier of misinformation, mistrust, and lost opportunities.

Five roles were described in an earlier part of this chapter: resource manager, demonstrator, watchdog, weather forecaster, and interpreter. *Most* technical managers have these roles to carry out, but few work under the conditions that the MOP faces. The resources managed are not directly connected with the firm's products and services and therefore are accounted for as overhead items rather than as expenses directly related to profit formulation. Thus it is difficult for the firm to put a value on many of the resources the MOP has to administer.

While demonstrating appropriate use of these resources within the DP department is not difficult, it is difficult to demonstrate how they fit into the profit picture, since contributions are all indirect. MOPs may be asked to make particular use of resources that cannot be appropriately used in that fashion.

Savings, which accrue from well-working systems, arise only if the system is used correctly—and then the saving is usually the displacement of workers. Typical would be the usual handling of a request for newer, smart terminals. Since they don't do anything more than the dumb ones in terms of producing income, it is difficult to argue that the terminals are needed. Programmers often therefore use 1960s technology for 1980s work. That software production would be more reliable because of the better display facilities and that the programmer would be able to work more comfortably, relieved of the need to wait for printed listings, is not understood outside the DP Department.

Because programmers have some unique traits, the watchdog role is interesting and frustrating. Programmers don't normally respond to the same incentives (and threats) that production workers do, as discussed in Chapter 5. But management is prepared to react only in standard ways to situations that in other departments would be considered absurd. Consider the problem of programmers working too hard! It is practically impossible to tear the involved programmer from his or her terminal. Access to screens is jealously guarded. What other workers arrange for others to tickle their machines while they take a coffee break for fear of losing a line because of timeout? What other workers assume they will be able to work at 3:00 A.M. and demand that as part of the working conditions? What other workers regularly ask for machines they don't understand? Would a lathe operator want a new, more complicated lathe every month? Would the building superintendent appreciate being told that split shifts are available if wanted?

Management's usual response to complaints of this sort are, "Gee, that's terrific. I wish the slowpokes in final assembly had that kind of spirit." What the organization sees as a superfunctioning unit is, of course, an individual doomed to burn out in a few years. Is management ever really ready to *limit* working hours?

So far as the weather forecaster role is concerned, it is doubtful that most executives are prepared to accept any but incremental advice from MOPs or from anyone in DP. First, changes in the DP area are expensive. Second, changes are rarely smooth, but rather require whole new, incompatible systems to be installed while hundreds of people use the old one. Although there have been some advances in system modification on line, large systems generally fail in large ways, and they fail exactly when they shouldn't: when they are being changed. Almost everyone in upper management has had the bad experience of hearing that some needed data or report was unavailable because "the new system has a few bugs in it." This bad history is the third reason why upper management will rarely respond favorably to well-thought-out advice. In fact, most organizations are not set up to receive changes other than those defined narrowly within the existing system.

Finally, the job of interpreting the firm's goals to programmers is hampered by the lack of information MOPs usually have about the firm's goals. With little experience outside DP and little empathy for problems arising in other divisions, MOPs are ill-prepared to interpret moves they don't understand themselves. Many MOPs feel burdened in any event by their management status and may wish to see the world through their terminal screens, which only makes the problem worse. There are, of course, many MOPs with a broad organizational view who welcome management responsibilities.

These are willing to act as interpreters, but unfortunately come up against the "12 o'clock curtain" that separates them from their management colleagues in other departments. They aren't invited to lunch, meetings, or bull sessions in other departments, and when they do show up, the others wonder why.

Hence, MOPs are generally going to be frustrated in their attempts to fill the roles set out for them because DP in general and programming specifically are isolated from the firm socially, vocationally, and educationally.

## 6.4. THE BOUNDARIES OF TECHNICAL MANAGEMENT

In playing these roles, the MOP should be aware of the boundaries of the roles. Specifically, a MOP's efforts should be concentrated in four areas, each pertaining to an interface between the programming group and the rest of the firm (see Figure 6.6):

1. The interface between the programmer and the analyst needs constant attention: the analyst is the equivalent in the programming group to the supplier to the firm.
2. The interface between the programmer and the user has traditionally been ignored or avoided. This is going to change as new development techniques migrate into the software shop. The MOP will be primary custodian of this interface.
3. The cost of error in using computers is quite high and errors are easy to notice and hard to pass the buck on; the buck stops with the MOP.
4. Technical arguments are valid only in technical arenas; as already discussed, these need to be translated into terms that others in the firm understand.

These four interfaces (analyst, user, technology, management) sit on the boundaries of the role of the MOP. Each has particular requirements, check tests, and correction strategies. The MOP must be skillful, tactful, and very systematic in maintaining them. In the following section, a brief discussion of each will be followed by some techniques for boundary maintenance in the software shop.

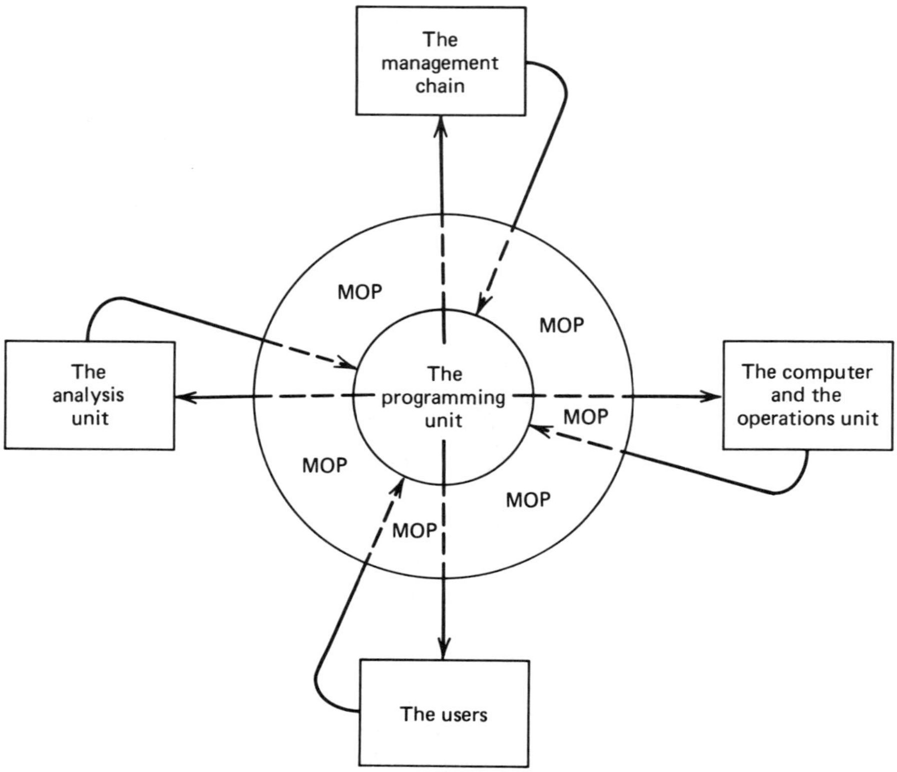


**FIGURE 6.6** The MOP as an interface in the organization.

### 6.4.1. The Interface with the Analyst

The *programmer–analyst interface* has traditionally been one of the most difficult to maintain harmoniously. This is so partly because the programmer cannot hide behind technical gobbledygook and partly because the assembly-line atmosphere of the typical, traditional development project has put great pressure on this interaction. Programmers and analysts are, almost by the nature of their working conditions, forced to argue about specs. Seen more closely, arguments arise for the following reasons:

1. The shop may not have well-defined hand-over procedures. In this case, no one is sure of where responsibilities lie.

2. Structured design techniques push development work later in the project cycle, thereby increasing the pressure on the MOP to accept specs when in doubt.

3. Programmers are not often trained in DP-Department-developed analysis techniques; analysts may be out of date with respect to programming techniques; each may arrogantly label the other's true concerns mere stubborness.

4. In some shops, information centers and end-user software have removed routine work, leaving only the most difficult projects to be handled by traditional means; by definition, difficult projects have difficulties, and agreement on specs is one of these.

5. Concerns in the analysis group and those in the programming group may not be compatible. For instance, turnover has been marginally higher in programming and management expertise (and confidence) may be lower. Programmers are younger than analysts and may require more direction (and thus clearer specs) than the more experienced analysts may be in the habit of supplying.

6. Pressure for increasingly complex demonstrations increases through the development cycle; the pressure to see something running is far greater than the pressure to see a spec.

7. Neither programmers nor analysts have a very wide view of the firm and its needs. Despite the fact that analysts are dealing with the organization in their work, in general they are tainted with the curse of DP: a narrow, technical, and technological view of the firm. Thus small conflicts may seem more important than they actually are.

8. Finally, DP management in general is not trained to confront internecine conflicts effectively, since the primary focus is on keeping the expensive machinery running. This is slowly changing. However, the short-term prospects for human relations training in DP is still poor, spotty, and limited to those who come from outside.

Some of the problems are structural and may respond only to a radical change in how software work is done. For instance, so long as programmers "grow up" to become analysts without any migration into the DP shop from user areas, no one in the development cycle will have a larger view of the firm and its goals. With continued emphasis on the technical,as opposed to the organizational, training of programmers, analysts, and their managers, this narrow view will continue to poison, unnecessarily, relations between programmers and their suppliers.

### 6.4.2. The Interface with the User

The *programmer–user interface* is the disaster film of software development. Each seems to avoid the other at any cost.

Programmers avoid users because (1) they don't really understand user problems, and (2) users have unrealistic expectations of what a programmer can do. Therefore, MOPs and others in DP management are loathe to assign programmers to speak with users except under the most controlled of conditions. This, in turn, contributes to the mutual stereotyping by these two groups.

In 1967, this writer had his first meeting with a "user." Not actually a user, this person seemed more like a griffin, with fangs, a roar that shook the building, and the carcasses of half-eaten programmers lying sheep-like about his office. After a stormy session, a phone call to my supervisor characterizing me as a "computernik" who should never be let out of his cell apparently finished my career as a user consultant, at least until the next time. What went wrong? Nothing, other than the fact that I understood not one thing about statistics and this statistician was so "ignorant" he didn't understand either FORTRAN or JCL!

Programmers are still coached in a language or two, a development system or two, a testing environment or two. Users continue to develop more and more intricate models requiring increasingly complex programming and databases. Breathless programmers struggling with compilers they've just learned are told not to say anything disruptive to terrified users facing numbers wrong in the fourth decimal place. Not perceiving moving parts in programs, users assume that the priests speaking incantations of APL and ADFA can exorcise the devil in seconds. Little wonder that MOPs handle these interactions themselves.

What's wrong with this situation?

1. Programmers should try not to meet users in an atmosphere of urgency, tension, or doubt. This is the best breeding ground for bigotry, as evidenced in every other sphere of human behavior.

2. Catching errors is not the same as creating works of art. Since users only see programmers when they are in cybernetic pain, doctoring skills, not art, are necessary. Most programmers don't have them—yet.

3. While programmer education is criminally narrow, the education of users vis-à-vis computers is even narrower, and often wrong. Users are trained in one, usually creaky system. Some may have taken a hated BASIC or FORTRAN course in college. They are users because they like their work in which computers are a *tool,* not the object of work. They have little motivation to learn about computers and even less to listen to others who care deeply about them. The occasional user who understands computers may well be a pain in the neck and a busybody. *This* situation has got to stop in modern business organizations.

4. Programmers are not well prepared to speak with users. Understanding the user's difficulty—the major task in maintenance—requires that the programmer understand the user's problem in its initial formulation. Usually only the analyst has had the preparation for this. It's unfair to expect the programmer to intuit this in 15 minutes.

5. A new type of skill is needed, and either the users or the DP staff will need to begin developing it. The computer interpreter is needed to clarify the ways of Turing to mere humans, and vice versa. Some firms are experimenting with computer service representatives. This is a good long-term goal. Others are opening information centers, but in many cases, as already mentioned, these merely siphon off the easy problems, leaving all the emergencies behind. Computer center bulletins, occasional courses, or even computer fairs will not help. Philosophically there is a separation of spirit and goals in the use of computers that will drive programmers and users apart. A radical alternative is needed. Martin hints that the problem will go away when programmers go away in the brave-new world of "programmerless programming." This writer feels otherwise. New management and organizational philosophies, exemplified (but not necessarily achieved) by Theory Z, may have the answer.These are discussed in Chapter 8.

### 6.4.3. The Interface with the Machine

The *programmer–machine interface* is also changing rapidly under the influence of software engineering and a movement toward fourth-generation languages. A variety of innovative techniques are removing "rote" programming from the software development shop. Certainly database technology and the almost universal availability of telecommunications have democratized access to computers. Everyone can be a programmer now. Even so conservative a constituency as Alberta, Canada, where this writer lives, has decided that computers-in-the-public-schools is the wave (fourth wave?) of the future and plans to install thousands in the next few years.

But along with this democratization comes the responsibility that goes with the right to access. The cost of technical error in complex systems is very high. Catching errors in early stages was the real impetus behind structured design. Those errors that do slip through are very expensive to fix. The MOP has increasingly more difficult responsibilities to see that increasingly more reliable software is produced. This tends, therefore, to focus the MOP's attention on reliability engineering, testing disciplines, and development environments, perhaps to the detriment of other aspects of the programmer's universe. As software becomes an increasingly important aspect of daily life outside the business data processing environment (as in microwave ovens, autos,information services to the home, and automation in the office), we can see increasing pressure on MOPs in the area of reliability. But there seems to be little work under way to improve the programmer–machine interface.

With few exceptions, programmers work no differently in developing programs in 1984 than they did in 1974. More use real-time on-line systems, more use debugging compilers and test harnesses, more use development packages such as IDF and database technology. But the task is essentially unchanged since 1974. A lot of work has gone into changing development methodology, especially with regard to systems analysis and design. Many have put forward, and many have resisted, structured programming as a sort of modern-day Latin for the high priests and priestesses of the bits. Yet structured programming is really a design technique.

No one is redesigning programming (other than attempting to eliminate it). Why, for instance, should programmers have to use JCL to test programs? Why should each terminal session assume that each logon is being requested by a first-year DP student? Where are the artificial intelligence applications to program development? Why is the concept of programming "style" still so primitive that only one book has been written with the word in its title? Why are programmers using 30-year-old languages (FORTRAN, COBOL) on 30-week-old machines? Why do we remain stuck on the idea of mutually incompatible languages in the first place? Why is programming so overwhelmingly procedural instead of specificational?

These and other questions remain unanswered because there is little interest in organizations and elsewhere in advancing the concept of "automatic calculation" (the "-ac" in ENIAC) beyond language translation. That is what programmers are hired for and that is what they will do. Until they do something else (or nothing, say Martin (1982) and Kraft (1977)), we will be stuck with MOPs who troubleshoot this interface.

### 6.4.4. The Interface with Management

The *programmer–management interface* has been discussed in some detail already. However, the most difficult aspect of maintaining this interface is not in interpreting the organization's goals to programmer—however difficult this may be—but in making valid and persuasive arguments about software and software development and maintenance resource needs. In other words, the important aspect of this interface is in interpreting the needs of the software development and maintenance group to management.

This interface is also characterized by changes that software and hardware technology progress has engendered in business. These trends have made the role of the MOP even more important as software use has extended to all corners of the firm. The trends are the following:

1. Data is becoming a salable product; software to use this data has likewise acquired a commerical value.
2. The use of computers has crept upward in the organization to individuals who, in the past, merely read reports produced by computers; now they request their own reports.
3. Computers are being made available directly to users through end-user software, prototyping, database management, architecture-based development, and so on.
4. The DP Department is becoming more democratic through computer services reps, specialized use training for programmers, unification of analysis and program development.
5. DP services are being sold to customers, suppliers, even competitors.
6. DP techniques are now used in other design areas, especially CAD and CAM.

Information has a value; companies accumulate a great deal of it over the years. Some may remain proprietary; other information may be valuable in marketing, manufacturing, and distribution of other's products.

For all this obviousness, the movement toward Decision Support Systems (DSS) and away from MIS has the benefit of applying computers more intimately and integrally to the firm's decision-making centers. In particular, it benefits the firm by showing that live data can be processed and presented in a variety of ways to decision-makers—it dispels the myth of DP as a mindless number-happy group. It also involves decision-makers intimately with the design process and builds a new kind of working relationship between the toolsmiths (programmers) and product consumers (decision-makers). The recent healthy marriage between DSS and office automation enables decision-makers to communicate their decisions more quickly. Here, too, the MOP can play a role in being responsive to the needs of management to have a particular style in addition to having particular display formats.

Point three merely restates the movement toward user-initiated and -developed applications programming. Estimates of the pervasiveness of this trend vary, but apparently, and predictably, some programming should move out of the software shop, if only because we already know so much about the structure of many applications that they are no longer challenging.

Democratization of DP may bring an end to the kinds of management structures with which we are familiar in DP, in particular the unnatural separation of analysis, programming, and operations. If this separation is bridged, the necessity for a segregated organization so prone to stereotyping may decrease. In this case, DP may assume more of a consulting role, similar to that played by management consultants in large firms.

Many firms, too, are discovering that their DP talent can be subcontracted to others. Some, such as Lockheed, run time-sharing services for bibliographic retrieval. Others offer their expertise in hybrid analog-digital computing. Many find their packages so well crafted that, in the case of accounting software, it is easily marketed to others without threat to the firm. The MOP is the natural entrepreneur in these cases, a role MOPs have seldom played successfully in their own organizations.

Finally, DP techniques have moved rapidly into manufacturing and design through CAD/CAM and into robotics for large-scale industrial applications. It is unlikely that this trend will reverse itself, even in a labor-rich post-1984 society. The ability to manufacture countless almost-identical objects with systematic variations and options is too great to hand back to "mere" humans. Whether or not this trend will be acceptable to those whose labors have been displaced remains to be seen. The managers of manufacturing concerns will continue employing robots and design terminals.

Hence, although DP has no real representation in management, there are a lot of opportunities for the MOP to make technical arguments that stick, if only because others outside the DP shop are making them, too.

## 6.5. ORGANIZATIONAL DEVELOPMENT PLANS

How can MOPs overcome these barriers? Is the 12 o'clock curtain going to remain with us? What strategies can the MOP employ to cope with an organization from which programming is relatively alienated?

There is no answer, although things are changing slowly. Greater numbers of younger managers have taken programming courses, although there is little evidence that a large proportion of them really understand what is unique about the job of being a programmer or a MOP. Nonetheless, programming is no longer the mystical practice it may have seemed in the 1960s and 1970s.

However, there is almost no movement on the opposite side. Programming is still a very narrow specialty; MOPs receive little in the way of management training or organizational seasoning; promotions are burdensome heaves into paperwork, and firms still do not see software as part of the profit picture. What can be done?

For younger MOPs, and especially for those contemplating promotions into MOP positions, there are a number of difficult strategies that can be followed. More details are provided in subsequent chapters, and only a summary is provided here.

The strategy consists of two parts. First, one needs to obtain experience outside DP. This gives the MOP a broader view of the organization's business, its products and services, its customer and clients, and its workers. There are many departments in which programming skills may prove useful, if the firm is willing to swap a measure of inefficiency for increased management effectiveness. Some of the areas are marketing, production scheduling, distribution, finance, R&D, long-range planning, and office automation. There is no empirical evidence that those trained as programmers will necessarily succeed in any of these areas.

However, it's obvious that the traits so desired in programmers and their managers, traits such as skill with symbols, language learning, memory, systematic and logical approaches, form important components of many user-area jobs. Consider this list:

1. *Marketing.* Data analysis, sales data reporting procedure development, decision-support system tool-building.
2. *Production.* Materials flow design, data entry procedure design, production report analysis.
3. *Distribution.* Materials flow design, data reporting procedure design, procedure description and debugging.
4. *Finance.* Decision-support system tool-building, report analysis and debugging.
5. *Long-Range Planning.* Data collection procedures.
6. *Research and Development.* Data analysis skills, logical design.
7. *Office Automation.* User reactions.

Here are many jobs that tap programming skills. It wouldn't hurt a MOP to remember his six months in marketing, her year in Production Quality Assurance and Control, his rotation through Finance, or her stint with Personnel. It also wouldn't hurt others to rotate through programming, but this is a topic for another book (Licker, 1985).

This broader experience must be coupled with a change in work philosophy if the MOP is to survive and remain effective into the twenty-first century. Because the DP community has now grown quite large (numbering in the several millions in the United States alone), the need to remain absolutely atop the technology must be backgrounded and replaced with a need to reconfigure symbolic and logical skills into packages that the firm understands. Above all, the MOP manages within an organization of people, task, and goals as well as one containing machinery, software, and projects. This shift of philosophy is going to signal the maturation of programming in the next century. Until then, programming will remain a branch of a service organization, with little possibility of being recognized as either a profession or a direct contributor to the firm's economic health.

One copes with organizations in only two ways:

1. *Withdrawal, or hiding.* In this case, the organization cannot find you. A typical MOP tactic, hiding quickly becomes mutual and habitual. In this case, organizational charts that really count never illuminate the depths of the data processing den.

2. *Integration, or exposure.* In this case, the individual embraces the firm. The typical grey-flannel executive adopts this tactic, which in the extreme makes it difficult to distinguish the person from the firm. "Playing organizational games" is the least distasteful aspect of this tactic—there are worse.

Obviously the day is far in the future when programmers embrace firms that don't produce software as their major product. This is one trend, however, that will continue, however slowly as already mentioned. For MOPs in these firms, no philosophy change is necessary; the firm has already "moved," so to speak, to the philosophical position held by the MOP.

In other ways, however, MOPs owe it to themselves to discover which of the values of the firm they do hold. This cannot be discovered if one is not open to finding out what the values are. Many firms are exactly as the myths described them. In these firms, even the President's son is uncomfortable. For many MOPs, survival is going to require getting more information about the beast they work for.

## 6.6. A NOTE ON POWER

Chapter 5 discussed five sorts of power with respect to directing a unit of programmers. However, power isn't always directed down the management chain. It can be exercised within the organization generally. In fact, the individual who is said to be powerful within an organization is not the person who manages a department with an iron fist (or a velvet glove), but the person who can get peers in other departments to agree with her or him and *get management moving*. In other words, the powerful MOP is the MOP who can effect changes, even quantum ones, from within (see Figure 6.7):

1. *Internal Growth.* Addition of human resources and equipment.
2. *External Growth.* Addition of products and markets.
3. *Redefinition.* Changes to the direction the organization as a whole is moving in.

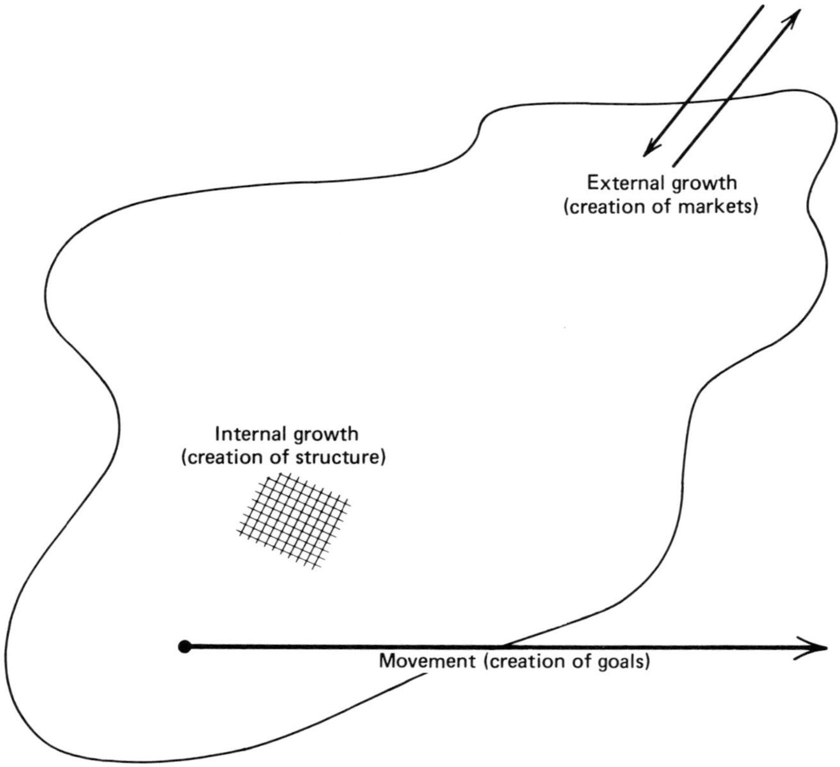


**FIGURE 6.7** Change areas for MOPs.

Much of our discussion so far has pointed out the difficulty the MOP has in arguing for internal growth. DP has traditionally, and somewhat grudgingly, been provided with many computers and much space by the firm. By Gibson and Nolan's (1974) thesis of the stages of DP growth, DP departments are in the mature stages of little growth relative to others and should expect slower internal growth. MOPs are so isolated from the firm's real business that their suggestions for external growth will not be credible. In any case, no one in a typical manufacturing concern would have an idea how to market and service software.

The third area, however, is one in which powerful MOPs may look to apply their expert and charismatic powers in an era of rapid change in technology. Most firms are finding computers and software pervading every division and every service department. Not only are authors of books like this attempting to insinuate programmers into the marketing department, but managers in the marketing department are demanding access to computer terminals of their own. Clearly manufacturing, design, office work, R&D (including market research), and finance are areas in which automation opportunities abound.

Direction, however, is lacking in these departments. Most managers there are limited to a course in BASIC. While many universities are experimenting with computer-based decision-support packages (IFPS, for instance) in management programs, the overwhelming majority of managers have little experience with computers in decision-making. This will change. Until it does, MOPs are the most knowledgeable in the firm with respect to the software aspects of the technology.

The enterprising MOP will interpret this last statement as an opportunity to demonstrate tact, judgment, and versatility, three attributes most prized in general management. The picture is completed when the MOP also demonstrates a knowledge of the work going on in other departments.

In other words, instead of concentrating on settling fights with the analysts and the vendors, the MOP should first try to understand the organization and then use his or her energies and great knowledge of software technology to start shoehorning the firm into the computer era. Then the title of this chapter can be changed to "Managing Organizations from Programming."

## 6.7. PUTTING OUT FIRES: CASE STUDIES

In the short term, however, the MOP will have many organizational fires to put out. This section discusses these through case studies which concern tactics for handling these situations:

1. Matching staff demands with organizational goals.
2. Resolving conflicts over use of computer resources.

### 6.7.1. Case 1. Fighting Words: Kate and Harvey, Round 2

When we last saw Kate and Harvey, Kate had threatened Harvey with going to Sam Underhill. Harvey had silently sworn to build a dossier of Kate's misdeeds to present to Sam, too. Both moves are poor, because Harvey and Kate's problems are not really with each other, but with the organization. □

As pointed out in this chapter, programming and analysis often disagree because they are set up to disagree. The problems stem from a possible lack of procedures, pressure from structured design delays in implementation, mutual and long-standing misperception of concerns, pressures from difficult assignments, incompatible management concerns, lack of a broad perspective (mountains) for these squabbles (molehills), and a lack of training in conflict management. In other words, the problems are inherent in the way analysts and programmers have to interact.

What can be done either to avoid this problem or to patch things up now? First, Harvey and Kate must realize that their disagreement is *expected*, but not very *important*. It is expected because the two groups have little in common and in all realms of human behavior this brings conflict. But it is not very important because, from the organization's viewpoint, the disagreement is a fight over a fireplug; the firm is worried about profits and losses.

Second, they should realize that Underhill will do nothing for them. He has his own problems, and facing the structural difficulties here will only divert important human resources from his inability to respond to the organization's never-ending stream of requests. Kate and Harvey will have to settle their differences themselves.

What should they do now? They can agree to disagree. That is, they can agree that they cannot have complete agreement and get on with the job. They can agree to work on hand-over procedures, writing a contract if necessary. Why not? Treaties are written between warring nations; why not between a MOP and a MOA? They can begin to notice that specifications are not the be-alls and end-alls of systems development, that newer techniques may soon make both their groups obsolete, and that thus they should work together to consider alternatives to specs. They can work to arbitrate individual problems over specs, too. Since on the one hand the fight is over power (who has the power to change specs), they should agree to a standoff and look at the other side of the fight, which is what the appropriate interface between the two groups should be. It is not a page of words, it is the working relationship between Harvey and Kate. Their disagreement is putting the jobs of both units in jeopardy, a jeopardy increased by their inability to see each other's viewpoint. Before they ask Sam to arbitrate each disagreement, they should realize that this is their responsibility. The organization cannot respond to disturbances like this without insensitive action.

Finally, they should look for patterns of disagreement. Which kinds of specs get changed? Why are or should they be changed? Which specs should never be changed? If Kate really believes that specs are the word of the computer deity, then why is she giving them to a mere mortal to implement? Harvey should point this out; specs exist for communication. They obviously aren't working well here. Harvey can make a concession ("Say, Kate, why don't I keep track of my disagreements on this project and discuss them with you afterwards; then we'll look at what we can do to avoid problems next time"), in return for the demotion of specs to mere communication among mortals.

One last word of advice to both Harvey and Kate. Look at what the firm thinks about specs and how other departments use them. Similar disagreements arise any time specs have to pass a unit boundary, and obviously there isn't continuous warfare. Most organizations have settled these fights years ago with established procedures for handling disagreement. DP should also look at these procedures, because disagreements will not go away.

### *Case 2. Fighting Over Crusts of Bread*

Marg Blaine leads a team of two senior programmers and two junior programmers for a medium-sized food processing firm. Normally she's fairly even-tempered, but events of the past week have raised her blood temperature to just below boiling. And the irony is that she's mad at the person she gets along with best, so she feels guilty too.

It's a classic problem: too little computer time for too many projects. Marg's got her team spending 12 hours a day putting together a scheduling program for the factory's new canning line due to be installed in a few weeks. She's exactly on schedule, too, something that makes her particularly proud of her staff. But now it looks like she's going to miss her deadline and spoil what has been an excellent record over two years of managing her team.

Two weeks ago, her manager, Dorethy Huong, approved the installation of a new version of the operating system for Foodco's minicomputer. Marg went along with the idea, primarily because the release promised faster speed and more disk availability. What no one knew at the time was that the installation would take three weeks, during which time the mini would mostly be unavailable except from 9 A.M. to 5 P.M. "Mostly unavailable" because Marg's team of go-getters have to do development work during nonproduction time. So there's a grand conflict between Marg and her group on one side and the two systems programmers on the other.

Marg's programmers are angry and disappointed about the restriction. Although Dot's promised that some production time will be freed for development ("A few hours a day," said Dot), the staff is sure that this won't do. In addition, Marg's guess is that production time, too, will be cramped because of the need to finish processing backlogged data on production on the soon-to-be-removed canning line.

Marg feels poorly done by because of Dot's decision to go ahead with the system installation now. Yes, Marg was consulted and, yes, it's important to have the new system, but why now during the busiest part of Marg's most important project since joining Foodco? Maybe Marg should go and complain to the VP for Production and get Dot's mental juices flowing in the correct channels again. □

Here is an example of a good working relationship spoiled because a MOP doesn't understand why a decision was made. The situation is complicated by pressure from staff under Marg and her own technical judgment that the system change is inherently valuable.

As in the previous case, Marg feels left out of a decision she actually had a large part in making. Perhaps Dot hasn't taken the time to explain well why system installation is important before the new major application. Or perhaps Dot is simply making a "judgment call" and taking the responsibility upon herself when Marg also feels a great deal of responsibility. In either case, Marg is left to explain to her staff why a decision has been taken and how it will adversely affect their work.

Behind this lie a number of important organizational problems:

1. Marg doesn't understand why the *organization* needs the new system now, not next month.
2. Marg is quicker to respond to staff needs to get on with the

work than to organizational needs to have things working smoothly for the introduction of the new canning line.

3. Marg isn't looking beyond the immediate conflict over *computer time* to the broader organizational context of divisional needs not to fight over *production* facilities (i.e., canning lines).
4. Marg isn't yet prepared to confront her staff with difficult work schedules or to wrest from Dot promises of compensation for her staff for increased efforts and strain.

Each organizational problem has a solution. First, Marg should *rephrase her question* to Dot from "Why now?" to "Who gains?" in order to locate where the benefits lie. There are more players in this drama than Marg, her staff, and Dot. The entire production division will be affected. If Marg is seriously considering the dangerous step of approaching the VP for Production, she'd better have the names of the players firmly in mind.

Second, Marg needs to shift her *management philosophy* from narrow focus upon getting the work done with the proper tools to achieving organizational goals efficiently (a mere restatement of the first concept, but with a different focus). Yes, she should remain responsive to her staff, but not to their weakness in coping with the organization. Rather she should respond to their needs to work within the organization comfortably. She can put this philosophy into effect by beginning to explain to her staff how their software is used and how others outside her department view the computer and have come to depend upon it for reliable data, a reliability that would be threatened if system changes were made after introduction of the new canning line.

Third, Marg needs to understand *organizational politics*. If the firm doesn't produce canned fruit, no one gets paid. If Production hasn't sufficient reliable equipment, peaches and plums rot in rail cars for lack of processing. The installation of the new canning line intends to reduce bottlenecks in production (and the fights that happen *there* over a shortage of machinery). These fights are more important to the firm than short-term disagreement in Dot's department over a few billion microseconds of computer time.

Finally, Marg needs the *courage* to confront both her staff and Dot to mediate an agreement about her project timetable, about compensatory time off for her staff for 2 A.M. work, and about negotiating appropriate rewards for working under difficult conditions. Since there will not be enough jollies to go around for working under strong pressure, she's going to have to arrange for Dot, not Marg, to provide some rewards to her staff. In this, Marg will have to understand the pressures Dot is under to clean up her shop in preparation for the new canning line. DP is important in keeping that new technological wonder going, and Dot, too, is feeling pressure to produce, a pressure that Marg needs to recognize. Going around Dot to the Vice President can only anger her supervisor and further spoil their relationship.

Thus Marg needs to strengthen her interface roles: with her own management, with her staff, and with the two systems programmers. In doing this she can only strengthen her group by improving their ability to work with the organization.

## 6.8. CONCLUSION

As employees in organizations, MOPs must be aware of how organizations function. Five principles dictate an organization's activities: goal-seeking, self-regulation, openness, formal communication, and division of labor. Each affects the MOP and the role the MOP plays in the firm. The role is fivefold: to manage technical resources, to show others how to use those resources, to provide the organization with information on how well the programming unit is functioning, to advise the organization on software threats and opportunities, and to interpret organizational goals into work statements for the software shop.

In carrying out these activities, the MOP interfaces with four groups in the firm: analysts, users, operations, and the firm's management. Each presents the MOP with unique challenges. In meeting them, the MOP shares many of the challenges that all technical managers face. Some, however, are unique to MOPs. Foremost are the isolation the MOP experiences within the firm and the specific nature of the concerns a manager in a software production shop must have.

These challenges may be met in a variety of ways that require creativity and patience. As computer technology pervades management training, especially in universities, the "foreignness" of the MOP's field will decrease. While this slow trend takes hold, MOPs can attempt to broaden their experience outside DP and in the area of user applications. In addition, MOPs require a shift in their philosophy from a concentration on the needs of technology to the needs of the firm to employ computer technology.

By integrating their efforts more closely with those of the firm, the MOPs will discover that their true powers lie in redefining the goals of the firm rather than in causing greater growth in technological acquisitions. Since MOPs possess knowledge that is important to the firm, the employment of that knowledge will be critical in the closing years of the twentieth century. However, that knowledge will be directed less toward the development of specific software and more toward understanding software opportunities as specific organizational goals.

CHAPTER SEVEN

# CAREERS IN PROGRAMMING MANAGEMENT

## *Case 1. The Dead End Job*

Over the past six years, Rob Condon has changed jobs three times, moving from Programmer to Programmer-Analyst to first-line Supervisor to an official title of Manager of Software Applications Development. In this sequence, Rob's changed employers twice and more than doubled his salary. Six programmers work for Rob, who mainly directs work for the Finance Department. Most notably, the Software Applications Department developed a fine, in-house accounting system, and Rob has convinced his employer, a fabrics manufacturer, to market it to other firms.

Rob knows he's risen fast primarily due to a shortage of skilled managers in DP. He is a hard worker, has a B.B.A. and is taking some evening courses toward an M.B.A. He thinks he really understands organizations.

Unfortunately, he also feels he's boxed in by an unpromotable Director of DP. This fellow is a college chum of the President. He owes his tenure to having arrived 15 years ago with the first automated accounting system, the very one Rob replaced. Larry Goudreau is firmly entrenched as the company man, and Rob isn't going to be promoted to anything in DP in the near future.

In reviewing his career management decisions, Rob thinks he's made a mistake. Being a fast riser is only valuable in an organization open to innovation. But with Goudreau at the top, innovation will be at a glacial pace. Rob's experience is confined to DP and mostly to this accounting system. Fine products that he's made, but he's not an accountant and DP is his field. Maybe, he thinks, it's time to switch employers again. □

So far in this book, we've examined the four major day-to-day concerns of the technical manager in the nontechnical organization: the technology (Chapter 2), work itself (Chapter 3), personnel (Chapters 4 and 5) and the firm (Chapter 6). One additional management concern should be on the minds of MOPs, and that is the topic of this chapter: careers in programming management.

Programmers may be workaholics, but few can accuse them of wanting to climb the corporate ladder. Despite this fact, programmers are the most ambitious of all workers, because they desire constant technical challenge. Programmers need exposure to new languages, packages, and technology. They need new glass mountains to climb, and the smoother and taller the better. It seems that the only rewards they recognize or need are increasingly more difficult tasks.

Their managers, too, work in this kind of extreme reward-challenge-effort cycle, which differs a great deal from the normal challenge-effort-reward cycle of other employees (see Figure 7.1). But it is unlikely that MOPs will achieve many rewards of the type they desire from the usual bureaucratic management chain, for rewards here are those of organizational power. This usually translates into increased personnel management responsibility and increased delay in gratification from work done now. Programmers—and their managers—are trained from their first programming courses to seek gratification over the short term in the technology. The entire software industry seems designed to shorten *that* cycle to milliseconds.

Thus MOPs experience a contradiction. Being promoted means having to face challenges for which the MOP is ever less well prepared and being offered gratifications that lie farther in an increasingly overpopulated future. Since these sorts of promotions are in the

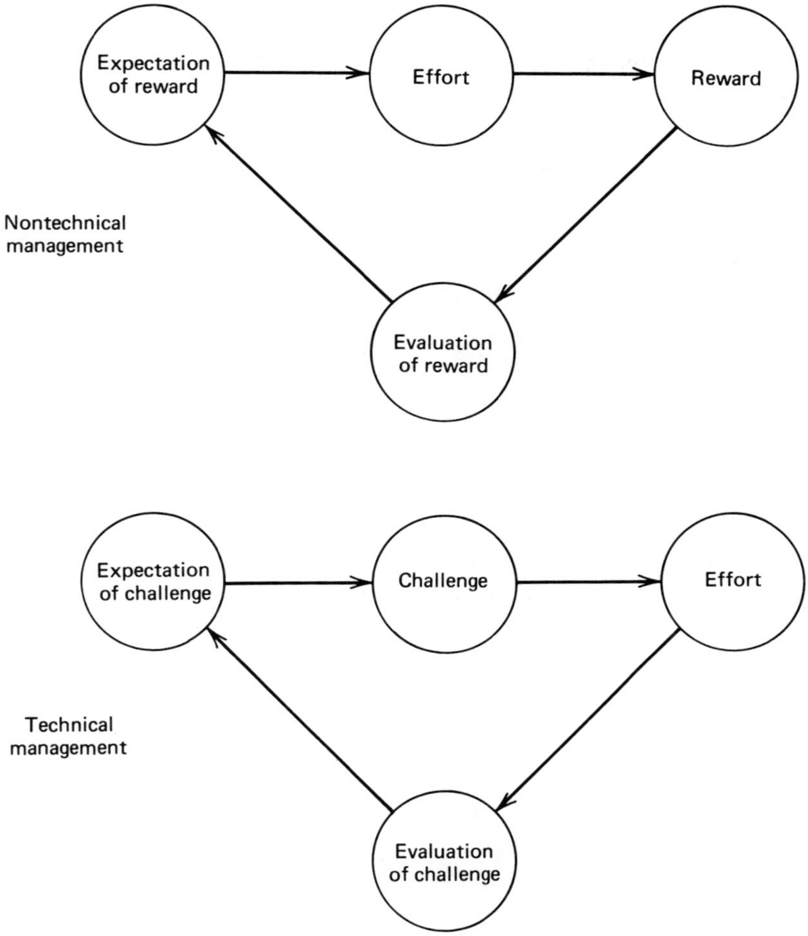


**FIGURE 7.1** Components of a career planning exercise.

realm of organizational life, which MOPs don't understand well anyway, they find themselves boxed in because of their skills, their inclinations, and their own definitions of "success."

*This* challenge is the focus of this chapter: how to organize and follow through on a career plan in DP management and beyond for the MOP who is wondering how he or she ever got into this mess.

There are many influences on a career of an individual. Many trends in the greater society influence the individual, and these are hard to predict and plan for. As Figure 7.2 illustrates, economic,

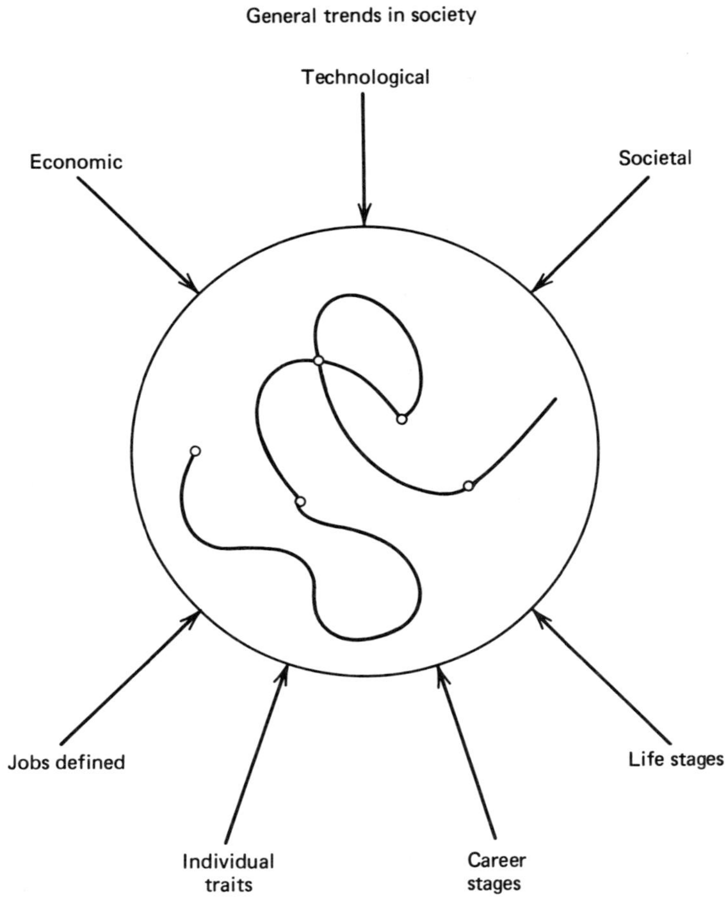


**FIGURE 7.2** Motivation in technical areas versus other professional areas.

technological, and societal trends are extremely important. However, the other influences, primarily the jobs available and defined for workers, individual traits, and career and life stages (Sheehy, 1976) seem to be more understandable and enter more clearly into career plans.

## 7.1. TRAINING FOR MANAGEMENT

Courses in management of programmers are almost nonexistent; books with this topic in the title are equally rare. While courses in DP management are offered at many universities and colleges in North America, the area of programmer management is as much a wasteland as television. An occasional short course or seminar is offered on motivation or some aspect of technical management (Chapters 2, 3, and 4 of this book include some of this material). Otherwise, the MOP learns by experience.

Even were such courses available, it is doubtful that MOPs would or could take them. By tendency and company policy, programmers are systematically denied access to the same sort of management training that shipping clerks can get when they express interest in becoming foremen. MOPs need, and should receive, grounding in management principles and administrative techniques if we are to avoid the robotification of programming management.

Currently, management training rests on the four pillars of on-the-job training, university preparation and retooling, in-house training, and consultants. The pros and cons of these are illustrated in Table 7.1. Of these, only consultants provide MOPs with a real window on the outside world. Only in-house training can give the MOP a window on the firm. Yet neither provides a rounded and in-depth view that the overworked MOP desperately needs to cope with crushing schedules and a mobile and highly strung workforce.

Training problems come up in three ways. First, many MOPs are also expected to program. If a DP manager has to choose between keeping programming MOPs up-to-date in ISDOS or up-to-date in organizational behavior, is there any doubt where the emphasis will be placed? Since DP managers have their backgrounds, too, in the hurry-up, chase-the-technology professions of computer operations and systems analysis, it's not surprising that they choose to keep their MOPs-who-program chasing the technology, too.

MOPs-who-program also face the problem of lack of time. Not only do they have killing schedules, but they have to stick to them, too. Failure to deliver software can mean their jobs. They have neither inclination nor time—and certainly no rewards—to pursue courseware rather than software.

A second set of problems dogs the heels of the nonprogramming MOP, the import from the Engineering Department or a systems analyst who hasn't seen COBOL since it was a twinkle in Grace Hopper's eye. These MOPs are under pressure not from their management but from their staffs to become conversant. Their programmers simply do not know how to speak with managers who can't respond with PERFORMs, DO-UNTILs, and IFTHENELSEs.

**TABLE 7.1. ADVANTAGES AND DISADVANTAGES OF THE MAJOR MANAGEMENT TRAINING TECHNIQUES**

| Training Technique | Advantages | Drawbacks |
|---|---|---|
| On-the-job | Availability<br>Appropriateness to current situation | Concentrates on coping only<br>Bad habits easily taught and learned<br>Not proactive, generally reactive<br>Unsystematic, disorganized |
| Universities, colleges | Expert instruction<br>Current<br>Flexible offerings (courses, seminars, short courses) | Takes a lot of time<br>Classroom situation may be uncomfortable<br>Very general<br>Limited offerings in personnel management for programming management |
| In-house | Pertinent to organization<br>Available<br>Less expensive (maybe) | Lack of follow-up<br>General to all managers<br>Longer courses may be expensive |
| Consultants, professional organizations | Current<br>Very knowledgeable | Expensive<br>Not concentrated on front-line managers<br>Crisis oriented<br>Hit-and-miss in choice of consultant<br>Not relevant to this organization |

Finally, the MOP-who-doesn't-program simply faces the lack of courseware to choose from for management in the software shop. Available choices might include Organizational Behavior, Marketing, Accounting, Personnel Management, Management Science, and Advanced Computer Project Management Techniques. Which is the most likely choice for the MOP who has a seven-year-old Computer Science degree?

There are problems with each source of training for MOPs. On-the-job training is given in "ordinary" circumstances in which new MOPs learn only how to cope with last year's problems from people who have learned coping rather than success. The most effectively taught and learned strategies are the bad habits that on-the-job "teachers" have taught themselves. On-the-job training for MOPs is an intellectual dead end.

University and college training is also less valuable for MOPs than it might be for others. Bachelor's degrees rapidly become obsolete; in any event, many of tomorrow's MOPs are being trained today only in programming, and this is the most rapidly obsoleted skill they can acquire. Advanced degrees, such as M.B.A.s and M.Sc.s are difficult for MOPs who have only narrow technical backgrounds and jobs that require 24-hour-per-day alerts. Short courses and seminars are either devoted to technical topics, are intended for general markets (at my university, the most popular extension course is in basic BASIC), or are aimed at general management, which is more familiar with management technique than MOPs may be. Software courses rarely mention management of programmers and their situations; management courses rarely mention programming. When you add the cost in time and money and the long delay in payoff, college work seems like a poor alternative.

In-house training suffers from the same problems as university courseware. Few smaller firms can offer *any* management courses. Those that do have them may provide a good introduction to the firm's paperwork, but there is rarely any time for covering personnel management or how to cope with the organization. In any event, a two-day management seminar is insufficient and there is rarely a follow-up to the courseware. Developing good in-house courseware is expensive.

Consultants may provide a great deal of management-related information and may relate a great deal of management-appropriate experience. But they are usually called in for crisis management and have little time to train MOPs in coping with the daily small crises of managing programmers. They are problem- rather than people-oriented; they are themselves typically people who abdicated organizational life for consulting. And finally, as outsiders, they rarely have an intimate view of the firm with which they are consulting.

In the face of this inadequacy, what can be done? The ideal would be to hire consultants in the area of management training who can specifically tailor courseware to MOPs. But few such individuals exist. These courses are not stock-in-trade for either management- or computer-consultants, although as the ranks of programmers swell, some of these firms are more willing to respond—expensively and slowly.

A small firm cannot afford an extended training program. It must, however, make the choice between the short-term payoff of specific—and relatively nontransferable—programming language familiarization and the long-term—and very transferable—skill-building in management. Management short courses and seminars are cheaper and a better long-term investment even for the small firm. If MOPs are ever to leave the "DP Ghetto" mentioned by Janet Crane (1982) in a recent *Datamation* article, they must stop merely receiving technological change and start learning how to impart to others the skills needed to cope with such change—a management course is a good beginning.

Larger firms should retool their in-house and contracted educational curricula and expand into the management and administration courses for MOPs. Their educational objectives are often confused by the underlying confusion DP Directors have about skill needs in their own departments, as a recent article by Simpson and Bettinger (in *The Journal of Systems Management)* and one by Reeves and Busson (1980) illustrate. DP managers feel the edges of the problem in lack of communication, planning, and motivation skills in their software development groups, but they continue to emphasize the short-term requirements in programming languages in their training programs.

Below is described a long-term—and admittedly expensive—training program for MOPs and MOPs-in-training. It attempts to combine emphasis upon the needs of individuals with the needs of the organization. Summarized in Figure 7.3, this list is as follows:

1. Technology for management (120 hours)
   a. Project management techniques
   b. Information resource management
   c. Use of computers in management and administration.
2. General management for MOPs (48 hours)
   a. Personnel management principles
   b. Organizational development in the DP shop
   c. DP shop standards.
3. Seminars in techniques of management and administration (32 hours)
   a. Programmer performance appraisal

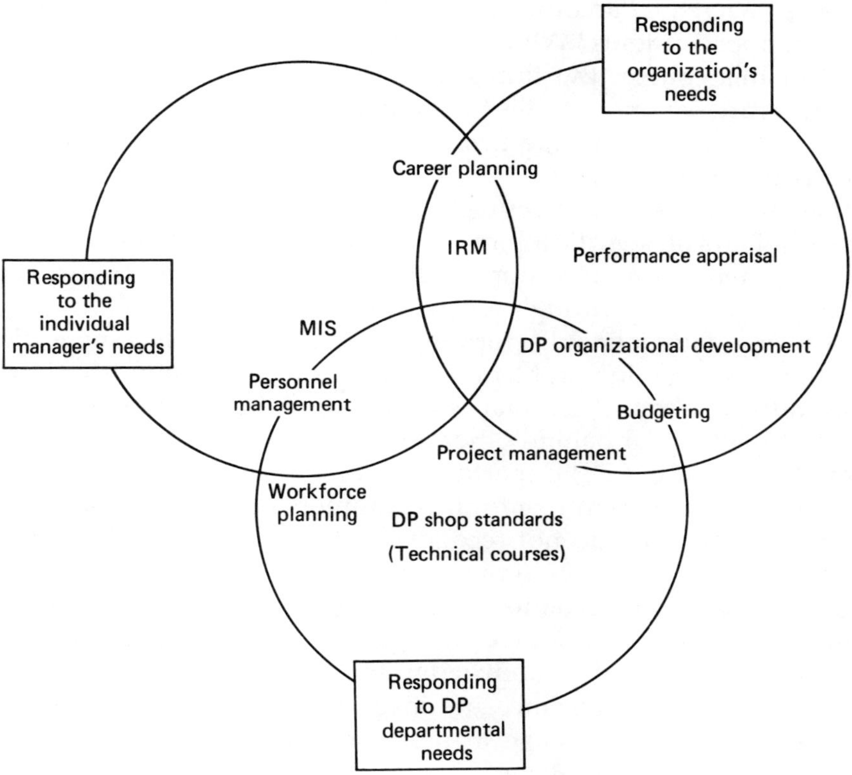


**FIGURE 7.3** A MOP training program.

b. DP project budgeting and administration

c. Career planning for programmers

d. Workforce planning and estimation.

The first tier consists of 40-hour groundings in project management, Information Resource Management (IRM) and MIS from the *user's* viewpoint, probably offered through universities. Project management techniques are necessary in any event. The IRM course seems a more appropriate topic for MOPs than the more familiar systems analysis course. It can help integrate much of the firm's concern for information of a variety of natures: DP, public relations, consumer product information, and procedures and standards.

The use of computers in management in administration concentrates upon the employment of applications that the software staff creates. What are "accounts receivable"? Who is supported by decision-support systems? Who uses computer-based models and what for? In this course, the firm's, rather than the DP Department's, interests are paramount. It is this course that specifically responds to the MOPs function in the firm of translating organizational statements into work plans.

General management courses in the second tier are seen as two-day seminars on specific topics, which are usually left to hit-and-miss development through rumor and habit formation. Much of the content of Chapters 2 through 6 is relevant to these courses.

The one-day seminar list forming the third tier is only a suggestion for the most pressing problems in supervision and administration in the software shop. Performance appraisal and budgeting in the DP Department lag far behind other departments. Few do these well in any event, but the DP Department distinguishes itself with its failures here. Career planning for programmers is irrelevant, of course, in those firms that do not recognize careers for programmers; the course is a contradiction in these companies. Workforce planning is rarely a discipline recognized outside the Personnel Department. Still, a traditionally workforce-shy group such as Programming could profit from the fund of knowledge the Personnel Department has built up over the years. Since, in Gibson and Nolan's (1974) sense, DP is reaching a mature stage in most firms and in many cases has plateaued in workforce levels, it is now possible to do rational workforce planning in DP.

In addition to these 200 hours of instruction—which closely conform to many post-bachelor certificate programs—MOPs should be given precisely the same details about the firm that other managers receive. This instruction should be followed up at regular intervals with diagnostic sessions. With this arsenal of education—equivalent to a semester of full-time university study—the MOP should be better prepared to begin a career in programming management than is possible with the current on-the-job training.

## 7.2. CAREER PLANNING FOR MOPs

Career planning is a method of planning paths through a field. In this section we examine the alternatives and choices in planning a career in programming management.

Are careers in programming management possible? Are there alternatives and choices to be made? Can these choices be made effectively or do we have to flip coins?

Until recently, the answer was probably no. Research and commentary indicated that, once in the software group, programmers were very likely stuck there, perhaps achieving a single promotion to a first-level supervisory, lead-programmer, position. Possibilities for promotion to DP Director were small since these positions typically went to those with backgrounds in operations or systems analysis. Often outsiders from the Accounting, Finance, or Engineering Departments were parachuted in.

Then, too, the number of management positions was very limited. A typical DP organization is broad, in structural terms, with large spans of control. Grid or matrix management provides a constant shuffle of individuals into and through projects without promotion to greater responsibilities. Figure 7.4 illustrates a typical career path for an individual in such a shallow organization.

Paths through general management, too, were quite limited. DP management is hardly a fertile breeding ground for executives. A service organization mandated to improve a particular system, DP does not enjoy organization-wide influence. Rather, it has to respond to organization-wide demands. This normally gives a DP manager a narrow technical experience with a broad range of frustrated individuals outside DP in functional area. This is not sufficient to achieve promotion into divisions not totally devoted to administration. Even in administrative divisions, the DP Director is competing with other Directors—in particular with those from Finance, Accounting, Personnel, Corporate Relations, and Long-Range Planning—who have broader experience in areas traditionally more pertinent to achieving promotions in administration.

How has this changed?

First, programmers are no longer satisfied with mere paper promotions, and have expressed this vocally in recent years. As labor costs have risen, industry pundits have raised the flag of human relations needs in the software shop. This need is best met with more and better management and the professionalization of administration in the shop. As DP becomes more complex and more closely resembles a firm-within-a-firm, possibilities of parachuting engineers and accountants in to lead this complex technical business are decreasing.

As DP shops have expanded (see Figure 7.5), spans of control have risen beyond the recommended three-to-five. Many MOPs have 10 or

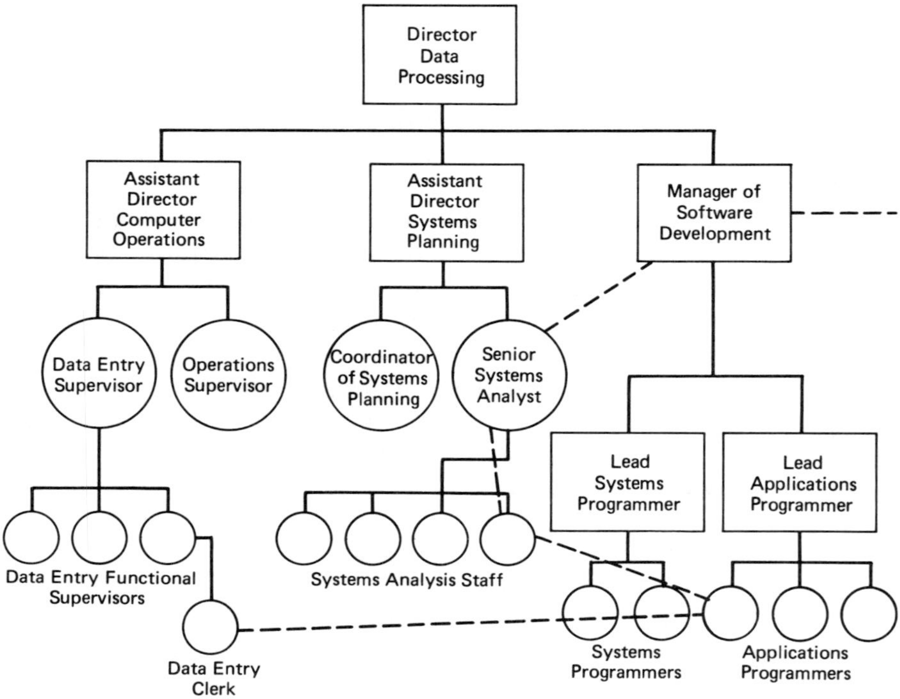


**FIGURE 7.4** Ten years in data processing.

more programmers to direct. Obviously many demands placed on them will not be met. The organization's response in other departments would be to bring in more managers; this rarely occurs in DP shops, but it's starting to happen.

Finally, DP Directors are gaining experience running big businesses for corporate customers. One of the hottest topics in DP administration is charge-back computations. CPU cycles, disk seeks, page accesses, and connect time to ports must be accurately and completely accounted for in DP budgets. This has motivated DP administrators to learn their businesses in ways many business managers are incapable of learning.

Partly this results from using the computer itself to observe its own resource utilization. Also, DP Directors more and more have business backgrounds that include B.B.A.s and M.B.A.s, with concentrations in Information Systems or Accounting. Parochialism within the shop is decreasing, at least at the top.

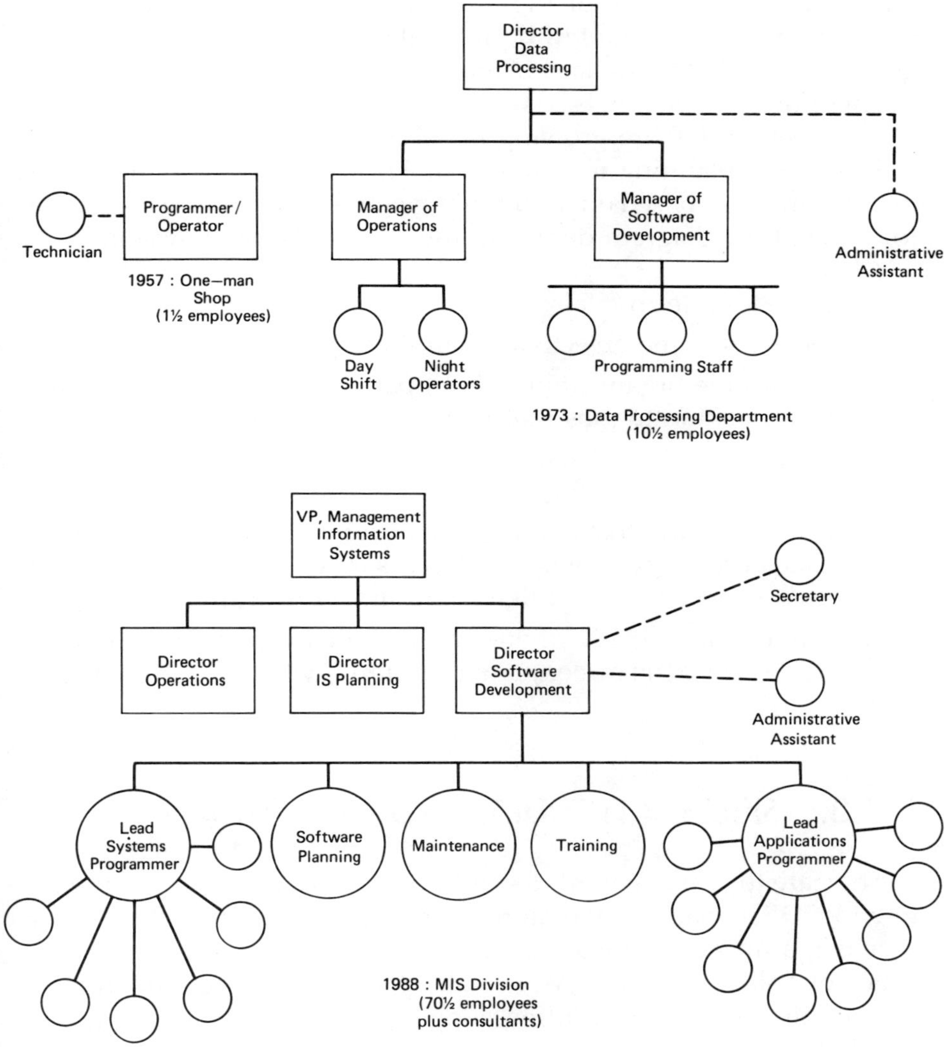


**FIGURE 7.5** The evolution of the data processing function.

Outside the DP Department, there is increasing awareness, as discussed in Chapter 6, of the value of information to the firm and the value of the DP Department to a long-term information resource strategy. Software sales, extra-corporate computer services, decision-support, and office automation are bringing DP into play not merely as a cost-control tactic but as a literal *profit center*, a source of income for the firm. Estimates of the value of the information-provision business are various, but few doubt that in the 1980s and 1990s it will grow to a decibillion-dollar business.

Therefore, the picture is changing. The possibilities for expanded, true, careers in DP are growing for MOPs.

The career planning method is similar to other long-range planning techniques, based on traditional systems analysis (see Figure 7.6 for a data flow diagram depicting the career planning system):

1. State long-term goals.
2. Derive specific objectives from these goals.
3. Determine organizational (job) paths that lead from the current position to jobs that meet those objectives (Figure 7.7).
4. Determine the skills, attitudes, and credentials needed to traverse this path.
5. Determine the cost in time, dollars, and effort to traverse each path and the possibility for success in following the path; and then choose the most likely and most rewarding path.
6. Pursue immediate activities on the chosen path and continuously revise the career plan from step 1 with new information.

## 7.3. SKILLS, ATTITUDES, AND CREDENTIALS

The gate to management doesn't normally open to the "software ghetto." DP management requires a broader view, especially in order to manage an equipment and personnel budget of hundreds of thousands of dollars annually. More skills, too, are necessary in budgeting, administration, accounting, long-range planning, and so forth.

What then are the appropriate skills, attitudes, and credentials to succeed in DP management? Based on research, experience, and common sense, this list emerges:

1. Communication skills.
2. Ability to see and describe problems.
3. Empathy and the ability to listen.
4. A broad view of the organization and its functions.
5. A feeling of responsibility.

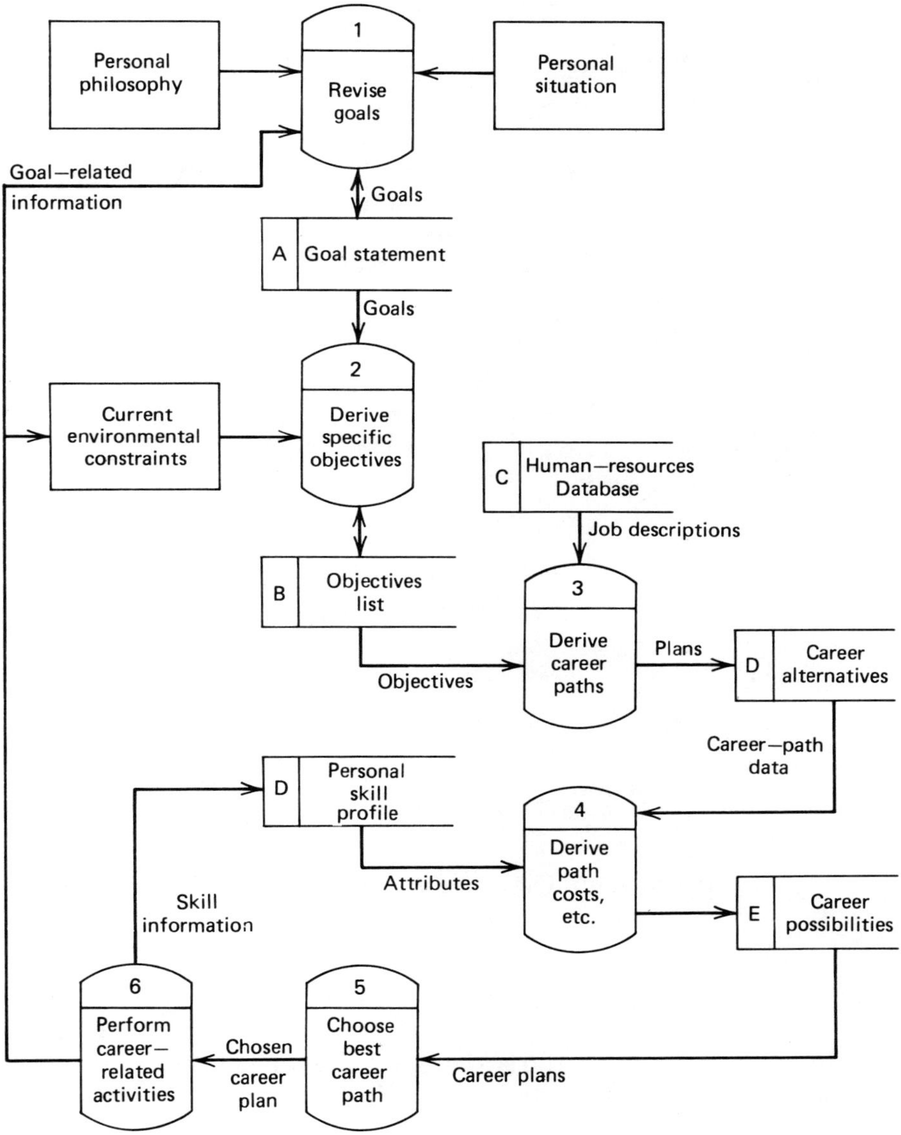


**FIGURE 7.6** Career planning data flow diagram.

6. Desire for success.
7. Patience—and flexibility.
8. Administrative skills in budgeting, human resources planning, and accounting.

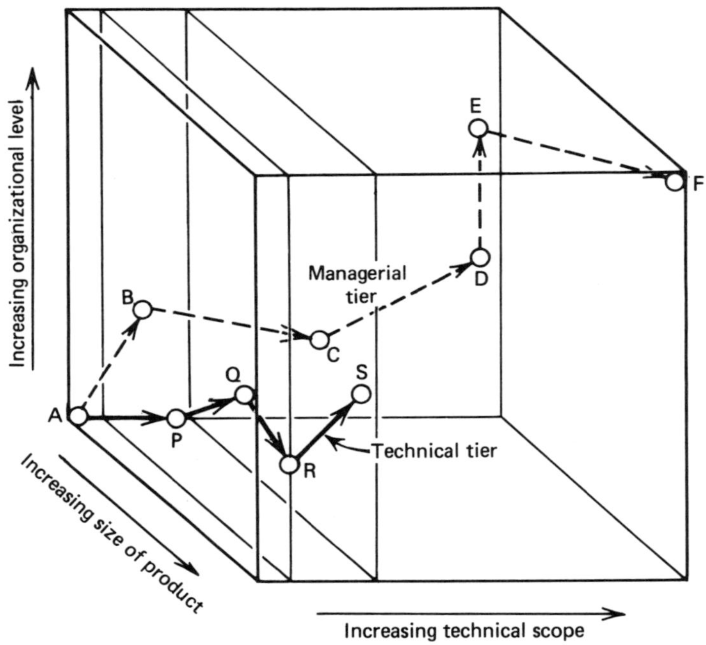


A : Trainee Operator
B : Lead Shift Operator
C : Lead Programmer
D : Senior Systems Analyst
E : Assistant Director, Systems Planning
F : MIS Director

P : Programmer Trainee
Q : Programmer
R : Senior Programmer
S : Manager of Programming

**FIGURE 7.7** Two DP careers in the career cube.

9. Courage.
10. Programming, but not necessarily programming languages.

In terms of experience, the successful DP manager needs, and will need increasingly in the future, the following:

1. Broad experience with the company's products and services.
2. Access to the current knowledge of organizational design, long-range-planning techniques, and the employment of computers in administration.
3. Advanced degrees, especially in business administration, MIS augmented by management science, and advanced degrees or training in accounting, finance, and personnel psychology.

## 7.4. AFTER SOFTWARE, WHAT?

Figure 7.7 illustrates typical DP careers. But what comes after DP? Where can a MOP go after a career in the software shop?

Figure 7.8 illustrates the three exits from software management positions. The first is to relinquish the management position to return to the software factory. Few ever take that exit due to obsolescence and avoidance of the appearance of failure. In many firms such voluntary demotions are impossible or are frowned upon.

The second is into entrepreneurship. Many employees have developed a hot product and left a firm to market it. Given the difficulty in patenting software inventions and given the facility with which look-alike software can be created, almost any capable programmer can create marketable software. The market potential is billions annually. A MOP with a few years' experience in management of a software shop can feel confident—given the skills this book discusses—in directing a software development and marketing firm for computer programs.

The third path out is to become a consultant. Often a MOP who feels uncomfortable with*in* a firm can leave and, phoenix-like, be reborn as a consultant who gets along quite well working *with* the firm as an equal. In this role, the former MOP can provide valuable guidance to smaller firms without good software development management and to larger firms spread thin in areas of planning and direction.

Whether or not a MOP can become an entrepreneur or a consultant is problematic. Skills needed to sell and consult are not normally developed and exercised in the software shop. In fact, in many cases, these are the specific skills lacking in programmers and MOPs, leading to the need to hire consultants. Sales work differs dramatically from programming. It requires exquisite interpersonal skills and the ability to put a point across to unwilling audiences, not ever-patient computers. It requires courage and perseverance of the type seldom seen in the software shop. Rewards are infrequent and delayed rather than frequent and immediate. Salary depends directly upon immediate work effectiveness, reflected in sales figures. In many ways, the idea of the typical MOP becoming an entrepreneur is absurd.

Consulting, too, draws upon skills MOPs have little opportunity to acquire and exercise. The consultant needs above all to be a listener who can pull back from the work at hand and place the information collected into a broader picture for the client. Consultants need

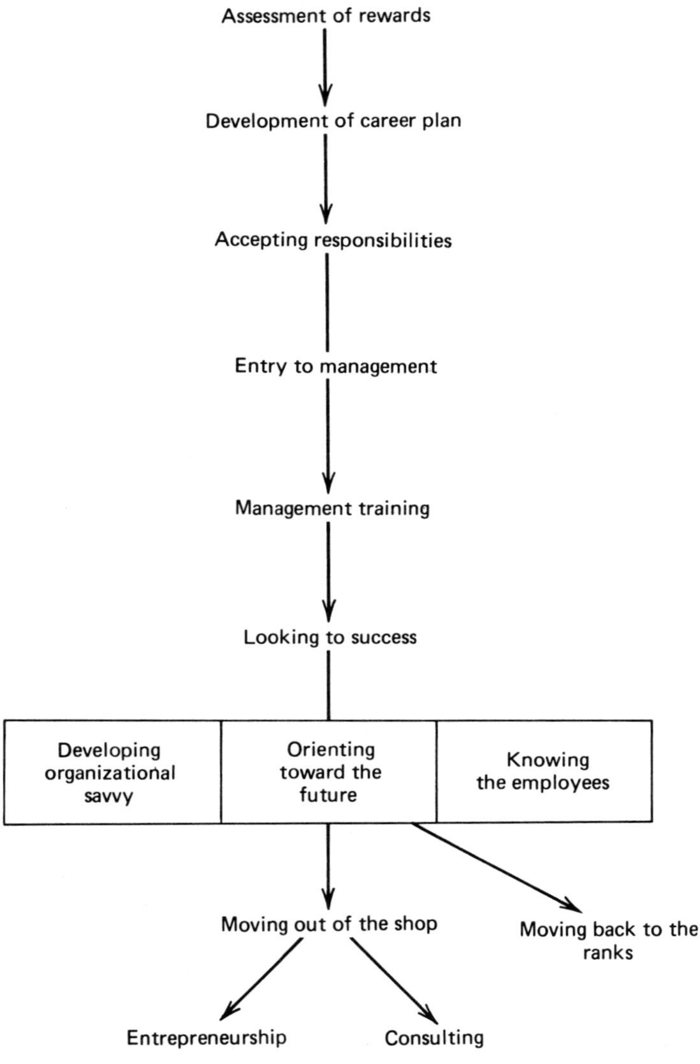


**FIGURE 7.8** Career activities for the MOP.

interpersonal skills and the ability to speak clearly and to the point. Client traits need to be evaluated quickly and accurately. A consultant cannot program a client. The best consulting is simply a restatement of the client's problems in clearer terms. MOPs who like to program may find consulting uncomfortable.

On the other hand, career paths out of software are not for the typical programmer but for the individual who finds the rewards of

MOP-ing insufficient in challenge. The rewards of sales and consulting are different, and the MOP who sets up a software house or a DP consulting firm is looking for those rewards beyond the technology.

Planning for these exit paths is more complex than preparing for a career within DP in a single firm because more skills are necessary and a lot of luck is involved. On the other hand, just being in DP is lucky today—ask teachers and social workers what *their* exit professions might be! The microcomputer revolution is creating markets for software. The rapid fall in hardware prices is making DP attractive to many firms who find hiring programmers unattractive. Larger firms find it expensive to maintain large DP staffs and constantly seek experienced outside help. Planning to acquire communication skills, patience, and tact to consult or sell may be the single best decision many MOPs will make while reading this book.

## 7.5. DEVELOPING A MANAGEMENT PHILOSOPHY

The final component of career planning is the development of an appropriate management philosophy. Without a traditional place in the organization and traditional work functions, DP careers have little to lean upon for intellectual, emotional, and spiritual guidance, other than personal resources. Making important long-term decisions is more than merely plugging values into an equation and coming up with a figure. One needs a feel for the decision and a confidence in the process.

There aren't major vocations to borrow from. MOPs will have to develop their own philosophies. In the coming two decades, programming will mature into a new kind of vocation. Those who have consistent and valuable philosophies will prosper; the others will remain confused.

What are the major components of a management philosophy appropriate to the management of programming? There are six of them:

1. Concern for technological change.
2. Interaction with consumers of computer products.
3. Entrepreneurship.
4. Attitudes toward fourth-generation workers.

5. Responsibilities toward constituencies.
6. Assumption of leadership in the DP field.

*Change is inevitable. Software is at the leading edge of the kind of changes society can expect in the next quarter century.* The information revolution, the third wave, the microcomputer revolution depend upon the availability of software as the key element in creation, distribution, and accounting for information. Those who produce—and those who lead those who produce—this software will be important players in this kind of change.

*Emphasis in software development must not fail to consider the ultimate users. System development methodologies must integrate producer and consumer of software products.* This restates Toffler's idea of "prosumer" in the third wave. In this concept, twenty-first-century consumers will produce large proportions of the products they need for their own use. It is a trend that counters the specialization of the Industrial Era and the principles of economy of scale and the law of supply and demand. Managers of software production need to include the consumer somehow in the production process.

*Software development efforts naturally result in saleable products whose value is determined in an open market.* In the past this market did not exist. Microcomputers are changing that, introducing the concept of the mass market for software and semisoftware, such as games. Managers of programmers must become entrepreneurial if software production is to become more than the handcrafting art it now is. Some would argue that the *status quo* is preferable to the software factory. The trends, however, are obvious, and better arguments can be made for retention of skilled artisans who make signed software *after* the marketplace has become healthy through the provision of enough software. Otherwise someone will design software sweatshops.

*Programmers are individuals, not interchangeable parts of software-producing machines. Dignity is almost as important as skill in the software shop.* Today programmers are either kooks or serfs, both without dignity. Kraft (1977) argues persuasively that the trend is toward the latter and that programming is ripe for deskilling. Others argue that programming is inherently a craft that cannot be managed in an industrial fashion. Meanwhile the nature of Western industry is itself changing, and the craft/factory distinction is becoming less important. Programming is the first fourth-generation vocation, not the last bastion of unwashed art. The sooner MOPs recognize this and develop management philosophies consistent with this *new* vocation, the happier we will all be. The key is the new kind of worker, the programmer.

*The natural constituency of the MOP is the organization itself rather than the computer or specific customers.* MOPs should direct their attentions toward the health of the firm rather than the strength of the firm's machinery. This merely repeats the emphasis of Chapter 6. The computer is beginning to change the structure of business in radical and unpredictable ways. The MOP leads this trend. MOPs who respond to favored customers only, or worse, fail to respond to any organizational players, do themselves a disservice. The organization and the computer have already been successfully married in office automation (from time to time a marriage counsellor is needed, however) and this shift should be apparent to MOPs, who ignore it at their own risk.

*Leadership is a quality that shouldn't be avoided. Software is the major player in computerization, not the poor sister. The MOP can lead and others can follow if appropriate leadership skills are allowed to emerge.* In the past, MOPs have shirked leadership responsibilities. This shows in all psychological studies of DP personnel. Few MOPs rise to be DP Director, and none become Presidents of nonsoftware firms. Leadership skills in the software shop can be made appropriate outside DP in the newly computer-conscious firm. However, this will require careful career planning.

Experiences that contribute to the development of individual variations of this philosophy include the following:

1. Experiencing change at the front lines in working for fast-track, high-tech companies.
2. Experimenting with prosumer-oriented development methodologies, such as prototyping and packages.
3. Developing software markets within the firm in committees or long-term planning projects.
4. Experimenting with alternative management styles, such as supportive management, participative management, Theory Z, or even MBO.
5. Working with the organization instead of despite it and trying to develop leadership skills in situations in which leadership is available, such as quality circles and long-range planning.

In other words, MOPs need to practice and value something other than straightforward directive leadership in a project management mode with milliseconds of time out here and there to put out fires. Individual philosophies will become important to MOPs as the profession matures in the future of programming, the topic of the next chapter.

## 7.6. CONCLUSION

A career that includes programming management is not a series of chance events. A successful career requires planning. Four major aspects are training, learning about the corporation, developing constituencies within the firm, and creating a management philosophy appropriate for computer technology positions.

The rewards of management are available for those who can successfully plan and carry out career decisions. These imply developing goals and objectives, learning about possible career paths, determining the costs and probabilities of particular paths, choosing among them, and carrying out appropriate actions. A career plan is regularly revised in pursuit of the goals.

As programmers move through their careers, significant decision points include whether to enter management, when to rotate to positions outside DP, and if (and how) to exit from software management. Choices depend upon skill profiles. One guiding principle in making choices will be the MOP's management philosophy. This should be based on considerations such as technological change, interaction with users, entrepreneurship, programmers as fourth-generation employees, responsibility to a constituency, and leadership in DP.

## 7.7. CASES IN CAREER PLANNING

### 7.7.1. The Dead End Job (Rob Condon on the Brink)

When we left Rob Condon, he was considering looking for another job to get out from under Larry Goudreau, a friend of the firm's president, Director of DP, manager of Rob Condon, and general roadblock to Rob's career.

Rob's career plan is poor simply because he doesn't have one. He is truly boxed in because his experience is narrow and because the firm lacks clearly defined career paths through and out of data processing. His options seem limited: leave or wait for Goudreau to retire. In the meantime, someone may take *Rob's* job from him.

Rob should have planned to acquire broader organizational platforms from which to advance. By concentrating on an area, such as building accounting packages, in which he has neither ambition nor credentials, he asks the firm to choose between himself and an organizational booster because of the narrow career ladder he has defined for himself. Of course Rob won't win promotion over Goudreau—and he won't replace him, either.

Rob has no constituency, either. Or so it seems. A careful look at this, however, reveals that Rob has opened the door for a career path he can define himself: software entrepreneurship. In fact, Rob is in an excellent position to define a new line of work for his firm and himself, since it is already interested in selling the accounting package to other firms. And while one accounting package may not be much of a product line, the fabrics manufacturing business is complex enough that integrated software packages for his firm's customers and suppliers may be a logical product for Rob's soft-and-dry-goods shop.

Rob should supplement his M.B.A. studies with a thorough grounding in the business of his firm. This should include manufacturing technology, marketing, distribution, advertising, commercial operations, and accounting specific to fabrics. From his position in the Finance Department, he can begin looking at the financial aspects of the business and expand from there. Above all, Rob must avoid concentrating only on software production and build his constituency elsewhere.

Acquiring training and constituencies are two of the three necessary elements of Rob's career planning. The third is to develop a management philosophy consistent with his career plan goals. Having drifted into management, seeking promotions for the sake of income, Rob has drifted in his career. He must develop some short- and long-term goals, perhaps including software entrepreneurship.

Of primary importance is how Rob will see himself handling change. Will he cause change in the firm or will he sit on the sidelines waiting to be called? Can he see profit for himself in selling software, or should he change jobs again in a search for an environment that matches his ideas? In other words, can he shape his current career meanderings to suit some goals, or does he have to wander in the career desert until he finds an oasis?

Rob will have to answer these questions:

1. What are my goals? Leadership, entrepreneurship, comfort?
2. If I choose entrepreneurship, what objectives does that imply? A sales position, pressure from the DP Department, pressure on the VP for Finance?
3. Will entrepreneurship provide me with the rewards I desire? Is entrepreneurship the only path left in this firm? Do other firms provide me with clearer paths to this goal?
4. Can I make it in software sales? What do I need to know to succeed? *Whom* do I need to get to know?
5. If I succeed, will I be able to move again? Can I plan from such a position or will I be trapped again?

Rob *can* detour and achieve his career goals, but first he has to have them—and plan to meet them.

### *Case 2. Horatio Programmer: A Success Story*

Karyn Middleton is VP of Information Systems for a medium-sized trucking firm in the midwest. Her responsibilities include the direct management of all computer operations and office automation activities in the head office and six district offices in Michigan, Illinois, Indiana, Ohio, and Kentucky. In addition, she is in charge of all information-related activities in the firm, including archiving of office information, public relations, telecommunications (including dispatching of trucks), and software marketing. Last month she inaugurated a trucker's information dataline, in which a nationwide linkup of trucking firms purchase information on trucking routes, emergency situations, inter- and intrastate trucking regulations, bids and requests for bids on government contracts, and advertisements by equipment manufacturers and service centers (and not a few trucker-oriented greasy spoons along interstate highways).

Karyn's especially proud of the dataline, because this was one of her pet projects. Since joining the firm 11 years ago as a manager of a small software group engaged mostly in writing software for dispatching and scheduling loadings, she's wanted to move on to having more responsibilities and to doing more things with the technology. Not content with merely implementing on a computer calculation done before by hand, she prodded her DP Director to look at third- and then fourth-generation software techniques and was instrumental in shifting many applications development activities to the users' side. This of course made her particular group redundant. However, she had long before this put into operation career plans for her workers (all of whom now have responsible positions in software management) and herself.

In particular, she noted a complete vacuum at the top of the firm with regard to information usage. Information came from a variety of locations, with less-than-perfect reliability, little consistency, and often no validity. The President was constantly dodging changes in regulation and the volatile energy market. Running a head office and several branches by phone proved difficult. While DP turned out fine applications for users who knew what they wanted, no one had seen opportunities for DP in upper management.

Karyn noted several other things and altered her personal philosophy to suit them. One was evidence that information overload was only a symptom of the subtle shift in the transportation business to a more reliable information base. The second was the disorganization brought about by software that only acted as a crutch to provide more, but not necessarily better, and quicker, but not necessarily more timely, information. Third, she saw that upper management wasn't necessarily silent about this problem, that it was actively seeking solutions. Fourth, she noted that she had no plans for her future, that she'd been satisfied with her promotions based on her technical skills. These skills included an ability to work with users who wanted to get involved in development of software to solve information problems.

Finally, she recognized that, while the DP shop was a hiding place for many shy people, having a DP background didn't automatically disqualify her to lead the firm through the minefield of late-twentieth-century cybernation. In fact, the skills she employed in leading her group well—communication, understanding the organization, empathy, an eye toward the future in software—were precisely those being rewarded by management.

She made her move. Because she desired to lead rather than

follow, she knew that the only paths available to her were outside DP and through the business of the firm. She took a risk and pressed for a transfer to the dispatching group (for which she had written programs earlier), and there supervised a team of analysts looking at dispatching systems. This choice was also guided by the probability that telecommunications, rather than DP, was going to form the nucleus of the new trucking business.

After a year there, she suggested to her manager that dispatching and telecommunications could profit from a bit of computerization and became project leader—from the *user* side—of a large pilot in digital dispatching. Since her plan included integrating computers with the business of the firm (trucking), she saw this project as central not only to achieving promotions, but also to getting to know as many aspects of the firm as possible.

When the project neared the tailing-off in expenses, she requested a transfer to a branch to supervise telecommunications from that end. Within six months, she'd streamlined branch dispatching and defined a new position, Coordinator of Communications. In this position, Karyn controlled not only the user side of dispatching (with the aid of several veteran dispatchers who were pleased with her ability to see their viewpoint and express it well to the firm), but also, through a stroke of luck, a small office automation activity—this last mostly word processing for business forms and letters.

With characteristic energy and foresight, Karyn set to work integrating word processing with telecommunications. In doing this, she inherited several programmers on this project. Some of their products looked general in nature and she tried, successfully, to market the products back to the computer vendor. This in turn led to other marketing efforts. Although she wasn't allowed to sell the dispatching system, she did become aware of the needs of other truckers to share information about roads, dangers, regulation, and technology. Her career plan put emphasis upon broadening organizational skills and, as well, organizational scope.

Working outside the firm enabled Karyn to adopt a view of the firm's environment of regulators, customers, vendors, and freight. The title contained the word "communications," and Karyn was later given responsibility over public relations as well as the phone system. Humorously she was referred to as the "company switchboard." In fact, because her goal was to employ technology in as many profitable ways as possible, she saw a benefit here, too. As "company switchboard," she could put her finger quite well on company affairs, both internal as well as external. This brought her into contact with upper management on a daily basis. Although writing speeches for the company President wasn't one of her responsibilities, she did have the opportunity to suggest a number of company-wide computer-communication projects. One of them was a dataline for truckers, but one firm couldn't support the system.

After some negotiation, the President had given the go-ahead to build the network in conjunction with the Trucker's Association. Karyn's planning and initiative had paid off. Her firm became know for its innovative use of technology in the service of transport, and with this came increased organizational responsibilities for dispatching software to the scene. She'd realized her goals in five years. □

To be fair, success stories are easy to write and hard to make into reality. In Karyn's case, the critical elements were ambition, communication, and career planning. She had a vision of herself leading the technology and the people who use it. She could place things into appropriate contexts and saw them in appropriate proportions. She took risks leaving DP and in taking on non-DP responsibilities later in her career. But above all, she drew, and redrew her career plans. That this fairy tale leaves no dead bodies behind may be slightly unreal. However, there is no *necessity* to be mean. A manager who challenges and prepares her workers for challenge is one who is building a constituency within the firm. A manager who can take DP ideas and sell them elsewhere builds up just as important a constituency outside the DP organization. Karyn had all the necessary skills in gargantuan measure. Most MOPs can expect small successes rather than Horatio Alger stories. Still, there's no gain without any planning—ask a gambler.

CHAPTER EIGHT

# THE FUTURE OF PROGRAMMING MANAGEMENT

The emphasis in this book has been on current practice in software development management and the career development of individual MOPs. Previous chapters have focused upon management techniques in direction of work, individuals, and groups within technical organizations. This chapter focuses upon more general and future directions in the software industry. While individual futures are extremely important, prognostication concerning the industry is an important element, too, of career planning on a long-term basis. Since "long-term" in this industry often means three years, several elements of project and personnel management may well require accurate industry prognostications, too. At the time of writing this, the author is about to embark upon a three-year project computerizing a social service office. Imagine the difficulties predicting software and hardware development needs this far in advance!

Chapter 8 examines two extreme predictions for the future of programming. The first, usually termed "pessimistic," is the "sweatshop" view of programmers turning out nearly identical low-level versions of standardized software on engines akin to the kinds of machines now employed in factories. The second, often thought of as "optimistic," posits a "cottage industry" of programmer-artisans who produce specialized, special-ordered software by hand, crafting it to the user in some as-yet-dreamed totally user-sensitive fashion akin to the weaver, the potter, and the painter. These overly extreme views are the beginning points for discussion of the future of software.

Three individual generic futures are explored for specific kinds of programmers: the applications programmer (which may include, of course, COBOLists), the systems programmer, and the scientific programmer. There are reasons to believe that, in general, futures for these groups may differ in ways important for those now choosing to pursue careers in programming management.

A short recap of the past history and a shorter recap of the future history of programming is then offered by this writer as the resolution of the two trends. As with many other resolutions, the actual implementation depends critically upon both technological advance and the state of the economy in information-consuming countries. The actual form of programming in the closing years of the twentieth century may bear no resemblance to today's structures.

Finally, programming management is examined critically and specifically to lay the foundwork for a *survival and advancement plan* for MOPs, to complement the *career and organizational development plans* offered in previous chapters. With these three plans, the new MOP will be well equipped to define, pursue, and achieve career goals within software-producing organizations.

## 8.1. CURRENT TRENDS

Six trends are apparent in the programming field; each has important implications for those who manage programmers.

1. *The scope of applications is increasing.* Programmers are increasingly called upon to apply their talents in areas that are intellectually inaccessible to them. These include complex business modeling, office automation and real-time communication, gaming and simulation packages, artificial intelligence and robotics, and arcane scientific areas such as biotechnology, image enhancement, and subatomic physics. There have always been business programmers and scien-

tific programmers, but the content of the programs have typically been computerized analogues of well-defined algorithms. Into the twenty-first century, we will no longer be able to count upon the native skills of programmers to provide understanding of what it is they are doing with the algorithms. New development techniques bring programmers into closer contact with clients; reliability considerations, especially for real-time systems, overwhelm the "dumb" programmer, who, like dumb terminals, may suffer from being unable to do "local" processing of the alogorithm. In short, as scope increases, chances for depth decrease and management problems skyrocket.

2. *Software opportunity areas are growing.* Even now, there are five important applications fields that didn't exist as recently as five years ago. In some cases networking, micro- and personal-computing, database and data-administration, user-friendly software and decision-support, and software engineering of the product itself have been either recently defined or introduced into the training regimen of programmers. Regardless of the prediction for the industry in general, the increasing sophistication managers and marketeers develop with computers will overlay several levels of product upon existing "flat" programs, developing specialization areas that didn't exist previously. Database grew from a realization that file access procedures needed to be made available at both command and program level. Micro-computing was initiated for research reasons but became a mass market playroom because of games, which had been the toys of the backroom kids for years. Decision-support and user-friendly software developed because of the necessity to migrate the software out of the technical shop. Similar movements are noticeable now through information centers, architecture-based software development, and CAD/CAM. Even ignoring the "golly-gee-whiz" literature of the trade mags, the implications for managers are enormous. The need MOPs have to leave the shop is growing; if visits are not to become exile, MOPs will have to learn how to manage software markets, too.

3. *The range of programming jobs is widening.* Four job thrusts in particular are now noticeable. Package tailoring, software and management consulting in computers, computer-based management, and information resources management are old tasks repackaged into new jobs. Some programmers now can look foward to spending their entire careers in tailoring general-purpose packages to specific

business requirements. In a way, the package becomes the programming language. Many programmers are now identified as MARK-IV or CICS programmers; the language is really a package. Software consulting is a venerable occupation, but now it includes more than merely contracting to produce a program. Rather, such consultants are increasingly called upon to plan, execute, and evaluate a migration from one software system to another. Computer-based management—a replacement of MIS—essentially uses software to provide a view of the firm through a green screen and a powerful dialogue manager, again "programming" in a borrowed suit of clothes. "IRM" is a new term encompassing almost all of the previous. Add to this the sure appearance of officeware programmers, the small-but-growing cadre of decision-support toolsmiths and consulting firms that specialize in teaching others how to uses packages such as Lotus 1-2-3™, and the picture of programming as an expanded profession emerges clearly.

4. *Emphasis on coding is decreasing.* Despite the cries from business people for more expert COBOL programmers, the trend is clearly toward lessening emphasis on coding skills among the increasingly professionalized and higher level programmers. Code-generators, use of VHL languages and fourth-generation languages (4GLs), the curious reintroduction of the tail-finned nonprocedural RPG as the sleek European-styled VisiCalc™, the great interest in interactive planning-based systems (including DSS), and the movement toward programmerless programming underscore this trend. Just as early chauffeurs were expected also to be mechanics, so too were programmers expected to know the hardware, then later only languages to manipulate the hardware. The trend is obviously toward programmers who only manipulate programs through brain-torque-increasing tools.

5. *The ability of education sources to keep up with demand is falling.* Except for cannon-fodder grunt programmers, turned out in great numbers by community colleges and technical institutes, higher education is failing to provide business, government, and science with sufficient and sufficiently prepared software experts. Such an expert is abreast of hardware and software developments, is motivated to apply that knowledge in another discipline (business, government, science), and is willing to run after the technology subsequent to employment. Too few get through the universities, too few are given a broad and deep education outside languages, too many fall behind

the technology. Obsolescence in this field is so rapid that a 10-year tenure qualifies one for the label of "veteran." As programmers "die" at increasingly younger ages, colleges and universities will fall further and further behind.

6. *A two-class programmer society is growing.* This is Philip Kraft's (1977) contentious hypothesis. Basically, he proposes that university-trained analysis-bound programmers will dominate a second group of community- and technical-college-trained applications programmers. The first group has the will and skills to rise out of the programming ranks, leaving it increasingly deficient in individuals who are motivated by programming rather than money. He predicts an increasingly unionized, alienated, and computer-illiterate "underclass." Relations between the two classes will not be friendly. MOPs will be chosen from the university-trained group, which will be allowed true professionalization; others will become expendable when they become 10-year "vets." This trend is only barely noticeable now. However, the recent recession of 1981–1983 demonstrated for the first time that programmers, too, could be laid off, that software is as vulnerable to economic winds as ladies' ware.

## 8.2. THREE INDIVIDUAL FUTURES

These current trends may not continue, of course. It is unlikely, however, that many of them will be reversed. In fact, according to some industry pundits, several will be accelerated, especially the loss of emphasis on coding and the increasing areas for opportunities in software.

Where are these trends leading us? Toward which of the two extreme views are we actually heading? The next section examines the future history of three programmers as mini case studies in the face of these trends.

### 8.2.1. The Applications Programmer

With a feeling of relief, Gary "Goofy" Doge opened the wrappings on the latest, and last, shipment of ACOS (A Can of Software). There it was, in living color, the last link in the complex GeCorpIs that the Software Shop had been carefully constructing over the past two years. Goofy had managed the group, when there was a group. Now it was just Goofy and a trainer, Michael "Micky" Mowers, who had been a crackerjack programmer two years ago but who had discovered a bit more job security in training executives in how to set up GeCorpIs "Bodies" to manage the shadow corporations now making up General Corporation's international structure.

Because GeCoprIs made it easy to suggest and create software, there was no longer any need for an applications staff. Those whom Goofy used to direct, 16 programmers and a slew of secretaries and clerks, had found jobs in operating areas or had moved on to other shops, but of course jobs were hard to find. Goofy had carefully briefed his workers on the implications of GeCorpIs and the philosophy behind its nonprocedural, programmer-free operation. Of course, there were still a few systems programmers around because things always needed fixing, but Goofy was sure their tenure was going to be short, too.

As application backlog increased beyond two years and programmers became increasingly difficult to train to produce the kind of reliable software GenCor needed, GenCor directors initiated a task force that developed the operating specs for GeCorpIs. "Humanware" is what they had termed it, but the viewpoint in the basement was that it implied programmerless programming. Dr. Paul ("Pluto") Popilos, President of GenCor, said it made good sense to move applications out of the specialized shop into the ranks of the corporation. Besides, he pointed out that some specialized applications were showing lifespans of less than six months, far too short to bring a programmer up to productive levels. A brief fling with ADF III and EasyTrieve IV proved happy, but incomplete. Pluto wanted a true fourth-generation system, and Mickey and Goofy had little choice other than to concur since most other larger multiglomerates were following the same star.

Now, two years later, Goofy and Mickey have opened the last segment of the development system ACOS. Within weeks or days the memo would arrive formally eliminating the Software Shop from GenCor. From 600 programmers to 8 isolated groups of 3 or 4 systems tenders in 2 years: this is little cause to celebrate, but for Goofy and Mickey there is some wheat amid the chaff. Mickey will move into Corporate Training, to manage a small group charged with migrating all of training onto recorded interactive digital media using GeCorpIs. Goofy has been promoted to Sales Manager, GenSoft, a spun-off software marketing subsidiary of GenCor. GenSoft is mostly concerned with marketing GeCorpIs look-alikes to smaller businesses in affordable packages. Goofy's located two programmers and a sales type to help him lead the group. He's moving next month to his new office in the corporate center known as BusiniLand. □

### 8.2.2. The Systems Programmer

Systems programmers have always been unique. From the first moment of life of the stored program computer ENIAC to today's megalithic distributed and virtual operating systems, systems programmers have stood apart from their colleagues in applications and scientific work. Systems programmers are the true descendants of the engineers who built the first systems. Only systems programmers truly understand *how* software gets the job done. Only systems programmers control all the keys, have access to all the data, and have the right to ask system operators to pull a unit down for maintenance—or for fun. Because of their special knowledge and the grave dependence the DP center has upon them for normal operation and enhancements, systems programmers have always been special and protected.

Apparently this special status is now threatened. The Multics operating system was written in PL/I and for the first time one did not have to know the actual machine language to be a systems programmer. The boundaries between systems programming and other work are being fuzzed by semiapplications such as teleprocessing on the one end and microcomputing on the other. The former allows nontechnical programmers to manipulate expensive equipment rather directly through packages such as CICS. The latter makes every programmer an engineer, an operator, and a systems programmer.

The traditional closeness of systems programmers and system operators is threatened by the increasing automation of computer operation itself and by the redundancy and complexity provided by telecomputing.

Then, too, companies such as Bell Labs and Microsoft have discovered that even operating systems can be commercial products. Just as market pressures are changing the shape of applications programming, we can expect similar pressures to influence the kids in the room off the back room. Already CP/M and MS/DOS are available on dozens of micros; it may be migrating into the mini market soon. UNIX is moving in the opposite direction. IBM has brought out so many versions of OS/360 over the years that volumes could be written on it. Some say that Multics is a world unto itself, that even its systems programmers don't understand it. Predictions of sentient operating systems (such as in the *Medusa Conspiracy* and the film "War Games") may be farfetched, but users of Multics sometimes feel that "It" is watching the users as closely as it watches its printers. Can systems programmers maintain their mystique in this sort of world?

They are the true high priests of programming. Unlike their applications counterparts, who come either from a general business program or a science background, systems programmers are developed from two sources: computer science training and operations areas. Opportunities for operators to buy they way out of the pit are going to diminish as computer operations become increasingly complex and the need for security rises. Many firms will discover that fraud can be reduced by keeping operators away from the system through several layers of software security; they may implement similar measures for systems programmers, too. University programs, on the other hand, can supply only a few systems programmers each year. Becoming a systems programmer is not automatic upon receipt of the sheepskin, either. Months of pouring over dumps, examination of listings, and classes are required for confirmation. Each operating system must be beseeched in a unique language with appropriate invocations. Knowledge of one operating system does not qualify the programmer for priesthood in another one.

Managing systems programming is also uniquely challenging. Certain traits of applications programmers become exaggerated in the systems staff, particularly the isolation characteristic of the software shop and the concentration upon maintenance. After all, systems programmers' "users" are themselves programmers. The highly bred, narrowly focused efforts of systems programmers are not conducive to migration into the firm at large. Few other systems in the firm resemble those of the digital computer's operating system. There is literally no uncontrolled aspect of operating system other than the users, traffic on a dial-in communications network, and lightning. The users (i.e., programmers) are easily tamed and highly predictable in the aggregate, though irritable when excited. Managers of systems software shops need attend only to the technology.

In the future, management of systems shops will slowly come to resemble today's applications shops. There is an apparently natural progression of programs, data, and applications from "flat," untextured command-level work to leveled, multitextured, programmed work, mirroring the early history of stored-program computation itself. This principle means that, when managers were handcrafting reports with pencil and paper, systems programmers were wiring boards. When managers moved to requesting reports from the MIS department, systems programmers were using assemblers to build systems, piecing them together with rudimentary editors, link-loaders, and listing and dumping programs. When managers now move to writing their own reports in EasyTrieve and APL, systems programmers will be programmers who "apply" themselves to systems-type work using systems-building languages. This writer has designed an office automation language (LAMP) that empowers the building of a constant stream of offices that formerly had to be handcrafted at the operating system level. Those who last year hand-built office systems bit-by-bit will next year create volumes of office-ware on programming machines.

Managing systems efforts will therefore look a great deal like managing today's applications efforts. Systems programmers will look less like engineering high priests and priestesses and more like members of the programming choir. Computer Science degrees will still be necessary, one imagines, but probably not sufficient training for "systems" that include people as part of their component set. The texture of the operating systems of the 1990s and beyond will not be so predictable.

### 8.2.3. The Scientific Programmer

Scientific programmers, like their systems counterparts, have sat apart from applications programmers for years. Their specialized training in mathematics, physics, chemistry, biology, and aeronautics places them nearer their clients than applications programmers are. Most scientific programmers have come through a scientific education or vocation and *then* added programming skills, but the bulk of business programmers migrate in the opposite way. Needless to say, free flow of information between scientific programmers and their users is easier than that between business applications programmers and their customers.

Then, too, there is the question of shared goals and ethics. Scientific programmers may well be scientists themselves. At the very least, they have spent a lot of time with scientists. There is less disdain of computer science degrees, too, in the science programming shops than in a business programming environment.

These differences imply a difference in futures. We can expect an easier migration of scientific programming to scientific users because this migration has always occurred freely. Scientific programming is also more numerically oriented, based upon the easily communicated language of mathematics, which forms the theoretical basis of computer science. In a phrase, scientific programmers fit into their users' milieus far more easily than business programmers fit into their users'.

The trends pointed out in the previous sections will not leave scientific programming unaffected, but they certainly do not spell the kind of dislocation that will hit the business software shop. In some areas, particularly the programming of large on-line military and research systems and in artificial intelligence (part of the so-called "fifth-generation computing" movement), there will always be scientific programmers. Many of these will be hacks and many will be phased out. But scientific programming has *already* withstood three decades of end-user programming. Most scientists feel comfortable programming in BASIC, APL, and FORTRAN, and are ready for more.

### 8.2.4. Summary

These sections make rather specific predictions, many of which—like many predictions—will be wrong. However, the trends clearly spell out a great change in business application programming, particularly for *new development* but also for *maintenance*. The change may well appear only as a gradual shift in level, with a corresponding response to these challenges by MOPs. Or it may come suddenly, perhaps through government regulation (ADA is causing its own revolution) as the information revolution becomes important to governments. To look at either evolution or revolution in more detail, let's review the overall past and future history of software briefly.

## 8.3. PAST AND FUTURE HISTORY OF SOFTWARE

This history is divided into four segments, roughly corresponding to four technological generations. It's "rough" because fourth-generation technology hasn't been officially announced and because most third-generation languages are merely recyclings of second-generation ones. Few programmers working today would notice that the FORTRAN DO statement, with its strange test-after-loop construction, is modeled after the transfer-on-index-register instructions of the 700/7000 series of computers IBM produced in the 1960s. The structure of the COBOL language does not resemble the way business operates so much as the structure of business forms common in the late 1950s. PL/I strongly mirrors the capabilities of the early System/360s. Few languages, in fact, are designed independently of specific technological or work environments.

Software history segments this way:

1. *Pre-1946: Hard-Wired.* The programmer as engineer.
2. *1946–1956: Soft-Wired.* The programmer as craftsperson.
3. *1956–1975: Firm-Ware.* The programmer as factory hand.
4. *1975–1990??: Air-Wars.* The virtual programmer.

Prior to ENIAC, all computers had their "programs" semi-hard-wired through patch panels or similar connectors. The programmer had to know electronics well, for the programmer was often called upon to repair the very expensive and unreliable equipment on which he or she worked.

Between 1946 and 1956, programming was done in either machine language entered through punched card or paper tape or through autocoders, the forerunners of assemblers. Autocoder was one step above patching a panel by hand—the origin of the term "patch" meaning a correction. Debugging often meant sitting at the console looking at the lights. Much of what had to be known about a program could be gleaned from the console, noting the speed of the output typewriter or card punch.

Phase three of programming saw the evolution of operating systems to oversee computer operations. The programmer was kicked out of the machine room; a programmer's engineering skills and operating dexterity were no longer needed. Programmers, removed from the scene, worked through operating system requests, which in turn regulated their behavior. In the early years of this phase, programmers worked on several applications in order to mesh human work habits with those of the machine. But by the end of phase three, a programmer could sit down on Monday morning and not arise until Friday evening, working on a single program in a time-sharing mode.

During this time, the operating system treated the programmer as merely another, less predictable, I/O device. To MOPs, programmers, whose salaries were growing rapidly, became cost items.

The fourth phase of programming is still in its infancy. The virtual programmer began working in the early 1970s, using among other systems, CMS—the Cambridge Monitor System. This provided each programmer with his or her own pre-1956 machine and with a variety of post-1956 language processors or an operating system to watch over that programmer alone. In this way, the virtual environments of the 1980s mimic the very personal and technical environments of the 1940s and 1950s. But in truth, the virtual programmer is a creature of the operating system, which in turn doesn't care whether or not the operator of the virtual machine is a human (i.e., a programmer or user) or a device (a code generator, a committee, a player piano, a random number generator, or a telemetry device). The virtual programmer may "own" a "machine" but in a very real sense the machine owns the programmer.

Phillip Kraft (1977) notes that structured techniques make it possible to specify quite minutely just what gets programmed. Pseudocode specs may have some flexibility left to which the programmer can apply creative talents, but not much. Programmers A and B may work on related modules without knowing it. They communicate only through strict calling sequences and predefined vocabularies, which neither clarify the application nor inform the programmer of its purpose. It is entirely possible to work on every module of an application and never understand what its purpose is, what value it is to anyone, and how near completion it is. Testing is done by other specialists, who have access to your code through the virtual operating system. Work assignments are dealt out through a stored program of work activities, increasingly monitored through an automated project management system. While both these trends are ethically neutral, probably helpful, and certainly efficient, in many ways the programmer has little control of his or her work when shops are organized along these lines, and little motivation other than salary to do his or her best work.

Management, however, becomes far easier as humans are increasingly treated as extensions of their programmable tools. Subdivided work is easier to cost out. Small, standardized work units are easier to assign and account for. Arguments are fewer, and those that do occur are more easily arbitrated if communication among assignments is in a standard vocabulary.

The disadvantage is that programmers working in this sort of environment may, despite their reportedly low social need strength, still not be quite hermits. If programmers are in general younger and have more poorly developed social skills, the compartmentalization brought on by software-engineered environments may only exacerbate their lack of social skills. If, as Kraft fears, an increasingly class-distinguished programmer society is developing, then only very adept MOPs will succeed in avoiding a plantation atmosphere in the software shop.

Kraft also postulates a trend toward routinization or trivialization of programming work in the virtual environment. For programmers, any transformation from art into artifice would mean a concentration upon economies of scale, upon the production of the most efficient software development environment to produce reliable software at the lowest cost. Perhaps there will be widespread unemployment in the programming ranks by 1995. My prediction would be the opposite. Software will become, in some as-yet-unpredicted way, a commodity like soap, transistor radios, and stock transaction data. Many more people will be employed in the software fabrication business. These people will not, however, be university graduates from Kankakee but rather quick-and-dirty trained software engine operators from Kuala Lumpur and La Paz. It will become too expensive to pay a university graduate to crank out variations on a program. Instead, programmers will be recruited in those countries eager to skip industrialization. Software for ovens, cars, boats, lights, television, data entry and retrieval, electronic games, personal communicators, agriculture, merchandizing, security, and office automation will be turned out by tens and hundreds of thousands of individuals who know only enough BASIC-88 or FOCUS to get by.

Managers of these programmers will run factories. They will need to know how to set and keep a schedule, how to detect a "machine" that cannot be fixed, when to excuse a worker for an afternoon to get his or her teeth fixed, and what to do about alcoholic employees—in other words they will face the same kinds of challenges factory foremen have always faced. Since neither the MOP nor the programmer will ever physically see a computer mainframe, alienation will be a big obstacle to productivity. Chapters 3 through 7 will be irrelevant for these MOPs because they'll never be promoted above a foreman's elevation and will never have an opportunity to view either the technology or the organization.

Those who do not survive Kraft's deskilling holocaust will have to have three qualities:

1. General management skills and entrepreneurial values.
2. Expertise in a content area of value to the firm.
3. Skill in managing the remaining computer resources.

Since MOPs will be merely more efficient programmers who never see the technology itself and who have access only to a segment of the virtual computer system, the chances of advancement or even survival are slim in Kraft's extreme prediction.

In general, many shops will have to become S.W.E.A.T. (software engineered adjustment techniques) shops simply because the economics of programs-as-commodity will demand it. The appearance of a nascent software industry begins to demonstrate this. Early software houses were heavily staffed with university-trained engineers and professional programmers who created and marketed their own products. But today's software customers are increasingly interested in a version of a package rather than true custom software. Marketing to those customers requires the ability to code variations and enhancements of the standard well-designed software. University-trained engineers and professional programmers don't want to do this.

Neither do you.

The future of the software industry is a bit rosier than Kraft would paint it, however. Whereas the rest of our resource-based society is debating the new-growth, no-growth controversy (which paradoxically and ironically rejects "dirty" industries like steel plants in favor of "clean" industries like S.W.E.A.T. shops), the software industry itself has never had the distinction of facing that issue. All software is "clean" and all programmers are clean-cut white-collar workers. The controversy in the software industry is whether or not there *is* such an industry in the face of the astronomically quickly rising ratio of labor to capital costs in computation.

The controversy spins about this axis: if development costs are so high, you must be doing something wrong. Look at the productivity of farmers, secretaries, and Japanese auto workers. *They* produce much for little. *You* can't even produce an approximate cost estimate. If we give you better tools, you should be able to do your jobs better, if only we knew what tools to use.

The problem is becoming ever more difficult because cheaper computing means even more computers and a greater need for people who seem not to be very productive. The search for an answer to the productivity "crisis" seems to lead naturally to the same solution that has raised productivity for the previously cited farmers and Japanese auto workers, namely automation. But what do we automate, when we hardly understand what a programmer does? And if we do automate, should we automate the automation? And then what do we do with the programmers who will automatically be laid off, their paychecks automatically pink slipped by our automatic billing systems? And if we do lay some of them off, what do we do with those left employed?

Three prognostications arise:

1. The proliferation of computers in society will mean that software becomes like other mass publishing industries.
2. The increasing power of computers will mean that programming can be off-loaded onto users just as automatic transmissions and electric starters meant that chauffeuring could be off-loaded onto owners.
3. The increasing flexibility provided by the chip means that new kinds of "programming" jobs will arise, which only superficially resemble those of today.

In fact, these three prognostications are the theses of this book. Yes, some programming will resemble Harlequin romances while other will (hopefully) resemble Pulitzer Prize writing. Off-loading of programming will alleviate the push toward the S.W.E.A.T. shop while, where off-loading cannot be made to work, S.W.E.A.T. shops will appear, providing opportunities for new workers with a lower level of sophistication. And finally, many new programming jobs will arise, among which we will see these:

1. Officeware analysts.
2. Games programmers.
3. Organizational programmers.
4. Industrial programmers working on robots.

In other words, the trends will not produce either extreme, but in the cauldron of Western industrial society programming will mature and be absorbed as a "usual" job, while those who either excel or wish not to will be employed at the ends of the scale, as entrepreneurs and specialists and consultants or as drones and officeware tenders.

The MOP in all cases will need plans to survive.

## 8.4. A SURVIVAL AND ADVANCEMENT PLAN FOR MOPs

If you are currently a MOP or if you are wondering if you'd like to advance into a supervisory position in the programming shop, consider these words of advice:

1. Plan to advance as a means of survival.
2. Fall out of love with computers and into love with information resources.
3. Plan your past carefully.
4. Learn to make yourself available and valuable to the organization of the 1990s.

In organizations, there is only growth. Otherwise there is nonsurvival. Yes, there are people in governments and businesses who have learned nothing in 20 years and others who have done the same thing for 40 years or more. But you are in a changing field in which no one is really sure of what is "proper." This means that tomorrow your work can be deemed "improper" or unproductive, and out you go. Or you could strike it rich and get promoted without wanting a increase in responsibility simply because DP management needs a body in the supervisory ranks.

Computers are going to disappear from your intellectual environment. Already, two to five years out of university, half of what you learned is out of date. You've already given up following the literature on distributed processing and telecommunications. Simulation languages will be the next to go. In no other field are as many new specializations created each decade as existed in all of previous history. By 1990 no one will even be able to tell you where the computer is and you certainly won't have the plastic card that admits you to the room. You can only love the technology you're near, and for you it's the technology of information resources; the technology to gather, store, peruse, format, and distribute information. In the final analysis, you're only using the computer because it's available. In 1900 they used ledger cards. In 1900 BC they used scribes. In 1999 you might be using biocomputers.

Your past in most cases dictates your future; choose a past carefully by planning your career in DP management. Chapter 7 provides guidelines for career planning, even in a rapidly changing career environment. The evidence is that DP managers are going to be generalists and are going to need general skills to prosper in the organizations of the end of the twentieth century. By the time you wish to advance, your past should include a variety of experiences and several of them should be outside DP. Avoid, too, DP organizations that seem interested only in bringing in more technology without the managerial expertise or motivation to use the technology better. The chances are that whatever technology you use in 1985 will be obsolete by 1990; your experience in installing, debugging, and training for this equipment may prove worthless. Instead, your past should include a great deal of organizational work to provide you with a broad view of what the firm does. This experience is valuable if only because organizations don't change as rapidly as technology.

Finally, in gathering this experience, be on the lookout for opportunities for your specific background to profit the firm. DP is more than processing input to make output today. The firm needs a smoothly functioning information resource. Turn your talents to making that resource into a potent contributor to the firm's economic health. As communication and computation converge even more in the 1980s, your experience in DP will become increasingly convertible into other areas, in particular manufacturing, office automation, corporate planning, distribution, and R&D.

In two other ways you are already equipped to advance in the organizations of the 1980s and 1990s, ways that others who wish to become executives may lack. First, you are already employing computer systems in management, even if it is only to track projects. Your workers regularly employ computerized equipment (by definition) and you know how to respond to the demands this equipment places upon you. When it doesn't work you know whom to call and what to ask for—or you can "fix" it yourself. You are used to working with levels of abstract concepts and the concept of programmability is your daily meat. In other words, whereas other managers would have to break out of the "command-level mold," you are already planning for programs. The typical supervisory-level job involves only carrying out someone else's plans (which makes the manager a microprocessor responding to a program). You are familiar with creating programs yourself. Of all the managers at the supervisory level in firms, you uniquely reverse the order of supervision: you are given a general description of a single product and produce a step-by-step program as a response. Others are given step-by-step production programs and are expected to produce identical products. You are already an executive in a very real sense, an operating system for the software shop. Thus you are a step ahead of others who would like the chance to operate in this mode.

In another way, too, you possess intellectual equipment that prepares you well for the coming two decades. Early in your career you developed "reconfiguration skills." These are skills that allow you to look at a problem statement and a list of available resources and to reconfigure those resources to solve the problem. You are not stuck in a single mental mode for problem-solving simply because your stock-in-trade from the days of your first BASIC program has been reconfiguring problems in a variety of ways. What, after all, is a program other than a reconfiguration of basic machine resources sequenced properly to solve a problem? At successively higher levels, too, you have learned how to reconfigure: reconfiguring modules and subroutines, reconfiguring job control language and preparing JCL macros for others to consume, and reconfiguring these macro operations to produce a variety of efficient ways to sort, merge, break out, detail, list, compare, and redefine data in a variety of structures. Years before anyone gave a name to database managers you understood the difference between the name of an item and its value, and you understood the difference between an interpretive processor and a compiler, differences that mattered 500% in efficiency.

Reconfiguration skills are valuable outside the DP shop, too. Often resources, such as labor, are incorrectly or inefficiently assigned and need to be reshuffled. Then, too, reconfiguring tasks over time so that a critical path is not delayed is often the difference between success and failure in management. Experience gathered in the software shop in making programs run efficiently is directly transferable to other realms in which resources are less easily controlled.

This, of course, spells out the danger in letting the MOP bull loose in the executive china shop without training. We merely want to underscore that the raw talent is already there in MOPs who have practiced these skills for years. Choosing a past that exercises the skills in the other, not-so-controllable ways provides the organizational seasoning on the managerial repast.

The survival and advancement plan is thus summed up in the following phrase:

Pick your past carefully.
Learn computation rather than programming.
Apply your skills to things of value to the firm.
Note that survival means advancement.

Wield your computer in attacking management problems.
Executive jobs go to those who plan.
Learn and apply reconfiguration skills.
Lean on your skills, but exercise them outside DP, too.

## 8.5. CONCLUSION

This book has been organized about those eight points. Chapters 1 and 7 showed the MOP that executive jobs go to those who plan and follow through on those plans. Chapter 2 discussed the application of computer skills to management problems and how to reconfigure them to suit management exigencies. In Chapter 3, we saw how these skills are then applied directly in work management.

Chapters 4 and 5 shifted the focus to managing programmers, helping secure not only survival for the MOP but important personnel management skills, which are necessary for advancement in any firm. In Chapter 6, we looked at the firm as a system that responds to its own needs, among which are the application of computation to its information needs. The next chapter helped you begin picking your past carefully and opened up the possibility of expansion outside traditional DP areas.

Finally, this chapter has outlined a survival and advancement plan for MOPs into the twenty-first century, the software century in which those who know the technology need only learn how to show it to others in order to lead.

# BIBLIOGRAPHY

Aron, J. D., *The Program Development Process*. Reading, MA: Addison-Wesley, 1974.

Auerbach Publishers, Inc. *Computer Programming Management*. Pensauken, NJ: Auerbach, 1981.

Awad, E. M., "Prediction of Satisfaction of Systems Analysts, Programmers." *Data Management* **15**(1), 12–18 (1977).

Baker, T., "Chief Programmer Team Management of Production Programming." *IBM Systems Journal* **11**(1), 56–73 (1972).

Bartol, K., "Building Synergistic EDP Teams." Proceedings, 15th Conference, ACM SIG-CPR, pp. 18–30, August 1977.

Bartol, K., "Professionalism as a Predictor of Organizational Committment, Role Stress, and Turnover: A Multidimensional Approach." *Academy of Management Journal* **22**(4), 815–821 (1979).

Bartol, K., "Managing Information Systems Personnel: A Review of the Literature and Managerial Implications." *MIS Quarterly* **6**(5), 49–70 (1982).

Beeler, J., "Seminar: Meaningful Work, Job Interest Top Priorities in Boosting DP Productivity." *ComputerWorld* **14**(14), 9 (April 7, 1980).

Benbazat, I. and I. Vessey, "Programmer and Analyst Time/Cost Estimation." *MIS Quarterly* **4**(2), 31–43 (1980).

Berrisford, T. and J. Wetherbe, "Heuristic Development: A Redesign of Systems Design." *MIS Quarterly* **3**(1), 11–19 (1979).

Blake, R. and J.. Mouton, *Building a Dynamic Organization Through Development*. Reading, MA: Addison-Wesley, 1969.

Bostrom, R. and K. Kaiser, "Personality Differences within System Project Teams: Implications for Designing Solving Centers." Proceedings, 18th Conference, ACM SIG-CPR, pp. 248–285, June 1981.

Brandon, D., *Data Processing Organization and Manpower Planning*. New York: Van Nostrand Reinhold, 1974.

Brooks, F., *The Mythical Man-Month: Essays in Software Engineering*. Reading, MA: Addison-Wesley, 1975.

Bybee, D., "Why DP Managers Are Disliked." *ComputerWorld* **16**(14), 67–68 (1982).

Bylinsky, G., "EDP Managers Put on Business Suits." *Fortune* **98**(9), 68–75 (November 6, 1978).

Carey, T. and R. Mason "Productivity Experiences with a Scenario Tool." Research Report CIS 81–001, Department of Computing and Information Science, Wilfred Laurier U., Waterloo, Ontario, 1981.

Carlyle, K., "Programmer's Job Service Averages 18 Months." *ComputerWorld* **15**(13), Special Report, p. 19 (March 30, 1981).

Chadwin, M. and E. Cross, "Japanese Management Style Right for DP?" *Journal of Systems Management* **34**(3), 6–9 (1983).

Cherlin, M., "The Toll of Turnover." *Datamation***27**(4), 209–212 (1981a).

Cherlin, M., "Burnout: Victims and Avoidances." *Datamation* **27**(7), 92–99 (July 1981b).

Chesebrough, P. and G. Davis, "Planning a Career Path in Information Systems." *Journal of Systems Management* **34**(1), 6–13 (1983).

Cheyney, P. and N. Lyons, Information Systems Skill Requirements: A Survey." *MIS Quarterly* **4**(1), 35–43 (1980).

Cooke, L. and J. Companiello, "The Programmer/Analyst Is an Endangered Species." *ComputerWorld* In-Depth **14**(36), 1–8 (Sept. 8, 1980).

Couger, J. D. "Circular Solutions." *Datamation* **29**(1), 135 ff. (1983).

Couger, J., and R. Zawacki, "What Motivates DP Personnel?" *Datamation* **24**(9), 119–122 (1978).

Couger, J. D. and R. Zawacki, "Compensation Preferences of DP Professionals." *Datamation* **24**(11), 96–102 (1978).

Couger, J. D. and R. Zawacki, *Motivating and Managing Computer Personnel*. New York: John Wiley, 1980.

Couger, J. D., R. Zawacki, and E. Opperman, "Motivation Levels of MIS Managers Versus Those of Their Employees." *MIS Quarterly* **3**(3), 47–56 (1979).

Crane, J. "The Changing Role of the DP Manager." *Datamation* **28**(5), 97 ff. (1982).

Crossman, T., "Taking the Measure of Programmer Productivity." *Datamation* **28**(5), 144–147 (1982).

Dooley, A., "Employee Relations Touted as No. 1 Priority." *ComputerWorld* **14**(46), 23 (November 10, 1980).

Dooley, A., "Turnover: Myth or Impediment to Managers?" *ComputerWorld* **15**(8), 4 (February 23, 1981).

Dubrin, A., *Human Relations: A Job-Oriented Approach* (2nd ed.). Reston, VA: Reston Publishing, 1978.

Dyer, L. (Ed.), *Careers in Organizations: Individual Planning and Organizational Development*. Ithaca, NY: New York State School of Industrial and Labor Relations, 1976.

Elliott, C., "Qualities of a Data Processing Manager." *Data Management* **13**(1): 35–37, 1975.

Enger, N., "Communication Skills Required by Computer Professionals." Proceedings, 18th Conference, ACM SIG-CPR, pp. 80–89, June 1981.

Fitz-enz, J., "Who Is the DP Professional?" *Datamation* **24**(9), 125–128 (1978).

Francl, C. and W. Lin, "The Gravy Train Derails." *ComputerWorld* **14** (46), In-Depth, 1–6 (November 10, 1980).

Frost, W. and C. Vaughan, "Within Context—The Application of Team Concepts to Work Teams." 15th Conference, ACM SIG-CPR, pp. 1–17, August 1977.

Gall, J., Systemantics: *How Systems Work and Especially How They Fail*. New York: Pocket Books, 1975.

Gibson C. and R. Nolan. "Managing the Four Stages of EDP Growth." Harvard Business Review **52**(1), 76–88,1974

Godair, E. and A. Staub, "Quality Circles (A People Building Concept) in a Data Processing Environment." Proceedings, 18th Conference, ACM SIG-CPR, pp. 323–351, June 1981.

Gunther, R., *Management Methodology for Software Product Engineering*. New York: Wiley, 1978.

Halstead, M., *Elements of Software Science*. New York: Elsevier North-Holland, 1977.

Herzberg, F., B. Mausner, and B. Snyderman, *The Motivation to Work*. New York: Wiley, 1959.

Hoard, B., "Panel Decries Lack of Training for Managers." *ComputerWorld* **14**(20), 28 (May 19, 1980a).

Hoard, B., "Study: It's Not Money That Motivates DPers." *ComputerWorld* **14**(21),16, May 26, (1980b).

Hoard, B., "Management Found Top Source of Discontent." *ComputerWorld* **14**(49), 8 (December 1, 1980c).

Hoard, B., "Management Ignorance Blamed for Staff Blues, Turnover." *ComputerWorld* **14**(49), 1, 8 (December 1, 1980d).

Hoard, B., "Study Says Managers Dense About What Moves DPers." *ComputerWorld* **15**(6), 1, 6 (February 9, 1981).

Hoard, B., "DP Turnover Blamed on Lack of Career Paths." *ComputerWorld* **17**(2), 8, January 10, (1983).

Howden, W. "Contemporary Software Development Environments." *Communications of the ACM* **25**(5), 318–329 (1982).

Hunsacker, P. and A. Alessandra, *The Art of Managing People*. Englewood Cliffs, NJ: Prentice-Hall, 1980.

Idema, T., "Systems Career Path Development." *Journal of Systems Management* **29**(4), 30–35 (1978).

Ives, B. and M. Olson, "Manager or Technician? The Nature of the Information Systems Manager's Job." *MIS Quarterly* **5**(4), 49–63 (1981).

Jackson, J. and Keaveny, T., *Successful Supervision*. Englewood Cliffs, NJ: Prentice-Hall, 1980.

Johnson, J. "A Working Measure of Productivity." *Datamation* **23**(2), 106–110 (1977).

Jones, T. C., "Measuring Programming Quality and Productivity." *IBM Systems Journal* **17**(1), 39–63 (1978).

Karlins, M., *The Human Use of Human Resources*. New York: McGraw-Hill, 1981.

Kirchner, J., "Responsible Career Planning Begins at Home, DPers Told by Federal Personnel Expert." *ComputerWorld* **14**(18), 15 (May 5, 1980).

Kraft, P. *Programmers and Managers: The Routinization of Computer Programming in the United States*. New York: Springer-Verlag, 1977.

Krauss, L. *Administering and Controlling the Company Data Processing Function*. Englewood Cliffs, NJ: Prentice-Hall, 1969.

Kugel, H. "How to Improve Programmer Evaluation (Performance Reviews)." *Canadian Datasystems* **14**(9), 44, 49 (1982).

Lazer, R. and W. Wikstrom, *Appraising Managerial Performance: Current Practices and Future Directions*. New York: Conference Board, 1977.

Lederer, A., "Going Outside—Or—Why Buy a Programmer When You Can Rent One for Less?" Proceedings, 18th Conference, ACM SIG-CPR, pp. 352–370, June 1981.

Lehman, J., "How Software Projects Are Really Managed," *Datamation* **25**(1), 119–129 (1979).

Licker, P., "The Japanese Approach: A Better Way to Manage Programmers?" *Communications of the ACM* **26**(9), 631–636, 1983a.

Licker, P., "On Beyond 'Z': Japanese Style Might Seuss Us Just Fine." *Journal of Systems Management* **34**(10), 10–13, 1983b.

Licker, P., "DP/Company Interaction: Is Job Rotation the Answer?" *Journal of Information Systems Management*, 1985, (forthcoming).

Locander, W., H. Napier, and R. Scammell, "A Team Approach to Managing the Development of a Decision Support System." *MIS Quarterly* **3**(1), 53–63 (1979).

Martin, J., *Application Development without Programmers*. Englewood Cliffs, N.J.: Prentice-Hall, 1982.

McGregor, D., *The Human Side of Enterprise*. New York: McGraw-Hill, 1960.

McLean, E., "End Users as Application Developers." *MIS Quarterly* **3**(4), 37–46 (1979).

Metzger, P., *Managing a Programming Project (2nd ed.)*. Englewood Cliffs, NJ: Prentice-Hall, 1981.

Mintzberg, H., *Impediments to the Use of Management Information*. New York: National Association of Accountants, 1974.

Moan, F., "Does Management Practice Lag Behind Theory in the Computer Environment?" *Academy of Management Journal* **16**(1), 7–23 (1973).

Moore, J. A. Framework for MIS Software Development Projects." *MIS Quarterly* **3**(1), 29–38 (1979).

Osborn, R., "Theories of Productivity Analysis."*Datamation* **27**(9), 212–216 (1981).

Ouchi, W., *Theory Z*. New York: Avon, 1982a.

Ouchi, W., "Theory Z: An Elaboration of Methodology and Findings." *Journal of Contemporary Business* **11** (2), 83–92, (1982b).

Powers, R. and G. Dickson, "MIS Project Management: Myths, Opinions, and Reality." *California Management Review* **15**(3), 147–156 (1973).

Ramsgard, W., *Making Systems Work: The Psychology of Business Systems*. New York: Wiley-Interscience, 1977.

Reeves, G. and R. Bussom, "Information Systems Curricula: Business Versus Academic Viewpoints." *Information & Management* **3**, 227–235 (1980).

Robbins, S., *Organizational Behavior: Concepts and Controversies*. Englewood Cliffs, NJ: Prentice-Hall, 1979.

Rosenberg, M. "He Would Take a Different Route to the Top Today," *ComputerWorld* **13**(36), 1, 8 (September 3, 1979).

Rosenberg, M. "Job Moves Can Have Pitfalls, Article Warns." *ComputerWorld* **14**(31),5 (August 4, 1980).

Scheidt, F., J. Hunter, R. McKenzie, and T. Muldrow. "Impact of Valid Selection Procedures on Work-Force Productivity."*Journal of Applied Psychology* **64**(6), 609–626 (1979).

Schneiderman, B., *Software Psychology: Human Factors in Computer and Information Systems*. Cambridge, MA: Winthrop, 1980.

Senn, J. "A Management View of Systems Analysts: Failures and Shortcomings." *MIS Quarterly* **2**(3), 25–42 (1978).

Sheehy, G., *Passages*. New York: Bantam, 1977.

Sheil, B., "Power Tools for Programmers." *Datamation* **29**(2), 131– 133, 136, 138, 142, 144 (1983).

Shoor, R., "Supervisor Job Called Toughest in World." *ComputerWorld* **14**(48): 2 (December 1, 1980).

Shoor, R., "Human Resources Called "Real Crisis" of DP." *ComputerWorld* **15**(12), 21 (March 23, 1981).

Simpson, C. and C. Bettinger, "Are Computer Science Degrees Necessary in Business DP?" *Journal of Systems Management* **33**(4), 29–33 (1982).

Slaughter, G., "Manager's Role in Improved DP People Communications, Motivation and Management (MRM)." Bethesda, MD: Gary Slaughter Corporation, undated.

Snyders, J. and M. Lasden, "Managing Programmers to Work Harder and Happier." *Computer Decisions* **12**(10), 34–35 (October 1980).

Stevens, B., "Probing the DP Psyche." *ComputerWorld* **14**(29), 25 ff., (July 28, 1980).

Stone, J., "Managers Seek Loyalty First, Reader Says." *ComputerWorld* **13** (28), 21 (July 9, 1979).

Stone, J., "Second-Class Image Hurts DPers." *ComputerWorld* **14**(16), 25 (April 21, 1980).

Tanniru, M., and S. Taylor, "Causes of Turnover among Data Processing Professionals—Some Preliminary Findings." Proceedings, 18th Conference, ACM SIG-CPR, pp. 224–247, June 1981.

Toffler, A., *The Third Wave*. New York: Morrow, 1980.

Unger, B. and S. Walker, "Improving Team Productivity in System Software Development." Proceedings, 15th Conference, ACM SIG-CPR, pp. 104–115, August 1977.

Walston, C. E. and C. Felix, "A Method of Programming Measurement and Estimation." *IBM Systems Journal* **16**(1), 54–73 (1977).

Walton, R. "Social Choice in the Development of Advanced Information Technology." *Human Relations* **35**(12), 1073–1084 (1982).

Ward, T., *Computer Organisation, Personnel and Control*. London: Longman, 1973.

Wasserman, A. and S. Gutz, "The Future of Programming." *Communications of the ACM* **25**(3), 196–206 (1982).

Weinberg, G. *The Psychology of Computer Programming*. New York: Van Nostrand Reinhold, 1971.

Willoughby, T. "Computing Personnel Turnover: A Review of the Literature." *Computer Personnel* **7**(1–2), 11–13 (1977).

Wilson, G. "Workforce Strategies: Hire, Win, Hire, Lose." *Data Management* **19** (12),27 ff. (1981).

Winkler, C., "Panel Suggests Ways of Hanging onto DPers." *ComputerWorld* **14**(42),12 (October 13, 1980).

Woodruff, C. "Job Satisfaction of Data Processing Personnel." *Computer Personnel* **7**(4), 5–7 (1978).

Woodruff, C. K., "Data Processing People: Are They Satisfied/ Dissatisfied with Their Jobs?" *Information & Management* **3**(6), 219– 225 (1980).

Wooldridge, S., *Project Management in Data Processing*. New York: Petrocelli/Charter, 1976.

Yeh, R. (Ed), *Current Trends in Programming Methodology, Vol 1: Software Specification and Design*. Englewood Cliffs, NJ: Prentice-Hall, 1980.

Yourdon, E., *Structured Walkthroughs*. Englewood Cliffs, NJ: Prentice-Hall, 1980.

Yourdon, E., *Software Development Methodology*. New York: Yourdon, 1982.

Zientara, M., "Honesty, Pay, Challenge Cited as DPers' Needs." *ComputerWorld* **14**(21), 7 (May 26, 1980).

Zloof, M. M., "Query-by-Example: A Data Base Language." *IBM Systems Journal* **16**(4), 324–343 (1977).

Zloof, M. M., "Office-by-Example: A Business Language That Unifies Data and Word Processing and Electronic Mail." *IBM Systems Journal* **21**(3), 272–304 (1982).

# INDEX